Collected Poems in English

JOSEPH BRODSKY was born in Leningrad (St Petersburg) in 1940 into a Russian-Jewish family. He left school when he was fifteen and began writing poetry three years later. He lived a year (1964–5) in exile in the Arkhangelsk region of northern Russia. In June 1972 he became an involuntary exile and settled in the United States. He received the Nobel Prize for Literature in 1987 and served as Poet Laureate of the United States in 1991 and 1992. He died in 1996.

Collected Poems in English

by Joseph Brodsky

OxfordPoets

CARCANET

Acknowledgements

The poems in this volume are either written in English or translated from the original Russian by or with the author.

Including translations by: Jonathan Aaron, Peter France, Jamey Gambrell, Paul Graves, Anthony Hecht, George L. Kline, David McDuff, David MacFadyen, Jane Ann Miller, Howard Moss, Alan Myers, David Rigsbee, Barry Rubin, Harry Thomas, Derek Walcott, Daniel Weissbort and Richard Wilbur.

The editor gratefully acknowledges her debt to Maria Brodsky, Alexei Grinbaum, Gennady Komarov, Viktor Kulle, Jainee McCorroll Edward Mendelson, Barry Rubin, Jon Stone, Alexander Sumerkin, Tomas Venclova, Masha Vorobiov, and especially Professor Lev Loseff for their help with this book. Thanks also to Ms Wislawa Szymborska and Mrs Zbigniew Herbert for permission to reproduce Joseph Brodsky's translations of poems by Ms Szymborska and Mr Herbert.

'A History of the Twentieth Century (A Roadshow)' first appeared in *Partisan Review* Vol. Liii, No. 3 (1986); Joseph Brodsky's translation of 'Tristia' by Osip Mandelstam first appeared in *Confrontation*, #27-28 (1984); 'Lines for the Winter Recess' and Brodsky's translation of 'Two Poems from 1916' by Marina Tsvetaeva first appeared in *The New Yorker* on 4 May 1992 and 17 October 1983, respectively, and are reprinted by permission.

First published by Farrar, Straus and Giroux, New York, 2000

Published in Great Britain in 2001 by
Carcanet Press Limited
4th Floor, Conavon Court
12-16 Blackfriars Street
Manchester M3 5BQ

A CIP catalogue record for this book
is available from the British Library

ISBN 1 903039 55 X

The publisher acknowledges financial
assistance from the Arts Council of England

Printed and bound by Antony Rowe Ltd, Eastbourne

Contents

Editor's Note

This volume contains all the poems by Joseph Brodsky that appeared in book form in English under his supervision during the author's lifetime, in their last known versions, as well as several poems he was enthusiastic about but unable to accommodate in his books. It consists largely of translations from his original Russian, made by the author or in collaboration with different translators; there are also a number of poems composed directly in English and several translations of poems by others.

Brodsky's own organization of his books, which is roughly but not strictly chronological, has been preserved, with one exception: the long poem "Gorbunov and Gorchakov," which was originally appended to *To Urania* because of delays in translation, has been moved forward, to reflect its chronological place in the author's work.

We have chosen to identify the translators and collaborators in the notes. In this we follow the author's decision, in *So Forth*, to acknowledge translators separately from the poems, which we understood as an invitation to the reader to consider the poems as if they were original texts in English; we beg the indulgence of Brodsky's translators, to whom he often expressed his admiration and gratitude.

The author was able to render into English about a third of his mature work in Russian, which was published concurrently in six volumes under the Ardis imprint, with Carl and Ellendea Proffer. These six volumes have recently been collected and annotated by Professor Lev Loseff for the *Biblioteka poeta* series of Russian poets, to which this volume is heavily indebted. All of Brodsky's work in both languages is being gathered by Russian and American scholars for a bilingual complete works.

The present volume will also be supplemented by two collections of translations now in preparation. First, a new, expanded edition of *Joseph Brodsky: Selected Poems*, translated by George L. Kline, which appeared in the United States and England in 1973 and which includes more of the poems the author wrote in the Soviet Union before his emigration in 1972.

And second, translations by other hands of poems in Russian written after 1972 that Brodsky was unable to see through translation during his lifetime.

Brodsky took an active hand in the translation of his own work into English. He believed strongly that a poem's verse structure should be rendered in translation, and to this he applied the dictates of his own very particular ear. (In Russian he is recognized as one of the most original prosodic stylists of his time.) As he was both author and translator, he was able to reach for solutions that were unavailable to another translator. Many of these translations were reworked extensively by the author in the course of publication, and all of them (with the possible exception of "Gorbunov and Gorchakov") bear the mark of his authorial hand.

They also bear the mark of his long affinity for English, a language he had admired since his early youth. Although Brodsky remained a Russian poet first, his unique relationship to his adoptive language, filled with vigor and affection, brought forth a body of work resting somewhere between translation and original creation, internally coherent, rich in linguistic and prosodic invention, and quickened by the spirit that had made him a great poet in his native Russian. If, as Brodsky wrote, a writer's biography is in his twists of language, an important chapter of his own story resides in these poems, exactingly rendered into his beloved second tongue.

ANN KJELLBERG
New York, 1999

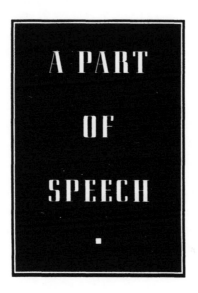

A PART

OF

SPEECH

.

TO MY MOTHER
AND FATHER

Six Years Later

So long had life together been that now
the second of January fell again
on Tuesday, making her astonished brow
lift like a windshield wiper in the rain,
  so that her misty sadness cleared, and showed
  a cloudless distance waiting up the road.

So long had life together been that once
the snow began to fall, it seemed unending;
that, lest the flakes should make her eyelids wince,
I'd shield them with my hand, and they, pretending
  not to believe that cherishing of eyes,
  would beat against my palm like butterflies.

So alien had all novelty become
that sleep's entanglements would put to shame
whatever depths the analysts might plumb;
that when my lips blew out the candle flame,
  her lips, fluttering from my shoulder, sought
  to join my own, without another thought.

So long had life together been that all
that tattered brood of papered roses went,
and a whole birch grove grew upon the wall,
and we had money, by some accident,
  and tonguelike on the sea, for thirty days,
  the sunset threatened Turkey with its blaze.

So long had life together been without
books, chairs, utensils—only that ancient bed—
that the triangle, before it came about,
had been a perpendicular, the head

of some acquaintance hovering above
two points which had been coalesced by love.

So long had life together been that she
and I, with our joint shadows, had composed
a double door, a door which, even if we
were lost in work or sleep, was always closed:
     somehow its halves were split and we went right
     through them into the future, into night.

[1968]

Anno Domini

The provinces are celebrating Christmas.
The Governor-general's mansion is bedecked
with mistletoe, torches smoke by the entrance.
In the lanes the people press and lark around.
A merry, idle, dirty, boisterous
throng crowds in the rear of the mansion.

The Governor-general is ill. He lies
on a couch, wrapped in a shawl from Alcazar,
where he once served, and his thoughts turn
on his wife and on his secretary
receiving guests downstairs in the hall.
He is not really jealous. At this moment

it's more important to him to retire
into his shell of illness, dreams, the deferment of
his transfer to the capital. And since
he knows that freedom is not needed
by the crowd at all to make a public holiday—
for this same reason he allows

even his wife to be unfaithful. What would
he think of if ennui attacks
did not plague him? If he loved?
A chilly tremor runs through his shoulders,
he chases these alarming thoughts away.
In the hall the merrymaking subsides

but does not end. Muddled with drink,
the leaders of the tribes stare glassily
into a distance now devoid of enemies.
Their teeth, expressive of their rage,

set in a smile that's like a wheel
held fast by brakes—and a servant

is loading them with food. In his sleep
a merchant cries out. Snatches of song are heard.
The Governor-general's wife and secretary
slip out into the garden. And on the wall
the imperial eagle, like a bat, stares down,
having gorged on the Governor-general's liver.

And I, a writer who has seen the world,
who has crossed the equator on an ass,
look out of the window at the hills asleep
and think about the identity of our woes:
the Emperor won't see him, I won't be
seen by my son and Cynthia . . . And we,

we here shall perish. Arrogance will not raise
our bitter fate to the level of proof
that we are made in the Creator's image.
The grave will render all alike.
So, if only in our lifetime, let us be various!
For what reason should we rush from the mansion,

we cannot judge our homeland. The sword of justice
will stick fast in our personal disgrace:
the heirs, the power, are in stronger hands . . .
How good that vessels are not sailing!
How good that the sea is freezing!
How good that the birds in the clouds

are too frail for such cumbrous frames!
For that, nobody is to blame.
But perhaps our weights will be
proportionate exactly to their voices.
Therefore, let them fly to our homeland.
Therefore, let them yell out to us.

My country . . . foreign gentlemen,
visiting Cynthia, are leaning
over the crib like latter-day magi.
The infant slumbers. A star glimmers
like a coal under a cold font.
And the visitors, not touching his head,

replace the halo by an aureole of lies,
and the Virgin Birth by gossip,
by the passing over of the father in silence . . .
The mansion empties. The lights on each floor die.
First one, then another. Finally, the last.
And only two windows in the whole palace

are alight: mine, where, with my back to the torchlight,
I watch the moon's disk glide
over the sparsely growing trees, and see
Cynthia, the snow; the Governor-general's, where
he struggles silently all night with his illness
and keeps the fire lit, to see his enemy.

The enemy withdraws. The faint light of day
barely breaking in the world's East,
creeps through the window, straining
to see what is happening within,
and, coming across the remnants of the feast,
falters. But continues on its way.

[January] 1968
Palanga

Autumn in Norenskaia

We return from the field. The wind
clangs buckets upturned,
unbraids the willow fringe,
whistles through boulder piles.
The horses, inflated casks
of ribs trapped between shafts,
snap at the rusted harrows
with gnashing profiles.

A gust combs frostbitten sorrel,
bloats kerchiefs and shawls, searches
up the skirts of old hags, scrolls them
tight up as cabbageheads.
Eyes lowered, hacking out phlegm,
the women scissor their way home,
like cutting along a dull hem,
lurch toward their wooden beds.

Between folds flash the thighs of scissors,
wet eyes blur with the vision
of crabbed little imps that dance on
the farm women's pupils as a shower flings
the semblance of faces against a bare
pane. The furrows fan out in braids
under the harrow. The wind breaks
a chain of crows into shrieking links.

These visions are the final sign
of an inner life that seizes on
any specter to which it feels kin
till the specter scares off for good
at the church bell of a creaking axle,
at the metal rattle of the world as it

lies reversed in a rut of water,
at a starling soaring into cloud.

The sky lowers. The shouldered rake
sees the damp roofs first, staked
out against the ridge of a dark
hill that's just a mound far off.
Three versts still to cover. Rain
lords it over this beaten plain,
and to the crusted boots cling brown
stubborn clods of the native earth.

1965

A second Christmas by the shore
of Pontus, which remains unfrozen.
The Star of Kings above the sharp horizon
of harbor walls. And I can't say for sure
that I can't live without you. As
this paper proves, I do exist: I'm living
enough to gulp my beer, to soil the leaves, and
trample the grass.

Retreating south before winter's assault,
I sit in that café from which we two were
exploded soundlessly into the future
according to the unrelenting law
that happiness can't last. My finger tries
your face on poor man's marble. In the distance,
brocaded nymphs leap through their jerky dances,
flaunting their thighs.

Just what, you gods—if this dilating blot,
glimpsed through a murky window, symbolizes
your selves now—were you trying to advise us?
The future has arrived and it is not
unbearable. Things fall, the fiddler goes,
the music ebbs, and deepening creases
spread over the sea's surface and men's faces.
But no wind blows.

Someday the slowly rising breakers but,
alas, not we, will sweep across this railing,
crest overhead, crush helpless screams, and roll in
to find the spot where you drank wine, took cat-
naps, spreading to the sun your wet

thin blouse—to batter benches, splinter boardwalks,
and build for future molluscs
a silted bed.

1971
Yalta

Homage to Yalta

The story to be told below is truthful.
Unfortunately, nowadays it's not
just lies alone but simple truth as well
that needs compelling argument and sound
corroboration. Isn't that a sign
of our arrival in a wholly new
but doleful world? In fact, a proven truth,
to be precise, is not a truth at all—
it's just the sum of proofs. But now
what's said is "I agree," not "I believe."

What troubles people in the atom age is—
much less than things themselves—the way they are
constructed. Like a child who clobbers dolly,
then wails on finding the debris inside,
we tend to take what lies in back of this
or that event as nothing less than that
event itself. To which there is a kind
of fascination, inasmuch as things
like motives, attitudes, environment,
et cetera—all this is life. And life
we have been trained to treat as if it were
the object of our logical deductions.

And sometimes all it seems we have to do
is interweave them—motives, attitudes,
environment, and problems—and events
will then take place; a crime, let's say. But no.
It's just an ordinary day out there.
It's drizzling, cars go rushing by. Inside,
a standard-model telephone (a clump
of cathodes, junctions, terminals, resistors)

is resolutely speechless. No event,
alas, takes place. On second thought, thank God.

The matter here described occurred in Yalta.
Of course, I'll make an effort to comply with
the view of truth I mentioned earlier—
that is to say, I plan to disembowel
that dolly. But I hope you will forgive
me, gentle reader, if I here and there
append to truth an element of Art,
which, in the last analysis, lies at
the heart of all events (though, to be sure,
a writer's art is not the Art of life,
it only forms a likeness).
                            Testimony
of witnesses will follow in the order
in which it was obtained. Herein lies an
example of how truth depends on art,
and not of art's dependence on the truth.

                            I
"He telephoned that evening and he said
he wasn't coming. He and I beforehand,
on Tuesday, had agreed that he'd drop by
my place on Saturday. Yes, yes, on Tuesday.
I'd called him and invited him to come.
'On Saturday' is when he said he'd see me.
The purpose? Simply that for quite a while
we'd hoped to sit and analyze together
a problem of Chigorin's. That was all.
Our meeting was to have no other 'purpose,'
to use your word. Unless, of course, you choose
to say that wishing to take pleasure in a
congenial person's company amounts to
a purpose. Still, you probably know better . . .
As luck would have it, though, he phoned that evening

and said he'd not be coming. What a shame
it was! I really would have liked to see him.
Distraught? Was that the word you used? Oh, no.
He sounded just the same as usual. But
of course, a telephone's a telephone;
although, you know, when you can't see a person
you focus on his voice a bit more sharply.
He didn't sound distraught . . . But then, the way
he phrased his words was always somewhat odd.
His speech consisted, on the whole, of pauses
that always made you feel uneasy, since
we ordinarily interpret silence
to mean a person's mind is busy working.
And his, in fact, was nothing but pure silence.
You'd soon begin to get a feeling of
your own dependence on this quietness,
and that would irritate a lot of people.
Oh, no, I knew it had resulted from
his shell shock. Yes, of that I'm very certain.
How else would you explain the fact . . . What's that?
That's right, he didn't sound at all distraught. But
of course, that's only judging by his voice.
There is one thing I'll say in any case:
that Saturday and earlier, on Tuesday,
he sounded just the same as usual. So
if something really happened to him then,
it wasn't Saturday, because he called!
That simply doesn't fit distraught behavior!
Take me: when I'm distraught, for instance . . . What?
The tenor of our conversation? Gladly.
The moment that I heard the telephone I
was there to pick it up. 'Good evening, it
is I; I owe you an apology. For,
as things turn out, I simply won't be able
to come today.' Oh, really? That's a shame.
On Wednesday, maybe? Should I call you up?
Offended? Why, for heaven's sake, of course not!

14

Until next Wednesday, then? 'Good night,' he answered.
That's right, it was at eight or thereabout.
When I hung up I cleared away the dishes
and took the board out. Last time, his advice
had been to try the Queen E-8 maneuver.
An odd and somewhat muddled move it was.
Nonsensical, almost. And not at all in
the spirit of Chigorin. Odd it was,
and senseless. Didn't change a thing, and therefore
it nullified the meaning of the problem.
In any game what matters are results:
a win, a loss, or even if a draw—
but nonetheless an outcome. His move, though—
it seemed as if it put the pieces in
some doubt about their very own existence.
I sat up with the board till late at night.
Perhaps the game may someday actually
be played like that. As far as I'm concerned,
however . . . Sorry, what was that you asked: does
the name mean anything to me? It does.
Five years ago the two of us broke up.
Yes, that's correct: we weren't ever married.
Was he aware of it? Most likely not.
It surely wasn't something she'd have told him.
What's that? This photograph? I'd make a point
of putting it away before he came here.
Oh, no! You needn't be apologetic.
The question is quite natural, and I . . .
How was it that I knew about the murder?
I got a call from her that very night.
Now there's a voice that really was distraught!"

II
"Last year I didn't see him very often,
but still, I saw him. Twice a month he'd pay
a visit, sometimes even not that often.
Except October, when he never came at all.

15

He'd usually call to let me know
ahead of time. A week or so beforehand.
In order to avoid a mix-up. I'm,
you know, in theater. Something unexpected
is always coming up. For instance, all
at once, a person's taken ill or leaves us
to make a film—and has to be replaced.
Well, basically, that sort of thing. Besides that—
besides, he knew that now I had become . . .
Why, yes. That's right. But how on earth did you know?
But after all, that is your métier.
However, this time things are, well, I'd say it's
a serious involvement. What I mean
by that is . . . Yes, and all that notwithstanding,
I still continued seeing him. Oh, how
can I explain it! He was rather odd, I
would say, and not like anyone. Of course,
yes, everyone is different from all others.
But he was very different from us all.
Yes, that's precisely what I found attractive.
When we were with each other, all around
us everything would cease existing. I mean
it all continued moving and revolving—
the world went on, he didn't block it out.
Love? No, that's not what all this talk has been
about! The world went on. But suddenly
the top of things—both moving and immobile—
was covered with a sort of film or, rather,
a coat of dust, which gave them all a kind
of senseless similarity. For instance,
you know, the way they paint the walls and ceilings
and beds all white in hospitals. All right, then.
Now try to form a picture of my room
all blanketed with snow. Peculiar, wouldn't
you say? But at the same time, don't you think
that furniture would only stand to gain

from such a metamorphosis? You don't? That's
a shame. Back then I used to think that sameness
was in reality the world's true surface.
I valued that sensation very dearly.
Yes, that's exactly why I never broke
things off. Just why should I have had to,
pray tell me, sever our relations? Should I
have left him for the captain's sake? Well, frankly,
that's not the way I see it. Certainly, he's
an earnest sort of person, even if
he is an officer. However, what
means most to me is that sensation! Really,
could he have given it to me? O God! I'm
beginning only now to understand
just how important that sensation was
to me! And furthermore, it's so peculiar.
Specifically? The fact that I myself
will now be just another tiny speck in
the universe. I, too, will now be tinged
with that same patina. And all the while I'll
be thinking I'm not like the rest! . . . Until
we realize that we can be repeated,
we don't know anything. It's awful, awful.

"Forgive me while I pour myself some wine.
And some for you? With pleasure. Don't be silly,
I won't think anything at all! Just when
and where was it we met? I don't remember.
I guess it was the beach. That's right, it was:
Livadia—we met there on the beach of
the health resort. Where else do people get
together in a hole like ours? But really,
you do know all about me, don't you! Still,
I know you'd never guess the words with which
we first became acquainted. What he said was
'I'm sure you find me quite obnoxious, but . . .'

17

The rest of what he said is not important.
A pretty good beginning, don't you think?
If I were you, I'd add it to my stock
of weapons. I can say that as a woman.
What do I know about his family?
Why, absolutely nothing. Well, I think he . . .
he evidently had a son—but where?
On second thought that's wrong, I've got it twisted:
the child's the captain's. Yes, a kid, a schoolboy.
Morose; but on the whole the image of
his father . . . No, I haven't got the slightest
idea about his family—or friends.
As I recall, he never introduced me
to anyone. Forgive me while I have
a little more. You're right: the evening's stifling.

"No, I don't know who killed him. What was that?
You must be kidding! He's a total washout.
The man was driven crazy by queen's gambits.
Besides, the two of them were friends. Now that
was something I could not explain: their friendship.
Inside that club of theirs they smoke so much
they easily can stink the whole South Shore up.
Why, no, the captain spent the evening at the
performance. Yes, of course, in mufti. I
can't stand their uniform. And afterward we
returned together.
                        We found him there
at my front entrance. He was lying in
the doorway. 'Just a drunk' was our assumption.
You see, our hall is rather dark. But then
I recognized the raincoat he was wearing.
The coat was white but smeared with mud. No, no,
that's right, he didn't drink. I know for certain.
Yes, evidently he'd been crawling. And
for quite a while. What then? Well, first we brought

him into my place, then we rang up the
police. Not me, the captain. I felt ill.

"Yes, this whole thing's a real nightmare. Oh,
you think so, too? I find that so surprising.
You know: it is your job and all. You're right,
I'm sure it's hard to get accustomed to it.
You're human, too, of course . . . I'm sorry!
I didn't put that very nicely . . . Yes,
please pour yourself another; none for me, though.
I've had enough. What's more, I haven't slept
well lately and rehearsal's in the morning.
Well, if it helps insomnia. You're certain?
In that case, just a swallow. Yes, you're right,
the atmosphere tonight is really stifling.
Oppressive, too. There's absolutely nothing
to breathe. Oh—everything just makes it hard.
The stuffiness. I'm suffocating. Yes.
And you? And you? You, too? You, too, then? Nothing—
there's nothing else at all I know. Oh, yes?
There's absolutely nothing I can tell you.
Say, what is it you want from me? What is it . . .
All right, now. Tell me, huh? What is it? What?"

III

"It's your opinion, then, that I'm obliged to
provide you explanations? Well, all right,
if I'm obliged, then I'm obliged. But mind you:
I'm bound to disappoint you inasmuch
as I most certainly know less about him
than you do. Even that much is enough, though,
to drive a person mad. But I suppose
that's not a threat to you, since you are . . . Yes,
that's absolutely true: I couldn't stomach
the character. I think you know the reasons.
And if you don't—it makes no sense at all

to get involved in explanations. That
especially holds true since in the end
what interests you are facts. So there you have it:
I openly admit it—I despised him.

"No, he and I had never met. I knew—
I knew that someone used to see her. Only
I didn't know exactly who, though. She,
of course, did not say anything to me. But
I knew! One didn't have to be a Sherlock
like you to know it. Average concern
was really all it took. Especially since . . .
But you don't know the sort of person she is!
Although she didn't talk about the guy,
that doesn't mean that she was hiding something!
She simply didn't want to see me get
upset—that's all it was. And anyway, there
was nothing, after all, to hide. As she
herself admitted when I cornered her, it
has almost been a year since anything
went on between them . . . What was that? I don't
quite understand. Did I believe her? Sure, I
believed her. Whether that was any consolation
is, frankly speaking, something else entirely.

"You may in fact be right. It's easier
for you to tell. But if a person says a thing,
it's not because he wants to be distrusted.
To me, the very movement in itself
of someone's lips is even more essential
than truth or falsehood; just the very movement
of lips contains more life than do the words
the lips are moved by. I have said that I
believed her. No! A certain something else was
involved. It's simply that I saw what she
was telling me. (I didn't hear it, mind you;
instead, I saw it.) Try to understand:

Before my eyes there stood a human being—
a speaking breathing, moving human being.
I didn't want to think it all a lie,
nor could I . . . You're amazed that even with an
approach like that I somehow still was able
to get four stars? They're very little stars, though.
I started out quite differently. The ones
who started with me have been wearing big stars
a long, long time already. Many even
have two. (In your account of this whole thing
be sure to add that I'm a failure, too; it
will help to make it sound more plausible.) I
repeat: I started differently. Like you, I
kept looking for skulduggery around
me everywhere. And, naturally, I'd find it.
It's in a soldier's blood: they're always out
to put one over on the brass . . . But then
one day in Košice, in '44, I
discovered this was stupid. Twenty-eight
of them were lying in the snow before
me, men I hadn't trusted—soldiers.
What? Why do I discuss this if it has
no bearing on the matter? I was only
attempting to reply to what you asked.

"Yes, I'm a widower. It's been four years now.
Yes, I have children. One, that is. A son.
Where was I in the evening Saturday? At
the theater. Afterward, I took her home.
Yes, he was lying there at her front entrance.
What? How did I react then? Not at all.
Of course, I recognized him. I had seen them
together once in the department store. They
were in the midst of buying something. That
was when I understood . . .
                    The fact is, we'd
run into one another now and then on

the beach. We both preferred the same location:
that spot—remember?—over by the fence.
And on his neck I'd always see those bruises . . .
the ones . . . oh, you know . . . So, then. Once
I spoke to him—most likely it was something
about the weather. Quickly he leaned over
in my direction and without a glance
at me he said: 'I just don't feel like talking . . .'
and only after several seconds passed
he added on: '. . . to you.' And all the while he
kept looking upward into space. Right then,
I swear to you, I could have murdered him.
My vision blurred, and everything was swimming.
I felt a scalding wave go rising through
my brain, and momentarily I think I
lost consciousness. When I regained my senses,
he'd reassumed that previous repose
of his, and then he'd covered up his face with
a newspaper. And meanwhile, on his neck I
could clearly see those marks—those darkish bruises . . .
No, I was not aware of who in fact
he was then. Luckily, I'd not yet met her.

"What then? Well, then I think he disappeared;
I somehow never saw him anymore at
the beach. And then an officers' reception
was given at the club, and that was when
I met her. Later on I saw them there—in
the store . . . and that was why I recognized him
at once that night, on Saturday. To tell you
the honest truth, in some way I was glad.
It might have otherwise gone on forever,
and every time, just following his visits,
she wasn't quite herself. But now I hope
that things will soon be going as they ought to.
At first it's bound to be a little hard,

but I for one can tell you: in the end
the murdered are forgotten. And, moreover,
it looks like we'll be leaving. I've been called
to the Academy. That's right, in Kiev.
Why, any theater there will hire her. And
my son is very friendly with her. Who
can tell? It's possible we'll have a child of
our own. As you can see, I'm—ha, ha, ha—
still . . . Yes, I do possess a handgun.
No, no, it's not a Stechkin; only my
old trophy from the war—a Parabellum.
Well, yes, I know the wound was from a gunshot."

IV
"That evening Pop shoved off and headed for
the theater. I stayed home myself with Granny.
Uh-huh, the two of us watched television.
My homework? It was Saturday, remember.
So we watched television. What was on?
I'm not so sure now. Maybe it was Sorge.
Yeah, Sorge, right! I didn't watch it to
the end, though. I had seen the thing already.
Our class once took a trip to see the film.
That's all . . . At what point did I go away?
Oh, at the part with Klausen and the Germans.
I mean, it was the Japs . . . and then they still
keep going in that boat along the shoreline.
Yes, it was sometime after nine o'clock.
For sure. I know because on Saturday
the supermarket closes up at ten, and
I felt like having ice cream. No, I looked
out through the window—after all, it's only
across the street. That's right, and then I felt
like walking. No, I didn't mention it
to Granny. Why? She would have started in
about a coat and hat and gloves—and that sort

of thing. Uh-huh, I wore a jacket. Not on
your life, not this; I wore my hooded one.
It's got a zipper.
                    Yes, I put it in
my pocket. No, no, no. I simply knew where
he kept the key . . . Sure, just for fun, of course!
No, not to be a show-off. Who would I have
shown off to? Late? Yes, right, and very dark.
What thoughts I had? I wasn't even thinking.
I guess that all I did was walk and walk.

"Huh? How was it I ended up there?
I don't remember . . . Well, I guess, because—as
you walk downhill the harbor always stays
in front of you. And so do lights in port.
Yeah, that's a fact, and you can try and picture
what's going on there. Anyhow, when you're
already on your way back home, it's nicer
to go downhill. Yes, quiet, and the moon
was out. Well, mostly, it was really gorgeous.
Pass by? No, no one happened to pass by me.
Not really, no. I didn't know the time. But
on Saturdays the *Pushkin* sails at midnight.
It hadn't left yet, though. Down there, astern,
they've got a lounge for dancing, and the windows
are stained glass. When you're way up there they look like
they're emeralds. Yeah, and then . . .
                                    I what? Of course not!
Her place is up above the park, while I,
I met him at the park, right by the exit.
Do what? Oh, tell you how I feel about her
in general? Oh, well, I guess—I think
she's very pretty. Yeah, and so does Granny.
And, well, she's sort of nice, she doesn't bug you.
It's all the same, though; I don't really care.
Oh, Dad'll work it out . . .

                              Yes, at the entrance.
Yeah, he was smoking. Sure, I asked for one,
but he refused and then . . . Well, anyway, so
   he said to me, 'Come on, now, beat it, willya?!'
A minute later—after I had walked
away about ten steps, or maybe farther—
beneath his breath he added, 'Scoundrel.' It
was very quiet then and so I heard him.
I really don't know what came over me!
Uh-huh, it felt like I'd been hit by someone.
And things began to swim before my eyes—
honestly I don't remember turning
and firing at him! But I know I missed:
he still was standing where he'd been before, and
I think he still was smoking. Then I . . . then . . .
I started screaming and I ran as fast as hell.
But he . . . well, he was standing there and . . .
                                        No one
had ever talked to me like that before!
So tell me: what was it I'd done? Just asked
for one. All right, a cigarette. So what if
it was? I know that smoking's bad. Yeah, sure,
but almost everybody smokes. And, really,
I didn't even feel like smoking! No,
I didn't plan to smoke it. All I wanted
to do was hold it . . . No! No, no! I didn't.
I didn't want to look grown-up. I said
I wouldn't have! But there, down in the harbor,
the lights were everywhere, like fireflies, too,
at anchorage . . . and here it also would've . . .
I can't explain it right . . . If you can help it—
please, don't tell Pop! He'll kill me . . . Yes, exactly.
I put it back. No, Granny was already
asleep. She hadn't even turned the set off.
The lines were flickering . . . Immediately,
I put it back immediately. Then I

got into bed! Don't tell my pop about it!
He'd murder me! Well, anyhow, I missed!
I missed—I didn't hit him, did I? Did I?!"

V

Name: such and such. Born: forty years ago.
State nationality. Unmarried. Children:
write "none." Preceding place of residence.
Is registered to live in. Where and when and
by whom deceased was found. List suspects.
As follows: three. So there it is—three suspects.
In general, the simple fact that one can
suspect three people of a murder is
extremely telling. Yes, unquestionably,
three people can perform the selfsame act.
Consume a roasted chicken, for example.
But this is murder. And the very fact that
suspicion fell on all of them provides
a guarantee that any of the suspects
was capable of murder. Consequently,
the whole investigation loses meaning—
because an inquest only tells you who
it was, but not that others couldn't do it . . .
Oh, come now! No! Get goose bumps? Fiddlesticks!
But on the whole, a man's ability to
commit a murder and, again, a man's
ability to probe it—even though there
exists a patent continuity
between them—aren't equivalent. That's certain.
Most likely, it's the impact of their closeness . . .
Oh, yes, indeed, it is—the whole affair's
lamentable . . .
               What's that? What's that you're saying?
You think the number in itself of those
on whom suspicion fell specifically
unites them, as it were, and in addition

26

in some way functions as an alibi?
That we can't hope to feed three people on
one chicken? Undeniably. And, as it
turns out, the murderer is not encompassed
within that circle, he's outside it. That
he's one of those who aren't in fact suspected!?
In other words, the murderer's the one
who doesn't have a motive for the murder!?
Yes, that's the way it happened this time. Yes,
you're quite correct . . . But that's . . .
                             why, that's . . . it's simply
an apologia for the absurd. An
apotheosis of the meaningless!
Delirium! So it turns out, then, that
it's logical. Hold on! Explain to me
the meaning of existence. Not a boy
emerging from the bushes in a jacket
who opens fire on you?! But if it's—if it's
so, why do we consider this a crime? And what
is more, investigate it! What a nightmare.
It turns out all our lives we're waiting to
be murdered, and thereby investigating
just proves to be a form of expectation,
and furthermore a criminal's not even
a criminal, and . . .
                   Sorry, I feel sick.
Come, let's go up on deck; it's stifling in here . . .
That's Yalta, yes. You see that—over there—
that building? No, a little higher, next to
the Monument . . . Just look how it's lit up!
It's pretty, isn't it? No, I can't tell you
how long they'll give him. No, that part of it
is not our business. It's the court's. Most likely
they'll give him . . . Sorry, at the moment I'm
not capable of focusing attention
on punishment. I just can't seem to breathe.

It's nothing, it'll pass. Yes, out at sea it
is sure to ease a bit. Livadia?
Right there. Yes, yes, that group of lights. Chic, isn't
it? Even in the night . . . I didn't hear you.
Yes, right, thank God. At last we're under way.

As the *Kolkhida* stirred a backwash, Yalta—
replete with all its flowers, palm trees, lights, and
vacationers still clinging to the doors of
already closed establishments, like flies
to lighted lamps—deliberately rolled
and started heaving to. A night above
the sea is different from a night above
dry land in just about the way a gaze
encountered in a mirror differs from
a gaze directed at another person . . .
And the *Kolkhida* put to sea. Astern
it left a foamy, hissing wake, and in
the midnight darkness the peninsula
was gradually melting. More precisely,
it was returning to the boundaries
of which our maps incessantly remind us.

[January-February] 1969

28

A Song to No Music

FOR FAITH WIGZELL

When you recall me in that land,
although this phrase isn't oracular—
a fact unthinkable for an
eye armed with tears as its binocular—

but just a fantasy whose string's
too limp for fishing out the very
date of this great event from ink-
like ponds of counting days; so when you,

beyond all seven seas, beyond
those lands whose sum is hardly shorter,
may, after all, recall me (though
I stress again: tears shrink the order

of everything except bygones)
nostalgically, in that Lord's summer,
and when you duly sigh (oh, don't
sigh), pondering the blinding number

of seas and fields flung out between
us, won't you notice something sadder:
i.e., the thing which led that train
of zeros was yourself.
                          A matter
quite likely of your hubris or,
more likely, of my own delusions,
or of the time not ripe yet for
our jumping to some brave conclusions:

still, it's surprising that a man
who fared so poorly as your guardian
against much lesser evils can
relieve you from this sighing burden.

The future is a form of dark;
compare it to a midnight's quiet;
there, in that future, too abstract
for us to have a right to eye it

together—which just proves that it
already has arrived, for we're
apart—so in this too concrete
future of ours that's clearly here,

and probably for long—a roar
of blizzard plus primeval howls
shrunk to words' status underscore
a wish to play at keeping house—

there, in that future, one thing will
console your heart or give some solace
—to that extent my voice is still
prophetic—to your mind, like stories

narrated by Scheherazade,
with the distinction that my fear
is rather posthumous while what
was hers dealt with plain death—so, dear,

let me now have, wagging my so-
called tongue of native asps, a try at
consoling you, while on the snow
their shadows make good Euclid triumph.

———

When you recall me in that land
on such and such day, month, Lord's summer,
beyond all seas and firmament
whose total I would hate to sum up

for it's much more than could be spent
by us, and having armed your pupil

with the said tear, take up a pen
and on a sheet of plain white paper

draw, like a buttress to the sky,
a perpendicular between two
quite humble points, for that's what, I
suppose, we will be shriveled into

by Time (who knows, by then we, both
invisible, may feel elation
at being famed at least as points)—
at any rate, a separation

is but a firmly drawn straight line,
and a date-hungry pair of lovers—
by that I mean your gaze and mine—
will climb up to the spheres where hovers

that perpendicular's sharp pin
(for, short of realms where angels wrangle,
there is no cave to hide them in);
and isn't that a fine triangle!

Let's analyze this figure which
would at another season force us
to wake up sweating, grab a switch,
tuck heads below the open faucet

to keep the mind from getting scorched
by horrid, all-consuming malice;
and if we both were saved from such
a fate and didn't drink this chalice

of jealousy, dark omens, lies,
spoils, comets, opiates, pure menace,
it was in order to entice
us in the end to sketch its semblance.

Let's analyze it. Time's upon
us: the embrace's stifling blindness
was in itself a pledge of an
invisibility that binds us

in separations: hid within
each other, we dodged space; our shoulder
blades played its borderline; I mean,
it couldn't hurdle them; small wonder

then that it smites a hundredfold
the treacherous—take pen and paper
(the latter symbolizing old
space here) and having found the proper

proportion—one may fancy all
space, since the world has limits, guarded
if not by some cherubic corps,
then by quite stratospheric ardent

emotion—having found it,
the straight line's (cutting us asunder)
proportion to the spacelike sheet,
and having spread an atlas under

this draft, break it into degrees,
then sacrifice that line to rigors
of their dense grid; and you will see
how life will overwhelm love's figures.

So let's presume the line's true length
is known to us, that it would feature
the given couple's lot, or, let
us be more accurate, a picture

of realms in which the two won't meet;
and if this estimate may enter

as a true one (alas, it may),
then, raised from this line's very center,

the perpendicular is but
a sum of these two piercing glances,
and due to their sheer force and jut,
the apex of our figure dances

within the stratosphere: it's quite
unlikely that their sum may ever
pitch higher, for each one's a side
of this isosceles endeavor.

Thus beams of two searchlights that prowl
advertently a hostile chaos
discover their elusive goal
crisscrossing far beyond night clouds;

the goal, though, isn't a target for
the soldiers: in its core, it's rather
a mirror where some would stare
while scared of looking at each other

directly; therefore, who else
but me, one side of that great figure,
should tackle for you this inverse
trite theorem where life, beleaguer-

ing our eyes with all kinds of
its certified scarecrows, gets formal
and tells us to determine now
our angle—in plain words: a corner.

That's what's been *given*. In a guise
of years, of all landscapes, or better
still, in a form of otherwise
unpalpable pervasive matter.

That's our meeting place. A spot
in clouds. A seraphic grotto.
A pergola in spheres. A sort
of corner—a good one, I ought to

admit: there is no one to seize
us hiding in those fleecy orchards
owned solely by our eyes:
the ultimate attempt to purchase.

In years that lie ahead—at best
we'll meet right after death—we'll surely
try to domesticate this nest
by lining it, in night shifts, duly,

with all the trash of lonely thoughts,
of things unsaid—with all that litter
which we'd pile up in our slots
so that it will, sooner or later,

acquire mass enough to strut,
a semblance of material substance,
a status of a star and that
intrinsic light which hardly suffers

because of clouds: for Euclid sees
to it himself that spheres encourage
two corners, alias angles, with
a third one. And it makes a marriage.

That's our *given* then. For quite
a while. Until we hit the coffin.
Apart. Out of each other's sight.
Though from that apex we'll be often

observed; perhaps too often: day
and night, and under either ceiling,

Eastern or Western. And we may
get quite enslaved by that all-seeing

eye finally. No matter how
securely real things imprison
the dark, put this bright pupil now
into your charts, before the risen

all-seeing eye has made out some
of our words! So separation
means our three sharp angles' sum,
while all its agony (let's ration-

alize) is just a product of
their mutual gravitation, which is
far stronger than the other stuff's,
than that of earth's with all its riches.

—————

Scholastics, you may utter. Yes,
scholastics, and a shameless hide-and-
seek game with grief. But look and guess:
a star above the sea horizon,

what is it but (permit this turn
so that you won't detect a surplus
of elevated style) a corn
rubbed by the light on space's surface?

Scholastics? Almost. Just as well.
God knows. Take any for a spastic
consent. For after all, pray tell,
what in this world is not scholastic?

God knows. It's rather late. I sink
deep into drowsiness. And winter's

demise in windows builds no link
to springtime. Like the cause that withers

bereft of its effect. My mind
swarms with odd numbers, angles, corners,
with your or my palm stroking my
or your cheekbone.
                    When you recall me
someday, recall the wrapped in black
night shrouds, hanging high, somewhere
out there, over Skagerrak,
accompanied by somewhat gayer

clear planets, shimmering with mist-
like distant light, a lone, name-lacking
star that in fact does not exist.
But this is what the Art of loving

or that of living's all about:
to see that flesh that nature hasn't,
and where the vacuum is, scout
for treasures and for omnipresent

winged female-breasted lions or
dark idols, rather small but able,
great eagles that foretell the score.
Much simpler, then, than all this labor

of making up these things, of spin-
ning promptly from both earth and water
their epidermis and so on,
to set in space a mere iota.

Point out into the midnight haze.
In which direction? Well, in either.
What matters is not what life has,
but just one's faith in what should be there.

Point your sharp finger in the dark:
there, like an alto left to harden
in highest pitch, should be a star;
and if it isn't up there, pardon

long similes, their worn supply;
like roosters that have missed their hour,
the mind, diminished badly by
our parting, simply tries to soar.

1970

37

The End of a Beautiful Era

Since the stern art of poetry calls for words, I, morose,
deaf, and balding ambassador of a more or less
   insignificant nation that's stuck in this super
power, wishing to spare my old brain,
hand myself my own topcoat and head for the main
   street: to purchase the evening paper.

Wind disperses the foliage. The dimness of old bulbs in these
sorry quarters, whose motto's "The mirror will please,"
   gives a sense of abundance supported by puddles.
Even thieves here steal apples by scratching the amalgam first.
Yet the feeling one gets, from one's own sweet reflection—this feeling I've
                                     lost.
   That's what really puzzles.

Everything in these parts is geared for winter: long dreams,
prison walls, overcoats, bridal dresses of whiteness that seems
   snowlike. Drinks. Kinds of soap matching dirt in dark corners.
Sparrow vests, second hand of the watch round your wrist,
puritanical mores, underwear. And, tucked in the violinists'
   palms, old redwood hand warmers.

This whole realm is just static. Imagining the output of lead
and cast iron, and shaking your stupefied head,
   you recall bayonets, Cossack whips of old power.
Yet the eagles land like good lodestones on the scraps.
Even wicker chairs here are built mostly with bolts and with nuts,
   one is bound to discover.

Only fish in the sea seem to know freedom's price.
Still, their muteness compels us to sit and devise
   cashier booths of our own. And space rises like some bill of fare.
Time's invented by death. In its search for the objects, it deals

with raw vegetables first. That's why cocks are so keen on the bells
chiming deafly somewhere.

To exist in the Era of Deeds and to stay elevated, alert
ain't so easy, alas. Having raised a long skirt,
    you will find not new wonders but what you expected.
And it's not that they play Lobachevsky's ideas by ear,
but the widened horizons should narrow somewhere, and here—
    here's the end of perspective.

Either old Europe's map has been swiped by the gents in plain clothes,
or the famous five-sixths of remaining landmass has just lost
    its poor infamous colleague, or a fairy casts spells over shabby
me, who knows—but I cannot escape from this place;
I pour wine for myself (service here's a disgrace),
    sip, and rub my old tabby.

Thus the brain earned a slug, as a spot where an error occurred
earns a good pointing finger. Or should I hit waterways, sort
    of like Christ? Anyway, in these laudable quarters,
eyes dumbfounded by ice and by booze
will reproach you alike for whatever you choose:
    traceless rails, traceless waters.

Now let's see what they say in the papers about lawsuits.
"The condemned has been dealt with." Having read this, a denizen puts
    on his metal-rimmed glasses that help to relate it
to a man lying flat, his face down, by the wall;
though he isn't asleep. Since dreams spurn a skull
    that has been perforated.

The keen-sightedness of our era takes root in the times
which were short, in their blindness, of drawing clear lines
    twixt those fallen from cradles and fallen from saddles.
Though there are plenty of saucers, there is no one to turn tables with
to subject you, poor Rurik, to a sensible quiz;
    that's what really saddens.

The keen-sightedness of our days is the sort that befits the dead end
whose concrete begs for spittle and not for a witty comment.
   Wake up a dinosaur, not a prince, to recite you the moral!
Birds have feathers for penning last words, though it's better to ask.
All the innocent head has in store for itself is an ax
   plus the evergreen laurel.

[December] 1969
Leningrad

Lithuanian Divertissement

FOR TOMAS VENCLOVA

I / Introduction
A modest little country by the sea.
It has its snow, an airport, telephones,
its Jews. A tyrant's brownstone villa.
A statue of a bard is there as well,
who once compared his country to his girlfriend.

The simile displayed, if not good taste,
sound geography: for here the southerners
make Saturday the day to go up north,
from whence, a little drunk, on foot,
they have been known to stray into the West—
a good theme for a sketch. Here distances
are well designed to suit hermaphrodites.

Noonday in springtime. Puddles, banked-up clouds,
stout, countless angels on the gables
of countless churches. Here a man
becomes a victim of a jostling crowd,
or a detail of the homemade baroque.

II / Liejyklos
To be born a century ago
and over the down bedding, airing,
through a window see a garden grow
and Catherine's crosses, twin domes soaring;
be embarrassed for Mother, hiccup
when the brandished lorgnettes scrutinize
and push a cart with rubbish heaped up
along the ghetto's yellow alleys,
sigh, tucked in bed from head to toe,
for Polish ladies, for example;

and hang around to face the foe
and fall in Poland somewhere, trampled—
for Faith, Tsar, Homeland, or if not,
then shape Jews' ringlets into sideburns
and off, on to the New World like a shot,
puking in waves as the engine churns.

III / Café Neringa
Time departs in Vilnius through a café door
accompanied by sounds of clinking forks and spoons,
while Space screws up its eyes from booze the night before
and stares at Time's slowly retreating spine.

A crimson circle, with its far side off,
now hangs moored in utter stillness over roof tiles
and the Adam's apple sharpens, quite as if
the whole face had shrunk to its sheer profile.

Obeying commands like Aladdin's lamp,
a waitress decked out in a cambric halter
saunters about with legs recently clamped
around the neck of a local footballer.

IV / Escutcheon
St. George, that old dragon slayer,
spear long lost in allegory's glare,
has kept in safety up till now
his sword and steed, and every place
in Lithuania pursues, steadfast,
his aim unheeded by the crowd.

Who now has he, sword clenched in hand,
resolved on taking? What he hounds,
a well-placed coat of arms blots out.
Who can it be? Gentile? Saracen?
The whole world, perhaps? If that's so, then
Vytautas knew well what he was about.

V / *Amicum-philosophum de melancholia, mania et plica polonica*

Sleeplessness. Part of a woman. A glass
replete with reptiles all straining to get out.
The day's long madness has drained across
the cerebellum into the occiput,
forming a pool; one movement and the slush
will feel as if someone, in that icy blot,
has dipped a sharpened quill that, after a pause,
deliberately traces the verb "hate"
in oscillating scribbles to reverse
the brain-wave pattern. Something lipsticked stuffs
the ear with lacerating lengthy words,
like running fingers through a hairdo stiff
with lice. Alone and naked in your sack,
you lie there, fallen from the zodiac.

VI / *Palanga*

Only the sea has power to peer *en face*
at the sky; and a traveler in the dunes
lowers his eyes and sips at his metal flask
like a king in exile, with no psalm-like tunes.

His house ransacked, flocks driven to foreign land.
Son hidden by shepherds inside a cave.
And before him lies just a hem of sand
but his faith's not enough for a walk on waves.

VII / *The Dominicans*

Turn off the thoroughfare, then into
a half-blind street, and once inside
the church, which at this hour is empty,
sit on a bench, adjust your sight,
and, afterward, in God's whorled ear,
closed to the clash of day's discord,
whisper four syllables, soft and clear:
    Forgive me, Lord.

1971

On Love

Twice I woke up tonight and wandered to
the window. And the lights down on the street,
like pale omission points, tried to complete
the fragment of a sentence spoken through
sleep, but diminished into darkness, too.

I'd dreamt that you were pregnant, and in spite
of having lived so many years apart
I still felt guilty and my heartened palm
caressed your belly as, by the bedside,
it fumbled for my trousers and the light

switch on the wall. And with the bulb turned on
I knew that I was leaving you alone
there, in the darkness, in the dream, where calmly
you waited till I might return,
not trying to reproach or scold me

for the unnatural hiatus. For
darkness restores what light cannot repair.
There we are married, blest, we make once more
the two-backed beast and children are the fair
excuse of what we're naked for.

Some future night you will appear again.
You'll come to me, worn out and thin now, after
things in between, and I'll see son or daughter
not named as yet. This time I will restrain
my hand from groping for the switch, afraid

and feeling that I have no right
to leave you both like shadows by that sever-

ing fence of days that bar your sight,
voiceless, negated by the real light
that keeps me unattainable forever.

[February] 1971

I Sit by the Window

FOR LEV LOSEFF

I said fate plays a game without a score,
and who needs fish if you've got caviar?
The triumph of the Gothic style would come to pass
and turn you on—no need for coke, or grass.
   I sit by the window. Outside, an aspen.
   When I loved, I loved deeply. It wasn't often.

I said the forest's only part of a tree.
Who needs the whole girl if you've got her knee?
Sick of the dust raised by the modern era,
the Russian eye would rest on an Estonian spire.
   I sit by the window. The dishes are done.
   I was happy here. But I won't be again.

I wrote: The bulb looks at the floor in fear,
and love, as an act, lacks a verb; the zer-
o Euclid thought the vanishing point became
wasn't math—it was the nothingness of Time.
   I sit by the window. And while I sit
   my youth comes back. Sometimes I'd smile. Or spit.

I said that the leaf may destroy the bud;
what's fertile falls in fallow soil—a dud;
that on the flat field, the unshadowed plain
nature spills the seeds of trees in vain.
I sit by the window. Hands lock my knees.
My heavy shadow's my squat company.

My song was out of tune, my voice was cracked,
but at least no chorus can ever sing it back.
That talk like this reaps no reward bewilders
no one—no one's legs rest on my shoulders.

I sit by the window in the dark. Like an express,
the waves behind the wavelike curtain crash.

A loyal subject of these second-rate years,
I proudly admit that my finest ideas
are second-rate, and may the future take them
as trophies of my struggle against suffocation.
   I sit in the dark. And it would be hard to figure out
   which is worse: the dark inside, or the darkness out.

1971

Nature Morte

Verrà la morte e avrà i tuoi occhi.

—CESARE PAVESE

I

People and things crowd in.
Eyes can be bruised and hurt
by people as well as things.
Better to live in the dark.

I sit on a wooden bench
watching the passers-by—
sometimes whole families.
I am fed up with the light.

This is a winter month.
First on the calendar.
I shall begin to speak
when I'm fed up with the dark.

II

It's time. I shall now begin.
It makes no difference with what.
Open mouth. It is better to speak,
although I can also be mute.

What then shall I talk about?
Shall I talk about nothingness?
Shall I talk about days, or nights?
Or people? No, only things,

since people will surely die.
All of them. As I shall.
All talk is a barren trade.
A writing on the wind's wall.

III

My blood is very cold—
its cold is more withering
than iced-to-the-bottom streams.
People are not my thing.

I hate the look of them.
Grafted to life's great tree,
each face is firmly stuck
and cannot be torn free.

Something the mind abhors
shows in each face and form.
Something like flattery
of persons quite unknown.

IV

Things are more pleasant. Their
outsides are neither good
nor evil. And their insides
reveal neither good nor bad.

The core of things is dry rot.
Dust. A wood borer. And
brittle moth-wings. Thin walls.
Uncomfortable to the hand.

Dust. When you switch lights on,
there's nothing but dust to see.
That's true even if the thing
is sealed up hermetically.

V

This ancient cabinet—
outside as well as in—
strangely reminds me of
Paris's Notre Dame.

49

Everything's dark within
it. Dust mop or bishop's stole
can't touch the dust of things.
Things themselves, as a rule,

don't try to purge or tame
the dust of their own insides.
Dust is the flesh of time.
Time's very flesh and blood.

VI

Lately I often sleep
during the daytime. My
death, it would seem, is now
trying and testing me,

placing a mirror close
to my still-breathing lips,
seeing if I can stand
non-being in daylight.

I do not move. These two
thighs are like blocks of ice.
Branched veins show blue against
skin that is marble white.

VII

Summing their angles up
as a surprise to us,
things drop away from man's
world—a world made with words.

Things do not move, or stand.
That's our delirium.
Each thing's a space, beyond
which there can be no thing.

A thing can be battered, burned,
gutted, and broken up.
Thrown out. And yet the thing
never will yell, "Oh, fuck!"

VIII

A tree. Its shadow, and
earth, pierced by clinging roots.
Interlaced monograms.
Clay and a clutch of rocks.

Roots interweave and blend.
Stones have their private mass
which frees them from the bond
of normal rootedness.

This stone is fixed. One can't
move it, or heave it out.
Tree shadows catch a man,
like a fish, in their net.

IX

A thing. Its brown color. Its
blurry outline. Twilight.
Now there is nothing left.
Only a *nature morte*.

Death will come and will find
a body whose silent peace
will reflect death's approach
like any woman's face.

Scythe, skull, and skeleton—
an absurd pack of lies.
Rather: "Death, when it comes,
will have your own two eyes."

X

Mary now speaks to Christ:
"Are you my son?—or God?
You are nailed to the cross.
Where lies my homeward road?

"Can I pass through my gate
not having understood:
Are you dead?—or alive?
Are you my son?—or God?"

Christ speaks to her in turn:
"Whether dead or alive,
woman, it's all the same—
son or God, I am thine."

[June] 1971

52

December 24, 1971

FOR V.S.

When it's Christmas we're all of us magi.
At the grocers' all slipping and pushing.
Where a tin of halvah, coffee-flavored,
is the cause of a human assault-wave
by a crowd heavy-laden with parcels:
each one his own king, his own camel.

Nylon bags, carrier bags, paper cones,
caps and neckties all twisted up sideways.
Reek of vodka and resin and cod,
orange mandarins, cinnamon, apples.
Floods of faces, no sign of a pathway
toward Bethlehem, shut off by blizzard.

And the bearers of moderate gifts
leap on buses and jam all the doorways,
disappear into courtyards that gape,
though they know that there's nothing inside there:
not a beast, not a crib, nor yet her,
round whose head gleams a nimbus of gold.

Emptiness. But the mere thought of that
brings forth lights as if out of nowhere.
Herod reigns but the stronger he is,
the more sure, the more certain the wonder.
In the constancy of this relation
is the basic mechanics of Christmas.

That's what they celebrate everywhere,
for its coming push tables together.
No demand for a star for a while,
but a sort of good will touched with grace

can be seen in all men from afar,
and the shepherds have kindled their fires.

Snow is falling: not smoking but sounding
chimney pots on the roof, every face like a stain.
Herod drinks. Every wife hides her child.
He who comes is a mystery: features
are not known beforehand, men's hearts may
not be quick to distinguish the stranger.

But when drafts through the doorway disperse
the thick mist of the hours of darkness
and a shape in a shawl stands revealed,
both a newborn and Spirit that's Holy
in your self you discover; you stare
skyward, and it's right there:

a star.

1972

To a Tyrant

He used to come here till he donned gold braid,
a good topcoat on, self-controlled, stoop-shouldered.
Arresting these café habitués—
he started snuffing out world culture somewhat later—
seemed sweet revenge (on Time, that is, not them)
for all the lack of cash, the sneers and insults,
the lousy coffee, boredom, and the battles
at vingt-et-un he lost time and again.

And Time has had to stomach that revenge.
The place is now quite crowded; bursts of laughter,
records boom out. But just before you sit
you seem to feel an urge to turn your head around.
Plastic and chrome are everywhere—not right;
the pastries have an aftertaste of bromide.
Sometimes before the place shuts down he'll enter
straight from a theater, anonymous, no fuss.

When he comes in, the lot of them stand up.
Some out of duty, the rest in unfeigned joy.
Limp-wristed, with a languid sweep of palm,
he gives the evening back its cozy feel.
He drinks his coffee—better, nowadays—
and bites a roll, while perching on his chair,
so tasty that the very dead would cry
"Oh, yes!" if only they could rise and be there.

[January] 1972

The Funeral of Bobò

I

Bobò is dead, but don't take off your hat.
No gesture we could make will help us bear it.
Why mount a butterfly upon the spit
of the Admiralty tower? We'd only tear it.

On every side, no matter where you glance,
are squares of windows. As for "What happened?"—well,
open an empty can by way of answer,
and say, "Just that, as near as one can tell."

Bobò is dead. Wednesday is almost over.
On streets which offer you no place to go,
such whiteness lies. Only the night river,
with its black water, does not wear the snow.

II

Bobò is dead; there's sadness in this line.
O window squares, O arches' semicircles,
and such fierce frost that if one's to be slain,
let blazing firearms do the dirty work.

Farewell, Bobò, my beautiful and sweet.
These teardrops dot the page like holes in cheese.
We are too weak to follow you, and yet
to take a stand exceeds our energies.

Your image, as I here and now predict,
whether in crackling cold or waves of heat,
shall never dwindle—quite the reverse, in fact—
in Rossi's matchless, long, and tapering street.

III

Bobò is dead. Something I might convey
slips from my grasp, as bath soap sometimes does.
Today, within a dream, I seemed to lie
upon my bed. And there, in fact, I was.

Tear off a page, but read the date aright:
it's with a zero that our woes commence.
Without her, dreams suggest the waking state,
and squares of air push through the window vents.

Bobò is dead. One feels an impulse, with
half-parted lips, to murmur "Why? What for?"
It's emptiness, no doubt, which follows death.
That's likelier than hell—and worse, what's more.

IV

You were all things, Bobò. But your decease
has changed you. You are nothing; you are not;
or, rather, you are a clot of emptiness—
which also, come to think of it, is a lot.

Bobò is dead. To these round eyes, the view
of the bare horizon line is like a knife.
But neither Kiki nor Zazà, Bobò,
will ever take your place. Not on your life.

Now Thursday. I believe in emptiness.
There, it's like hell, but shittier, I've heard.
And the new Dante, pregnant with his message,
bends to the empty page and writes a word.

[March] 1972

57

Letters to a Roman Friend

I

Now it's windy and the waves are running crisscross.
    Soon it will be fall, and nature's face will alter.
Shifts in these bright colors stir me more profoundly,
    Postumus, than changes in my lady's wardrobe.

To a certain point a girl can satisfy you—
    if you don't go farther than her knees or elbows.
But how much more joyous the unbodied beauty
    of an autumn wood: no kisses, no betrayals!

II

Postumus, I'm sending books, I hope you'll like them.
    How's Imperial Rome?—A soft bed, hard to sleep on?
How fares Caesar? What's he up to? Still intriguing?
    —Still intriguing, probably, and overeating.

In the garden where I sit a torch is burning.
    I'm alone—no lady, servant, or acquaintance.
Not the humble of this world, nor yet its mighty—
    nothing but the buzzing of an insect chorus.

III

In this graveyard lies a merchant out of Asia.
    He was clever, able, yet he passed unnoticed.
He died suddenly, of fever. Not to this end
    did he sail here, but to make a profit.

Underneath unpolished quartz there lies beside him
    an Imperial legionnaire, renowned in battle.
Target of a thousand thrusts, he lived till eighty.
    Rules here, Postumus, are proved by their exceptions.

IV

Birds aren't very bright, my Postumus, that's certain;
    but there's misery enough even for bird-brains.
If one's fated to be born in Caesar's Empire
    let him live aloof, provincial, by the seashore.

One who lives remote from snowstorms, and from Caesar,
    has no need to hurry, flatter, play the coward.
You may say that local governors are vultures.
    I, for one, prefer a vulture to a vampire.

V

I'm prepared, hetaera, to wait out this downpour
    in your company. But let us have no haggling.
Snatching silver coins from this, my covering body,
    is like ripping shingles from the roof above you.

This roof's sprung a leak, you say? But where's the puddle?
    I have never left a wet spot; no, not ever.
Better go and find yourself a proper husband:
    he will do it to your sheets and pay the laundry.

VI

Here we've spent—I swear it—more than half our lifetimes.
    As a slave—now white-haired—told me near the tavern:
"When we look around us, all we see is ruins."
    A barbarian perspective, though a true one.

I'm back from the mountains carrying fresh wildflowers.
    I'll get out a jug and fill it with cool water.
What's the latest from that Libya or wherever?
    Are we still engaged in all that desert fighting?

VII

Friend, do you remember our Proconsul's sister—
    rather skinny, though her calves were heavy?

You had slept with her . . . Well, she became a priestess—
    priestess, Postumus, with gods for her companions.

Come and visit me, and we'll drink wine together.
    Plums are ripe and bread is good. You'll bring the gossip.
I shall make your couch up in the star-swept garden
    and teach you to name our local constellations.

VIII

Soon, dear Postumus, your friend who loves addition
    will pay off his debt, his old debt, to subtraction.
Take my savings, then, from underneath my pillow—
    though not much, they'll pay the cost of my interment.

Post on your black mare to the House of Hetaeras
    hard against the wall of our provincial city.
Give each girl the sum for which she once embraced me:
    let them mourn me for the same amount of money.

IX

Dark green laurels on the verge of trembling.
    Doors ajar. The windowpane is dusty.
Idle chairs and the abandoned sofa.
    Linen blinded by the sun of noonday.

Pontus drones past a black fence of pine trees.
    Someone's boat braves gusts out by the promontory.
On the garden bench a book of Pliny rustles.
    Thrushes chirp within the hairdo of the cypress.

[March] 1972

Nunc Dimittis

When Mary first came to present the Christ Child
to God in his temple, she found—of those few
who fasted and prayed there, departing not from it—
      devout Simeon and the prophetess Anna.

The holy man took the babe up in his arms.
The three of them, lost in the grayness of dawn,
now stood like a small shifting frame that surrounded
      the child in the palpable dark of the temple.

The temple enclosed them in forests of stone.
Its lofty vaults stooped as though trying to cloak
the prophetess Anna, and Simeon, and Mary—
      to hide them from men and to hide them from heaven.

And only a chance ray of light struck the hair
of that sleeping infant, who stirred but as yet
was conscious of nothing and blew drowsy bubbles;
      old Simeon's arms held him like a stout cradle.

It had been revealed to this upright old man
that he would not die until his eyes had seen
the Son of the Lord. And it thus came to pass. And
      he said: "Now, O Lord, lettest thou thy poor servant,

according to thy holy word, leave in peace,
for mine eyes have witnessed thine offspring: he is
thy continuation and also the source of
      thy light for idolatrous tribes, and the glory

of Israel as well." Then old Simeon paused.
The silence, regaining the temple's clear space,

oozed from all its corners and almost engulfed them,
and only his echoing words grazed the rafters,

to spin for a moment, with faint rustling sounds,
high over their heads in the tall temple's vaults,
akin to a bird that can soar, yet that cannot
    return to the earth, even if it should want to.

A strangeness engulfed them. The silence now seemed
as strange as the words of old Simeon's speech.
And Mary, confused and bewildered, said nothing—
    so strange had his words been. He added, while turning

directly to Mary: "Behold, in this child,
now close to thy breast, is concealed the great fall
of many, the great elevation of others,
    a subject of strife and a source of dissension,

and that very steel which will torture his flesh
shall pierce through thine own soul as well. And that wound
will show to thee, Mary, as in a new vision
    what lies hidden, deep in the hearts of all people."

He ended and moved toward the temple's great door.
Old Anna, bent down with the weight of her years,
and Mary, now stooping, gazed after him, silent.
    He moved and grew smaller, in size and in meaning,

to these two frail women who stood in the gloom.
As though driven on by the force of their looks,
he strode through the cold empty space of the temple
    and moved toward the whitening blur of the doorway.

The stride of his old legs was steady and firm.
When Anna's voice sounded behind him, he slowed
his step for a moment. But she was not calling
    to him; she had started to bless God and praise Him.

The door came still closer. The wind stirred his robe
and fanned at his forehead; the roar of the street,
exploding in life by the door of the temple,
   beat stubbornly into old Simeon's hearing.

He went forth to die. It was not the loud din
of streets that he faced when he flung the door wide,
but rather the deaf-and-dumb fields of death's kingdom.
   He strode through a space that was no longer solid.

The rustle of time ebbed away in his ears.
And Simeon's soul held the form of the child—
its feathery crown now enveloped in glory—
   aloft, like a torch, pressing back the black shadows,

to light up the path that leads into death's realm,
where never before until this present hour
had any man managed to lighten his pathway.
   The old man's torch glowed and the pathway grew wider.

February 16, 1972

Odysseus to Telemachus

My dear Telemachus,
                    The Trojan War
is over now; I don't recall who won it.
The Greeks, no doubt, for only they would leave
so many dead so far from their own homeland.
But still, my homeward way has proved too long.
While we were wasting time there, old Poseidon,
it almost seems, stretched and extended space.

I don't know where I am or what this place
can be. It would appear some filthy island,
with bushes, buildings, and great grunting pigs.
A garden choked with weeds; some queen or other.
Grass and huge stones . . . Telemachus, my son!
To a wanderer the faces of all islands
resemble one another. And the mind
trips, numbering waves; eyes, sore from sea horizons,
run; and the flesh of water stuffs the ears.
I can't remember how the war came out;
even how old you are—I can't remember.

Grow up, then, my Telemachus, grow strong.
Only the gods know if we'll see each other
again. You've long since ceased to be that babe
before whom I reined in the plowing bullocks.
Had it not been for Palamedes' trick
we two would still be living in one household.
But maybe he was right; away from me
you are quite safe from all Oedipal passions,
and your dreams, my Telemachus, are blameless.

[March] 1972

64

An autumn evening in the modest square
of a small town proud to have made the atlas
(some frenzy drove that poor mapmaker witless,
or else he had the daughter of the mayor).

Here Space appears unnerved by its own feats
and glad to drop the burden of its greatness—
to shrink to the dimensions of Main Street;
and Time, chilled to its bone, stares at the clockface
above the general store, whose crowded shelves
hold every item that this world produces,
from fancy amateur stargazers' tel-
escopes to common pins for common uses.

A movie theater, a few saloons,
around the bend a café with drawn shutters,
a red-brick bank topped with spread-eagle plumes,
a church, whose net—to fish for men—now flutters
unfilled, and which would be paid little heed,
except that it stands next to the post office.
And if parishioners should cease to breed,
the pastor would start christening their autos.

Grasshoppers, in the silence, run amok.
By 6 p.m. the city streets are empty,
unpeopled as if by a nuclear strike.
Just surfacing, the moon swims to the center
of this black window square, like some Eccles-
iastes, glowering; while on the lonely
highway, from time to time, a Buick beams
its blinding headlights at the Unknown Soldier.

The dreams you dream are not of girls half nude
but of your name on an arriving letter.
A morning milkman, seeing milk that's soured,
will be the first to guess that you have died here.

Here you can live, ignoring calendars,
gulp Bromo, never leave the house; just settle
and stare at your reflection in the glass,
as streetlamps stare at theirs in shrinking puddles.

1972

1972

FOR V.G.

Birds don't fly through my skylight nowadays.
A girl, like a beast, guards her noble place.
If I chance to slip up on nobody's
cherrystone, I don't fall, since friction's
increased with the failed velocity.
The heart, like a squirrel in brushwood, is tossing up
ribs. And the throat celebrates the atrocity
of old age; lists its huge afflictions.

Aging! Hail to thee, senility.
Blood flows as slowly as chilly tea.
Limbs, former pride of the whole vicinity,
hurt my vision. And rather gingerly
I stuff the threatened fifth field of feeling—
when taking my shoes off—with cotton fillings.
The man with a spade is now a fitting
sight, as the knife said to the injury.

Rightly so! The body repents its proclivities.
All these singing, weeping, and snarled activities.
As for my dental cave, its cavities
rival old Troy on a rainy day.
Joints cracking loud and breath like a sewer,
I foul the mirror. It's premature
to talk of the shroud. But you may be sure,
those who'll carry you out besiege the doorway.

Well met, then, joyful, young, unfamiliar
tribe! Buzzing around my jugular,
time has discovered at last its singular
sweetmeat in my resilient cranium.
Thoughts are uncombed and a pogrom scours
my scalp. Like Ivan's queen in her tower,

all fibers sense the dark breathing powers;
I scramble the bedding but try to carry on.

Frightening! That's it, exactly, frightening.
Even when all the wheels of the train keep thundering
below your waistline, there is no faltering
for the flight of fancy. Like the amnesia-
stricken gaze of a graduate with his freckled face,
who confuses a bra with a pair of spectacles,
pain is weak-eyed and death in its speckledness
looks like the vague outlines of Asia.

All that I could have lost has been totally
lost. But also I've gained approximately
all those things I was in for. Oddly
enough, even a cuckoo's crooning in darkness
moves me little—let life be vilified
by her plangent notes, or affirmed and verified.
Aging is growth of a new but a very fine
hearing that only to silence hearkens.

Aging! The body reeks of mortality,
that is, of what's useless to life. From my metallic brow
the radiance cast over this locality
vanishes. And at noon a black searchlight harbors
in my sunken pupils. The strength, the gallantry
are stolen away from my muscles cowardly.
But I do not search for a gallows tree:
shameful to take on the Lord's own labors.

The point is, most likely, pure cowardice.
Fear. The technical side of the enterprise.
It's the imminent necrosis's menacing old device:
any erosion begins with willing,
the minimum of which is the heart, the basis
of stasis. Or so I was told while in that oasis
of school. Remove, dear chums, your faces!
Let me out into open valley!

I was much like the rest, that is, lived a similar
life. Would appear in halls with wisteria.
Drank a fair bit. Dragged my fool under the skin of a . . .
Used to take what was given. The soul didn't hanker for
what wasn't hers. Had a stable ground,
fashioned a lever. Or would produce a sound
from my hollow pipe fitting the space around.
What should I say before curtain fall?

Listen, my boon brethren and my enemies!
What I've done, I've done not for fame or memories
in this era of radio waves and cinemas,
but for the sake of my native tongue and letters.
For which sort of devotion, of a zealous bent
("Heal thyself, doctor," as the saying went),
denied a chalice at the feast of the fatherland,
now I stand in a strange place. The name hardly matters.

It's windy, dank, dark. And it's windy. Hence
midnight flings branches and leaves onto fence
and roof tiles. Now I can state with confidence:
here I'll live out my days, losing gradually
hair, teeth, consonants, verbs, and suffixes,
with this hat of mine ladling the ocean surface, as
with Prince Igor's helmet, just to reduce its size,
munching raw fish, behaving naturally.

Aging! The time of success. Of acknowledging
truth. Of its sullied linen. Of banishment. Of discouraging
pain. As for the latter, I neither nourish it
nor dismiss it. If it gets hard, annoying,
I'll yell out: self-restraint is just dumb and morbid.
As for now, I can take a bit more of it.
If an ember still glows inside this monolith,
it's not reason, just blood that keeps circling, going.

This song isn't the desperate howl of deep distress.
It's the species' trip back to the wilderness.

It's, more aptly, the first cry of speechlessness,
whose domain could be thought just a total feat
of sounds voiced by a once scarlet and
wet—now hardening into a moribund
more or less matter—strong vocal vent.
Change for the better. Or that's my view of it.

Lo! that's the point of my speech, I'm proud of making it:
of the body's conversion into a naked thing,
object—against a vast, vacant, and
empty space, be it lit up by so much fire.
Still, change for the best, since fright, horror, shudders
are alien to objects. So little puddles
won't be found under objects like under others,
even when your small object is to expire.

Just like Theseus out from the lair in the Minos ring,
coming up for air with the pelt of that menacing
beast, it's not a horizon I see but a minus sign
on my previous life. This line is clearly
keener than a hero's sword, and shorn off by its cutting blade
the dearest part. Thus they take away a costly blend
from the sober man, and salt from what's bland.
I feel like crying. But it's pointless, really.

Beat, then, the drum of your faith in shears
where the fate of all matter these days inheres.
Only a good-sized loss in the local spheres
makes a mortal equal to God. (This arching
observation is worthy of real emphasis
even in the view of amorous nakedness.)
Beat, see how much sticks and drums can take of this,
marching along while your shadow's marching.

[December 18] 1972

In the Lake District

In those days, in a place where dentists thrive
(their daughters order fancy clothes from London;
their painted forceps hold aloft on signboards
a common and abstracted Wisdom Tooth),
there I—whose mouth held ruins more abject
than any Parthenon—a spy, a spearhead
for some fifth column of a rotting culture
(my cover was a lit. professorship),
was living at a college near the most
renowned of the fresh-water lakes; the function
to which I'd been appointed was to wear out
the patience of the ingenuous local youth.

Whatever I wrote then was incomplete:
my lines expired in strings of dots. Collapsing,
I dropped, still fully dressed, upon my bed.
At night I stared up at the darkened ceiling
until I saw a shooting star, which then,
conforming to the laws of self-combustion,
would flash—before I'd even made a wish—
across my cheek and down onto my pillow.

[November] 1972
Ann Arbor

71

The Butterfly

Should I say that you're dead?
You touched so brief a fragment
of time. There's much that's sad in
the joke God played.
I scarcely comprehend
the words "you've lived"; the date of
your birth and when you faded
in my cupped hand
are one, and not two dates.
Thus calculated,
your term is, simply stated,
less than a day.

It's clear that days for us
are nothings, zeros.
They can't be pinned down near us
to feed our eyes.
Whenever days stand stark
against white borders,
since they possess no bodies,
they leave no mark.
They are like you. That is,
each butterfly's small plumage
is one day's shrunken image—
a tenth its size.

Should I say that, somehow,
you lack all being?
What, then, are my hands feeling
that's so like you?

Such colors can't be drawn
from nonexistence.
Tell me, at whose insistence
were yours laid on?
Since I'm a mumbling heap
of words, not pigments,
how could your hues be figments
of my conceit?

IV
There are, on your small wings,
black spots and splashes—
like eyes, birds, girls, eyelashes.
But of what things
are you the airy norm?
What bits of faces,
what broken times and places
shine through your form?
As for your *nature mortes*;
do they show dishes
of fruits and flowers, or fishes
displayed on boards?

V
Perhaps a landscape smokes
among your ashes,
and with thick reading glasses
I'll scan its slopes—
its beaches, dancers, nymphs.
Is it as bright as
the day, or dark as night is?
And could one glimpse—
ascending that sky's screen—
some blazing lantern?
And tell me, please, what pattern
inspired this scene?

VI

It seems to me you are
a protean creature,
whose markings mask a feature
of face, or stone, or star.
Who was the jeweler,
brow uncontracted,
who from our world extracted
your miniature—
a world where madness brings
us low, and lower,
where we are things, while you are
the thought of things?

VII

Why were these lovely shapes
and colors given
for your one day of life in
this land of lakes?
—a land whose dappled mir-
rors have one merit:
reflecting space, they store it.
Such brief existence tore
away your chance
to be captured, delivered,
within cupped hands to quiver—
the hunter's eye entrance.

VIII

You shun every response—
but not from shyness
or wickedness or slyness,
and not because
you're dead. Dead or alive,
to God's least creature
is given voice for speech, or
for song—a sign

that it has found a way
to bind together,
and stretch life's limits, whether
an hour or day.

IX

But you lack even this:
the means to utter
a word. Yet, probe the matter;
it's better thus.
You're not in heaven's debt,
on heaven's ledger.
It's not a curse, I pledge you,
that your small weight
and span rob you of tongue.
Sound's burden, too, is grievous.
And you're more speechless,
less fleshed, than time.

X

Living too brief an hour
for fear or trembling,
you spin, motelike, ascending
above this bed of flowers,
beyond the prison space
where past and future
combine to break, or batter,
our lives, and thus
when your path leads you far
to open meadows,
your pulsing wings bring shadows
and shapes to air.

XI

So, too, the sliding pen
which inks a surface
has no sense of the purpose

of any line
or that the whole will end
as an amalgam
of heresy and wisdom;
it therefore trusts the hand
whose silent speech incites
fingers to throbbing—
whose spasm reaps no pollen,
but eases hearts.

XII

Such beauty, set beside
so brief a season,
suggests to our stunned reason
this bleak surmise:
the world was made to hold
no end or *telos*,
and if—as some would tell us—
there is a goal,
it's not ourselves.
No butterfly collector
can trap light or detect where
the darkness dwells.

XIII

Should I bid you farewell
as to a day that's over?
Men's memories may wither,
grow thin, and fall
like hair. The trouble is,
behind their backs are:
not double beds for lovers,
hard sleep, the past,
or days in shrinking files
backstretched—but, rather,
huge clouds, circling together,
of butterflies.

Lagoon

FOR BROOKE AND STROBE TALBOTT

I

Down in the lobby three elderly women, bored,
take up, with their knitting, the Passion of Our Lord
    as the universe and the tiny realm
of the *pension* Accademia, side by side,
with TV blaring, sail into Christmastide,
    a lookout desk clerk at the helm.

II

And a nameless lodger, a nobody, boards the boat,
a bottle of grappa concealed in his raincoat
    as he gains his shadowy room, bereaved
of memory, homeland, son, with only the noise
of distant forests to grieve for his former joys,
    if anyone is grieved.

III

Venetian church bells, teacups, mantel clocks
chime and confound themselves in this stale box
    of assorted lives. The brazen, coiled
octopus-chandelier appears to be licking,
in a triptych mirror, bedsheet and mattress ticking,
    sodden with tears and passion-soiled.

IV

Blown by night winds, an Adriatic tide
floods the canals, boats rock from side to side,
    moored cradles, and the humble bream,
not ass and oxen, guards the rented bed
where the window blind above your sleeping head
    moves to the sea star's guiding beam.

V

So this is how we cope, putting out the heat
of grappa with nightstand water, carving the meat
   of flounder instead of Christmas roast,
so that Thy earliest backboned ancestor
might feed and nourish us, O Saviour,
   this winter night on a damp coast.

VI

A Christmas without snow, tinsel, or tree,
at the edge of a map- and land-corseted sea;
   having scuttled and sunk its scallop shell,
concealing its face while flaunting its backside,
Time rises from the goddess's frothy tide,
   yet changes nothing but clock hand and bell.

VII

A drowning city, where suddenly the dry
light of reason dissolves in the moisture of the eye;
   its winged lion, which can read and write,
southern kin of northern sphinxes of renown,
won't drop his book and holler, but calmly drown
   in splinters of mirror, splashing light.

VIII

The gondola knocks against its moorings. Sound
cancels itself, hearing and words are drowned,
   as is that nation where among
forests of hands the tyrant of the State
is voted in, its only candidate,
   and spit goes ice-cold on the tongue.

IX

So let us place the left paw, sheathing its claws,
in the crook of the arm of the other one, because
   this makes a hammer-and-sickle sign

with which to salute our era and bestow
a mute up-yours-even-unto-the-elbow
    upon the nightmares of our time.

X

The raincoated figure is settling into place
where Sophia, Constance, Prudence, Faith, and Grace
    lack futures, the only tense that is
is present, where either a goyish or Yiddish kiss
tastes bitter, like the city, where footsteps fade
    invisibly along the colonnade,

XI

trackless and blank as a gondola's passage through
a water surface, smoothing out of view
    the measured wrinkles of its path,
unmarked as a broad "So long!" like the wide piazza's space,
or as a cramped "I love," like the narrow alleyways,
    erased and without aftermath.

XII

Moldings and carvings, palaces and flights
of stairs. Look up: the lion smiles from heights
    of a tower wrapped as in a coat
of wind, unbudged, determined not to yield,
like a rank weed at the edge of a plowed field,
    and girdled round by Time's deep moat.

XIII

Night in St. Mark's piazza. A face as creased
as a finger from its fettering ring released,
    biting a nail, is gazing high
into that *nowhere* of pure thought, where sight
is baffled by the bandages of night,
    serene, beyond the naked eye,

XIV

where, past all boundaries and all predicates,
black, white, or colorless, vague, volatile states,
    something, some object, comes to mind.
Perhaps a body. In our dim days and few,
the speed of light equals a fleeting view,
    even when blackout robs us blind.

1973

The classical ballet, let's say, is beauty's keep
whose gentle denizens are moated off from feeling
prosaic things by pits filled up with fiddling,
and drawbridges are hoisted up.

In soft imperial plush you wriggle your backside,
as, thighs aflutter at the speed of shorthand,
a pearl who'll never make your sofa shudder
wings out into the garden in one glide.

We see archfiends in dark-brown leotards
and guardian angels in their tutus flaunting vision;
and then enough applause to rouse from sleep Elysian
Tchaikovsky and the other smarts.

The classical ballet! The art of better days!
When grog went hissing down with kisses ten a penny,
the cabs were tearing by, we sang hey nonny-nonny,
and if there was a foe, his name was Marshal Ney.

Gold domes were filling eyes of cops with yellow light;
a small plot gave you birth, the nest you lived and died in.
If anything at all went up sky-high then,
it was no railroad bridge but Pavlova in flight.

How splendid late at night, Old Russia worlds apart,
to watch Baryshnikov, his talent still as forceful!
The effort of the calf, the quivering of the torso
rotating round its axis, start

a flight such as the soul has yearned for from the fates,
as old maids cherish dreams while turning into bitches.

And as for where in space and time one's toe end touches,
well, earth is hard all over; try the States.

[1975]

On the Death of Zhukov

Columns of grandsons, stiff at attention;
gun carriage, coffin, riderless horse.
Wind brings no sound of their glorious Russian
trumpets, their weeping trumpets of war.
Splendid regalia deck out the corpse:
thundering Zhukov rolls toward death's mansion.

As a commander, making walls crumble,
he held a sword less sharp than his foe's.
Brilliant maneuvers across Volga flatlands
set him with Hannibal. And his last days
found him, like Pompey, fallen and humbled—
like Belisarius banned and disgraced.

How much dark blood, soldier's blood, did he spill then
on alien fields? Did he weep for his men?
As he lay dying, did he recall them—
swathed in civilian white sheets at the end?
He gives no answer. What will he tell them,
meeting in hell? "We were fighting to win."

Zhukov's right arm, which once was enlisted
in a just cause, will battle no more.
Sleep! Russian history holds, as is fitting,
space for the exploits of those who, though bold,
marching triumphant through foreign cities,
trembled in terror when they came home.

Marshal! These words will be swallowed by Lethe,
utterly lost, like your rough soldier's boots.
Still, take this tribute, though it is little,
to one who somehow—here I speak truth

plain and aloud—has saved our embattled
homeland. Drum, beat! And shriek out, bullfinch fife!

[June] 1974
London

Mexican Divertimento

FOR OCTAVIO PAZ

Cuernavaca

I

Beneath the tree where M., the Frenchmen's pet,
possessed his pearl of sluggish Indian blood,
a poet sits, who's come here from afar.
The garden's dense, like jewels closely set.
A thrush, like eyebrows knit, departs for food.
The evening air's a crystal chandelier.

The crystal, be it noted, smashed to sand.
When M. reigned here as emperor three years,
he introduced them: crystal, champagne, dancing.
For things like that pep up the daily round.
But then appeared the patriot musketeers
and shot poor M. A doleful, haunting

cry of the crane drifts out from dense blue shadows.
The local lads shake down a rain of pears.
Three snow-white ducks are swimming in the pond.
The ear picks out among the rustling shudders
of leaves the lingo tossed around as pairs
of souls converse in hell of things profound.

II

Dismiss the palms, let plane trees loom in view.
Imagine M. now laying down his pen;
he flings aside his silken gown and frets
and cogitates on what his kin would do—
Franz Joseph, fellow ruler over men—
and whistles plaintively: "Me and my marmot friend."

"Warm greetings, sir, from Mexico. My wife
went off her head in Paris. Now the palace
walls all resound with shooting, fire sprawls.
Now rebels, brother, choke the city's life.
(My marmot friend and I, we saw the places . . .)
Well, here guns are more in vogue than plows—

and who's to wonder; tertiary limestone
is just like brimstone, a heartbreaking soil.
Just add to that the equatorial heat.
So bullets are a natural ventilation.
Both lungs and kidneys sense this as they toil.
My skin is sliding off me—how I sweat!

Aside from which, I feel like coming home.
I miss the homeland slums, the homeland splendor.
Send current almanacs—I long for them!
This place will likely prove a goodly tomb
for me and for my marmot. Gorgeous sends her
due greetings to my royal brother. M."

III

July's conclusion merges with the rains
as talkers get entangled with their thoughts
—a thing of rather small concern to you;
back there the past means more than what remains.
A guitar twangs. The streets are out of sorts.
A passerby gets soaked and fades from view.

And everything's grown over, pond included.
Grass snakes and lizards swarm here, the tree crowns
bear flocks of birds, some laying eggs, some eggless.
What ruins all the dynasties, blue-blooded,
is surplus heirs replete with numbered thrones.
The woods encroach, and likewise the elections.

M. wouldn't know the place again. Each niche
is bustless now, the colonnade looks bundled,
and walls are sliding slack-jawed down the cliffs.
The gaze is sated, thoughts refuse to mesh.
The gardens and the parks become a jungle.
And "Cancer!" is what bursts out from the lips.

1867
Nocturnal gardens under slowly ripening mangoes.
M. dances what one day will be a tango.
His shadow twirls the way a boomerang does
  and the temperature's an armpit 98.
The iridescent flicker of a silver waistcoat;
and a mulatto girl melts lovingly like chocolate
while in a masculine embrace she purrs insensate,
  here—soft as wool, there—smooth as plate.

Nocturnal silence underneath the virgin forest.
Juárez, now the spearhead of, say, progress,
to his peons who never saw two pesos
  distributes rifles in the dark of night.
Bolts start their clicking, while Juárez on squared paper
puts little crosses, ticking off each happy taker.
A gaudy parrot, one who never makes mistakes or
  lies, sits on a bough and notes their plight:

Scorn for one's neighbor among those who sniff the roses
may be, not better, but more straight than civic poses.
But either thing gives quite a rise to blood and bruises.
  Worse in the tropics, here, where death, alas,
spreads rather quickly in the way flies spread infection,
or as a bon mot in a café draws attention,
where three-eyed skulls among the thickets rate no mention;
  in every socket—a clump of grass.

Mérida
A fan of palms surrounding
a tawny-colored town,
ancient tiles and gables.
Starting from the café, evening
moves into town. Sits down
at a deserted table.

In the ultramarine sky
now touched with golden tints
bells assault the ear
like a bundle of keys:
a sound, laden with hints
of comfort for the homeless here.

A point lights up close by
the cathedral's lofty tower—
Hesperus appearing.
Following it with his eye
filled to the brim with doubt
if not reproach, evening

downs his cup to the lees
(his cheekbones a touch florid),
pays the bill, adjusts
his hat brim over his eyes,
rises from his chair, unhurried,
and folds up his mussed

paper and leaves. The deserted
street makes to accompany
his lean black frame
through the somber mist. A concert
of shadows seems to waylay
him beneath an awning—a lame

rabble: plebeian manners,
blots, tattered loops and dents.
He throws off an onerous:
"Officers, gentlemen.
Betake yourselves hence.
The time is now upon us.

No time to lose, away!
You there, colonel, why, pray tell, is
onion on your breath?"
He untethers his dapple-gray
and gallops off at zealous
clip into the West.

Mexican Romancero

I
Good old Mexico City.
Marvelous place to kill an
evening. The heart is empty;
but Time still flows like tequila.

Façades, car flashes, faces
cut in half with mustaches.
The Ave. of Reforma forces
eyes to prefer the statues.

Under each one, in the gutter
with hands stretched to the traffic,
sits a Mexican mother
with her baby. A tragic

sight. Let the winning party
carve them both for a Statue
of Mexico, huge and portly.
To cast some shade in the future.

II

Something inside went slightly
wrong, so to speak—off course.
Muttering "God Almighty,"
I hear my own voice.

Thus you dirty the pages
to stop an instant that's fair,
automatically gazing
at yourself from nowhere.

This is, Father in Heaven,
a sad by-product of practice,
copper change for the given,
though it's been given gratis.

How far all this is from prayer.
Words cure no despair.
But a fish blind with hunger
can't tell the worm from the angler.

III

Palms, cactus, agaves. Slowly
sun rises where night has stored it.
Its smile—you might find it lovely,
but on a closer look, morbid.

Burned-out boulders. Gritty
soil, as fertile as a bolide.
Sun has a look of grinning
skull. And its rays are bonelike.

Naked-necked vultures carry on
their watch from a telegraph pole,
like hieroglyphs for carrion
in the dust-beaten scroll

of a highway. Turn right,
cactus will catch your sight.
The same on the left. And dead
rusty junk straight ahead.

IV

Good old Mexico City.
Delights in vocal power.
The band without any pity
grinds out "Guadalajara."

Enter this town. Enter
this mixture of styles and manners
of an unknown painter
framed by the heavy mountains.

Night. Coca-Cola's burning
message adorns the House
of Lawmaking. Beyond it
the Guardian Angel hovers.

Here he runs a risk
of being shot at random
and pinned to an obelisk
as a symbol of Freedom.

V

Heat retreats from the willow
to a single palm tree.
(I knew I existed while you
were near me.)

A fountain. A pockmarked, fine
nymph lends to its purr her ear.
(I saw all things in profile
while you were near.)

Tabernacles; the zero
of my thinking of Thee
grows. (Who was always there
when you were near me?)

A purple moon in its climb.
A quarter shrunk to a dime.
Midnight. (I didn't fear
dying while you were near.)

VI

Spreading itself out at last,
like delirium in dust,
the dirt road, sloping gently down,
brings you to Laredo town.

With your blood-swollen eyes,
wedging the knees as does
el toro to thrill a crowd,
you'll sag to the ground.

Life has no meaning. Or
it's just too long. The bore
of arguing lack of sense
stays with us, like that tense

of calendars on the wall.
Very useful. For all
plants, boulders, planets, etc.
Not for bipeds.

To Evgeny

In all the elements man is
but tyrant, prisoner, or traitor . . .
—PUSHKIN

I've been in Mexico, clambered up the pyramids.
Geometrically perfect solids,

dotted here and there on Tehuantepec isthmus.
I hope they really are the work of alien visitors,
since normally such things are raised by slaves alone.
And the isthmus is strewn with mushrooms made of stone.

Little gods of clay who let themselves be copied
with extraordinary ease, permitting heterodoxy.
Bas-reliefs with sundry scenes, complete with writhing bits
of serpent bodies and the mysterious alphabet
of a tongue which never needed a word for "or."
What would they say if they could speak once more?

Nothing at all. At best, talk of triumphs snatched
over some adjoining tribe of men, smashed
skulls. Or how pouring blood into bowls
sacred to the Sun God strengthens the latter's bowels;
how sacrifice of eight young and strong men before dark
guarantees a sunrise more surely than the lark.

Better syphilis after all, better the orifice
of Cortés's unicorns, than sacrifice like this.
If fate assigns your carcass to the vultures' rage
let the murderer be a murderer, not a sage.
Anyway, how would they ever, had it
not been for the Spaniards, have learned of what really happened.

Life is a drag, Evgeny mine. Wherever you go,
everywhere dumbness and cruelty come up and say, "Hello,
here we are!" And they creep into verse, as it were.
"In all the elements . . ." as the poet has said elsewhere.
Didn't he see quite far, stuck in the northern mud?
In every latitude, let me add.

Encyclopedia Entry
Magnificent and beggar land.
It's bounded on the west and east by beaches
of two blue oceans. In between are mountains,

thick forests, limestone plains, plateaus,
and peasant hovels. To the south lie jungles
and ruins of majestic pyramids.
Lying to the north, plantations, cowboys,
shading quite haplessly into the U.S.A.
Permitting us to dwell awhile on trade.

The chief exports here are marijuana,
non-ferrous metals, an average grade of coffee,
cigars that bear the proud name Corona,
and trinkets made by local arts and crafts.
(Clouds, I must add.) The imports are
the usual stuff and, naturally, rifles.
Possessing a sufficiency of these,
it's somewhat easier to take on the state structure.

The country's history is sad; however,
unique is not the word to use. The main
disaster was, as they insist, the Spaniards,
the barbarous destruction of the ancient
Aztec civilization—that's the local,
plain version of the Golden Horde complex.
With this distinction, namely, that the Spaniards
did grab, in fact, their little pile of gold.

It's a republic now. A nice tricolor
flag flutters high above the presidential
palazzo. The constitution is beyond
reproach. The text with traces of leapfrogging
dictators lies enshrined within
the National Library, secure beneath green bullet-
proof glass—it should be noted, the very same
as fitted in the President's Rolls-Royce.

Which permits us a glance clean through it to
the future. In the future, population,
beyond a doubt, will keep on growing. Peons

will rhythmically ply the hoe
beneath the scorching sun. A man in specs
will sadly leaf through Marx in coffee bars.
And a small lizard on a boulder, raising
its little head, will passively observe
up there in the blue

         a spaceship's passage.

1975

The Thames at Chelsea

I

November. The sun, having risen on an empty stomach,
hovers in a chemist's window on jars of soda.
The wind encounters a hurtle in every subject:
chimneys, trees, a man driven over the tarmac.
Gulls keep a vigil on fences, sparrows peck at the ground.
A transport without wheels crawls over the Thames
as though on a gray, idly wandering road.
Toward the right bank Thomas More aims
his eyes with the age-old desire and strains his mind.
The dull stare is itself more solid than the iron
of the Albert Bridge, and, to put it tersely,
it's the best way of getting out of Chelsea.

II

The endless street, making a sharp slant,
runs to the river, ending with an iron arrow.
The body scatters its steps on the walk from its rumpled pants,
and trees stand queuing up for the narrow
sturgeonlike waves; that's the only type
of fish the Thames ever is fit to offer.
A local rain darkens Agrippa's water pipe.
A man able to see a century into the future
would view a sooted portico
unspoiled by a pub sign hanging down below,
a line of barges, an ensemble of monotonous
drainpipe flutes, and, at the Tate, an omnibus.

III

London town's fine, especially in the rain,
which is not to be stopped by cloth caps or crowns.
In this climate only those who make
umbrellas have a chance to seize the throne.

On a gray day, when even a shadow has no strength
to catch up with your back, and the money is getting tight,
in a city where, dark as the brick may get,
the milk will always stand sedately white,
scanning the paper, one may read with care
the account of someone fallen under a car
and only the mention of the relatives' grief
makes one sigh "Well, it's not me" with relief.

                              IV
These words were dictated to me not by
love or the Muse but by a searching, dull
voice that had lost the swiftness of sound. I
replied, facing my bedroom wall:
"How did you live in those years?" "Like the 'h' in 'uh-oh.' "
"Would you describe your concerns?" "The price of a decent loaf."
"What in the world do you love most?"
"Rivers and streets—the long things of life."
"Do you remember the past?" "Yes, it was winter.
I went for a sleigh ride, caught a cold from the air."
"Are you afraid of death?" "No, it's the normal dark,
but even when you're used to it, you can't make out a chair."

                              V
The air lives a life that is not ours
to understand; it lives its own blue
windy life that starts overhead and soars
upward, ending nowhere. Looking out of the window, you
see spires and chimneys, rooftops of lead;
you see this: the beginning of a great, damp world
where a roadway, which reared us, heads
to its own premature end. Dawn curls
over the horizon. A mail truck clangs by.
There is no longer anything one can choose
to believe, except that while there's a bank on the right,
there's a left one, too: blessed news.

VI

London town's fine, the clocks run on time.
The heart can only lose a length to Big Ben.
The Thames runs to the sea, swollen like a vein,
and tugs strain their basses in Chelsea. London's fine.
If not in height, then in breadth it lumbers
as boundlessly as it can down by the river.
And when you sleep, the telephone numbers
of your past and present blend to produce a figure—
astronomical. And your finger turning the dial
of the winter moon finds the colorless, vile
chirp, "Engaged," and this steady noise
is clearer than God's own voice.

1974

A Part of Speech

I was born and grew up in the Baltic marshland
by zinc-gray breakers that always marched on
in twos. Hence all rhymes, hence that wan flat voice
that ripples between them like hair still moist,
if it ripples at all. Propped on a pallid elbow,
the helix picks out of them no sea rumble
but a clap of canvas, of shutters, of hands, a kettle
on the burner, boiling—lastly, the seagull's metal
cry. What keeps hearts from falseness in this flat region
is that there is nowhere to hide and plenty of room for vision.
Only sound needs echo and dreads its lack.
A glance is accustomed to no glance back.

The North buckles metal, glass it won't harm;
teaches the throat to say, "Let me in."
I was raised by the cold that, to warm my palm,
gathered my fingers around a pen.

Freezing, I see the red sun that sets
behind oceans, and there is no soul
in sight. Either my heel slips on ice, or the globe itself
arches sharply under my sole.

And in my throat, where a boring tale
or tea, or laughter should be the norm,
snow grows all the louder and "Farewell!"
darkens like Scott wrapped in a polar storm.

From nowhere with love the enth of Marchember sir
sweetie respected darling but in the end
it's irrelevant who for memory won't restore
features not yours and no one's devoted friend
greets you from this fifth last part of earth
resting on whalelike backs of cowherding boys
I loved you better than angels and Him Himself
and am farther off due to that from you than I am from both
of them now late at night in the sleeping vale
in the little township up to its doorknobs in
snow writhing upon the stale
sheets for the whole matter's skin-
deep I'm howling "youuu" through my pillow dike
many seas away that are milling nearer
with my limbs in the dark playing your double like
an insanity-stricken mirror.

A list of some observations. In a corner, it's warm.
A glance leaves an imprint on anything it's dwelt on.
Water is glass's most public form.
Man is more frightening than his skeleton.
A nowhere winter evening with wine. A black
porch resists an osier's stiff assaults.
Fixed on an elbow, the body bulks
like a glacier's debris, a moraine of sorts.
A millennium hence, they'll no doubt expose
a fossil bivalve propped behind this gauze
cloth, with the print of lips under the print of fringe,
mumbling "Good night" to a window hinge.

I recognize this wind battering the limp grass
that submits to it as they did to the Tartar mass.
I recognize this leaf splayed in the roadside mud
like a prince empurpled in his own blood.
Fanning wet arrows that blow aslant
the cheek of a wooden hut in another land,
autumn tells, like geese by their flying call,
a tear by its face. And as I roll
my eyes to the ceiling, I chant herein
not the lay of that eager man's campaign
but utter your Kazakh name which till now was stored
in my throat as a password into the Horde.

A navy-blue dawn in a frosted pane
recalls yellow streetlamps in the snow-piled lane,
icy pathways, crossroads, drifts on either hand,
a jostling cloakroom in Europe's eastern end.
"Hannibal . . ." drones on there, a worn-out motor,
parallel bars in the gym reek with armpit odor;
as for that scary blackboard you failed to see through,
it has stayed just as black. And its reverse side, too.
Silvery hoarfrost has transformed the rattling bell
into crystal. As regards all that parallel-
line stuff, it's turned out true and bone-clad, indeed.
Don't want to get up now. And never did.

You've forgotten that village lost in the rows and rows
of swamp in a pine-wooded territory where no scarecrows
ever stand in orchards: the crops aren't worth it,
and the roads are also just ditches and brushwood surface.
Old Nastasia is dead, I take it, and Pesterev, too, for sure,
and if not, he's sitting drunk in the cellar or
is making something out of the headboard of our bed:
a wicket gate, say, or some kind of shed.
And in winter they're chopping wood, and turnips is all they live on,
and a star blinks from all the smoke in the frosty heaven,
and no bride in chintz at the window, but dust's gray craft,
plus the emptiness where once we loved.

In the little town out of which death sprawled over the classroom map
the cobblestones shine like scales that coat a carp,
on the secular chestnut tree melting candles hang,
and a cast-iron lion pines for a good harangue.
Through the much laundered, pale window gauze
woundlike carnations and *kirchen* needles ooze;
a tram rattles far off, as in days of yore,
but no one gets off at the stadium anymore.
The real end of the war is a sweet blonde's frock
across a Viennese armchair's fragile back
while the humming winged silver bullets fly,
taking lives southward, in mid-July.

Munich

As for the stars, they are always on.
That is, one appears, then others adorn the inklike
sphere. That's the best way from there to look upon
here: well after hours, blinking.
The sky looks better when they are off.
Though, with them, the conquest of space is quicker.
Provided you haven't got to move
from the bare veranda and squeaking rocker.
As one spacecraft pilot has said, his face
half sunk in the shadow, it seems there is
no life anywhere, and a thoughtful gaze
can be rested on none of these.

Near the ocean, by candlelight. Scattered farms,
fields overrun with sorrel, lucerne, and clover.
Toward nightfall, the body, like Shiva, grows extra arms
reaching out yearningly to a lover.
A mouse rustles through grass. An owl drops down.
Suddenly creaking rafters expand a second.
One sleeps more soundly in a wooden town,
since you dream these days only of things that happened.
There's a smell of fresh fish. An armchair's profile
is glued to the wall. The gauze is too limp to bulk at
the slightest breeze. And a ray of the moon, meanwhile,
draws up the tide like a slipping blanket.

The Laocoön of a tree, casting the mountain weight
off his shoulders, wraps them in an immense
cloud. From a promontory, wind gushes in. A voice
pitches high, keeping words on a string of sense.
Rain surges down; its ropes twisted into lumps,
lash, like the bather's shoulders, the naked backs of these
hills. The Medhibernian Sea stirs round colonnaded stumps
like a salt tongue behind broken teeth.
The heart, however grown savage, still beats for two.
Every good boy deserves fingers to indicate
that beyond today there is always a static to-
morrow, like a subject's shadowy predicate.

If anything's to be praised, it's most likely how
the west wind becomes the east wind, when a frozen bough
sways leftward, voicing its creaking protests,
and your cough flies across the Great Plains to Dakota's forests.
At noon, shouldering a shotgun, fire at what may well
be a rabbit in snowfields, so that a shell
widens the breach between the pen that puts up these limping
awkward lines and the creature leaving
real tracks in the white. On occasion the head combines
its existence with that of a hand, not to fetch more lines
but to cup an ear under the pouring slur
of their common voice. Like a new centaur.

There is always a possibility left—to let
yourself out to the street whose brown length
will soothe the eye with doorways, the slender forking
of willows, the patchwork puddles, with simply walking.
The hair on my gourd is stirred by a breeze
and the street, in distance, tapering to a V, is
like a face to a chin; and a barking puppy
flies out of a gateway like crumpled paper.
A street. Some houses, let's say,
are better than others. To take one item,
some have richer windows. What's more, if you go insane,
it won't happen, at least, inside them.

. . . and when "the future" is uttered, swarms of mice
rush out of the Russian language and gnaw a piece
of ripened memory which is twice
as hole-ridden as real cheese.
After all these years it hardly matters who
or what stands in the corner, hidden by heavy drapes,
and your mind resounds not with a seraphic "do,"
only their rustle. Life, that no one dares
to appraise, like that gift horse's mouth,
bares its teeth in a grin at each
encounter. What gets left of a man amounts
to a part. To his spoken part. To a part of speech.

Not that I am losing my grip: I am just tired of summer.
You reach for a shirt in a drawer and the day is wasted.
If only winter were here for snow to smother
all these streets, these humans; but first, the blasted
green. I would sleep in my clothes or just pluck a borrowed
book, while what's left of the year's slack rhythm,
like a dog abandoning its blind owner,
crosses the road at the usual zebra. Freedom
is when you forget the spelling of the tyrant's name
and your mouth's saliva is sweeter than Persian pie,
and though your brain is wrung tight as the horn of a ram
nothing drops from your pale-blue eye.

1975–76

Lullaby of Cape Cod

I

The eastern tip of the Empire dives into night;
cicadas fall silent over some empty lawn;
on classic pediments inscriptions dim from the sight
as a finial cross darkens and then is gone
like the nearly empty bottle on the table.
From the empty street's patrol car a refrain
of Ray Charles's keyboard tinkles away like rain.

Crawling to a vacant beach from the vast wet
of ocean, a crab digs into sand laced with sea lather
and sleeps. A giant clock on a brick tower
rattles its scissors. The face is drenched with sweat.
The streetlamps glisten in the stifling weather,
formally spaced,
like white shirt buttons open to the waist.

It's stifling. The eye's guided by a blinking stoplight
in its journey to the whiskey across the room
on the nightstand. The heart stops dead a moment, but its dull boom
goes on, and the blood, on pilgrimage gone forth,
comes back to a crossroad. The body, like an upright,
rolled-up road map, lifts an eyebrow in the North.

It's strange to think of surviving, but that's what happened.
Dust settles on furnishings, and a car bends length
around corners in spite of Euclid. And the deepened
darkness makes up for the absence of people, of voices,
and so forth, and alters them, by its cunning and strength,
not to deserters, to ones who have taken flight,
but rather to those now disappeared from sight.

It's stifling. And the thick leaves' rasping sound
is enough all by itself to make you sweat.
What seems to be a small dot in the dark
could only be one thing—a star. On the deserted ground
of a basketball court a vagrant bird has set
its fragile egg in the steel hoop's raveled net.
There's a smell of mint now, and of mignonette.

II

Like a despotic Sheik, who can be untrue
to his vast seraglio and multiple desires
only with a harem altogether new,
varied, and numerous, I have switched Empires.
A step dictated by the acrid, live
odor of burning carried on the air
from all four quarters (a time for silent prayer!)
and, from the crow's high vantage point, from five.

Like a snake charmer, like the Pied Piper of old,
playing my flute I passed the green janissaries,
my testes sensing their poleaxe's sinister cold,
as when one wades into water. And then with the brine
of seawater sharpness filling, flooding the mouth,
I crossed the line

and sailed into muttony clouds. Below me curled
serpentine rivers, roads bloomed with dust, ricks yellowed,
and everywhere in that diminished world,
in formal opposition, near and far,
lined up like print in a book about to close,
armies rehearsed their games in balanced rows
and cities all went dark as caviar.

And then the darkness thickened. All lights fled,
a turbine droned, a head ached rhythmically,
and space backed up like a crab, time surged ahead
into first place and, streaming westwardly,

seemed to be heading home, void of all light,
soiling its garments with the tar of night.

I fell asleep. When I awoke to the day,
magnetic north had strengthened its deadly pull.
I beheld new heavens, I beheld the earth made new.
It lay
turning to dust, as flat things always do.

III
Being itself the essence of all things,
solitude teaches essentials. How gratefully the skin
receives the leathery coolness of its chair.
Meanwhile, my arm, off in the dark somewhere,
goes wooden in sympathetic brotherhood
with the chair's listless arm of oaken wood.
A glowing oaken grain
covers the tiny bones of the joints. And the brain
knocks like the glass's ice cube tinkling.

It's stifling. On a pool hall's steps, in a dim glow,
somebody striking a match rescues his face
of an old black man from the enfolding dark
for a flaring moment. The white-toothed portico
of the District Courthouse sinks in the thickened lace
of foliage, and awaits the random search
of passing headlights. High up on its perch,

like the fiery warning at Balthazar's Feast,
the inscription *Coca-Cola* hums in red.
In the Country Club's unweeded flower bed
a fountain whispers its secrets. Unable to rouse
a simple tirralirra in these dull boughs,
a strengthless breeze rustles the tattered, creased
news of the world, its obsolete events,
against an improvised, unlikely fence

of iron bedsteads. It's stifling. Leaning on his rifle,
the Unknown Soldier grows even more unknown.
Against a concrete jetty, in dull repose
a trawler scrapes the rusty bridge of its nose.
A weary, buzzing ventilator mills
the U.S.A.'s hot air with metal gills.

Like a carried-over number in addition,
the sea comes up in the dark
and on the beach it leaves its delible mark,
and the unvarying, diastolic motion,
the repetitious, drugged sway of the ocean,
cradles a splinter adrift for a million years.
If you step sideways off the pier's
edge, you'll continue to fall toward those tides
for a long, long time, your hands stiff at your sides,
but you will make no splash.

IV

The change of Empires is intimately tied
to the hum of words, the soft, fricative spray
of spittle in the act of speech, the whole
sum of Lobachevsky's angles, the strange way
that parallels may unwittingly collide
by casual chance someday
as longitudes contrive to meet at the pole.

And the change is linked as well to the chopping of wood,
to the tattered lining of life turned inside out
and thereby changed to a garment dry and good
(to tweed in winter, linen in a heat spell),
and the brain's kernel hardening in its shell.

In general, of all our organs the eye
alone retains its elasticity,
pliant, adaptive as a dream or wish.
For the change of Empires is linked with far-flung sight,

with the long gaze cast across the ocean's tide
(somewhere within us lives a dormant fish),
and the mirror's revelation that the part in your hair
that you meticulously placed on the left side
mysteriously shows up on the right,

linked to weak gums, to heartburn brought about
by a diet unfamiliar and alien,
to the intense blankness, to the pristine white
of the mind, which corresponds to the plain, small
blank page of letter paper on which you write.
But now the giddy pen
points out resemblances, for after all

the device in your hand is the same old pen and ink
as before, the woodland plants exhibit no change
of leafage, and the same old bombers range
the clouds toward who knows what
precisely chosen, carefully targeted spot.
And what you really need now is a drink.

V

New England towns seem much as if they were cast
ashore along its coastline, beached by a flood
tide, and shining in darkness mile after mile
with imbricate, speckled scales of shingle and tile,
like schools of sleeping fish hauled in by the vast
nets of a continent that was first discovered
by herring and by cod. But neither cod

nor herring have had any noble statues raised
in their honor, even though the memorial date
could be comfortably omitted. As for the great
flag of the place, it bears no blazon or mark
of the first fish-founder among its parallel bars,
and as Louis Sullivan might perhaps have said,

seen in the dark,
it looks like a sketch of towers thrust among stars.

Stifling. A man on his porch has wound a towel
around his throat. A pitiful, small moth
batters the window screen and bounces off
like a bullet that Nature has zeroed in on itself
from an invisible ambush,
aiming for some improbable bull's-eye
right smack in the middle of July.

Because watches keep ticking, pain washes away
with the years. If time picks up the knack
of panacea, it's because time can't abide
being rushed, or finally turns insomniac.
And walking or swimming, the dreams of one hemisphere (heads)
swarm with the nightmares, the dark, sinister play
of its opposite (tails), its double, its underside.

Stifling. Great motionless plants. A distant bark.
A nodding head now jerks itself upright
to keep faces and phone numbers from sliding into the dark
and off the precarious edge of memory.
In genuine tragedy
it's not the fine hero that finally dies, it seems,
but, from constant wear and tear, night after night,
the old stage set itself, giving way at the seams.

VI

Since it's too late by now to say goodbye
and expect from time and space any reply
except an echo that sounds like "Here's your tip,"
pseudo-majestic, cubing every chance
word that escapes the lip,
I write in a sort of trance,

I write these words out blindly, the scrivening hand
attempting to outstrip
by a second the "How come?"
that at any moment might escape the lip,
the same lip of the writer,
and sail away into night, there to expand
by geometrical progress, *und so weiter.*

I write from an Empire whose enormous flanks
extend beneath the sea. Having sampled two
oceans as well as continents, I feel that I know
what the globe itself must feel: there's nowhere to go.
Elsewhere is nothing more than a far-flung strew
of stars, burning away.

Better to use a telescope to see
a snail self-sealed to the underside of a leaf.
I always used to regard "infinity"
as the art of splitting a liter into three
equal components with a couple of friends
without a drop left over. Not, through a lens,
an aggregate of miles without relief.

Night. A cuckoo wheezes in the Waldorf-
Inglorious. The legions close their ranks
and, leaning against cohorts, sleep upright.
Circuses pile against fora. High in the night
above the bare blueprint of an empty court,
like a lost tennis ball, the moon regards its court,
a chess queen's dream, spare, parqueted, formal and bright.
There's no life without furniture.

VII
Only a corner cordoned off and laced
by dusty cobwebs may properly be called
right-angled; only after the musketry of applause

and bravos does the actor rise from the dead;
only when the fulcrum is solidly placed
can a person lift, by Archimedean laws,
the weight of this world. And only that body whose weight
is balanced at right angles to the floor
can manage to walk about and navigate.

Stifling. There's a cockroach mob in the stadium
of the zinc washbasin, crowding around the old
corpse of a dried-up sponge. Turning its crown,
a bronze faucet, like Caesar's laureled head,
deposes upon the living and the dead
a merciless column of water in which they drown.

The little bubble beads inside my glass
look like the holes in cheese.
No doubt that gravity holds sway,
just as upon a solid mass,
over such small transparencies as these.
And its accelerating waterfall
(thirty-two feet per sec per sec) refracts
as does a ray of light in human clay.

Only the stacked white china on the stove
could look so much like a squashed, collapsed pagoda.
Space lends itself just to repeatable things,
roses, for instance. If you see one alone,
you instantly see two. The bright corona,
the crimson petals abuzz, acrawl with wings
of dragonflies, of wasps and bees with stings.

Stifling. Even the shadow on the wall,
servile and weak as it is, still mimics the rise
of the hand that wipes the forehead's sweat. The smell
of old body is even clearer now
than body's outline. Thought loses its defined

edges; and the frazzled mind
goes soft in its soup-bone skull. No one is here
to set the proper focus of your eyes.

VIII

Preserve these words against a time of cold,
a day of fear: man survives like a fish,
stranded, beached, but intent
on adapting itself to some deep, cellular wish,
wriggling toward bushes, forming hinged leg-struts, then
to depart (leaving a track like the scrawl of a pen)
for the interior, the heart of the continent.

Full-breasted sphinxes there are, and lions winged
like fanged and mythic birds.
Angels in white, as well, and nymphs of the sea.
To one who shoulders the vast obscurity
of darkness and heavy heat (may one add, grief?)
they are more cherished than the concentric, ringed
zeros that ripple outward from dropped words.

Even space itself, where there's nowhere to sit down,
declines, like a star in its ether, its cold sky.
Yet just because shoes exist and the foot is shod
some surface will always be there, some place to stand,
a portion of dry land.
And its brinks and beaches will be enchanted by
the soft song of the cod:

"Time is far greater than space. Space is a thing.
Whereas time is, in essence, the thought, the conscious dream
of a thing. And life itself is a variety
of time. The carp and bream
are its clots and distillates. As are even more stark
and elemental things, including the sea
wave and the firmament of the dry land.
Including death, that punctuation mark.

At times, in that chaos, that piling up of days,
the sound of a single word rings in the ear,
some brief, syllabic cry,
like 'love,' perhaps, or possibly merely 'hi!'
But before I can make it out, static or haze
trouble the scanning lines that undulate
and wave like the loosened ripples of your hair."

IX

Man broods over his life like night above a lamp.
At certain moments a thought takes leave of one
of the brain's hemispheres, and slips, as a bedsheet might,
from under the restless sleeper's body clamp,
revealing who-knows-what-under-the-sun.
Unquestionably, night

is a bulky thing, but not so infinite
as to engross both lobes. By slow degrees
the Africa of the brain, its Europe, the Asian mass of it,
as well as other prominences in its crowded seas,
creaking on their axis, turn a wrinkled cheek
toward the electric heron with its lightbulb of a beak.

Behold: Aladdin says "Sesame!" and presto! there's a golden trove.
Caesar calls for his Brutus down the dark forum's colonnades.
In the jade pavilion a nightingale serenades
the Mandarin on the delicate theme of love.
A young girl rocks a cradle in the lamp's arena of light.
A naked Papuan leg keeps up a boogie-woogie beat.

Stifling. And so, cold knees tucked snug against the night,
it comes to you all at once, there in the bed,
that this is marriage. That beyond the customs sheds
across dozens of borders there turns upon its side
a body you now share nothing with, unless
it be the ocean's bottom, hidden from sight,
and the experience of nakedness.

Nevertheless, you won't get up together.
Because, while it may be light way over there,
the dark still governs in your hemisphere.
One solar source has never been enough
to serve two average bodies, not since the time
God glued the world together in its prime.
The light has never been enough.

X

I notice a sleeve's hem, as my eyes fall,
and an elbow bending itself. Coordinates show
my location as paradise, that sovereign, blessed
place where all purpose and longing is set at rest.
This is a planet without vistas, with no
converging lines, with no prospects at all.

Touch the table corner, touch the sharp nib of the pen
with your fingertip: you can tell such things could hurt.
And yet the paradise of the inert
resides in pointedness;
whereas in the lives of men
it is fleeting, a misty, mutable excess
that will not come again.

I find myself, as it were, on a mountain peak.
Beyond me there is . . . Chronos and thin air.
Preserve these words. The paradise men seek
is a dead end, a worn-out, battered cape
bent into crooked shape,
a cone, a finial cap, a steel ship's bow
from which the lookout never shouts, "Land ho!"

All you can tell for certain is the time.
That said, there's nothing left but to police
the revolving hands. The eye drowns silently
in the clockface as in a broad, bottomless sea.

In paradise all clocks refuse to chime
for fear they might, in striking, disturb the peace.

Double all absences, multiply by two
whatever's missing, and you'll have some clue
to what it's like here. A number, in any case,
is also a word and, as such, a device
or gesture that melts away without a trace,
like a small cube of ice.

XI

Great issues leave a trail of words behind,
free-form as clouds of treetops, rigid as dates
of the year. So, too, decked out in a paper hat,
the body viewing the ocean. It is selfless, flat
as a mirror as it stands in the darkness there.
Upon its face, just as within its mind,
nothing but spreading ripples anywhere.

Consisting of love, of dirty words, a blend
of ashes, the fear of death, the fragile case
of the bone, and the groin's jeopardy, an erect
body at seaside is the foreskin of space,
letting semen through. His cheek tear-silver-flecked,
man juts forth into Time; man is his own end.

The eastern end of the Empire dives into night—
throat-high in darkness. The coil of the inner ear,
like a snail's helix, faithfully repeats
spirals of words in which it seems to hear
a voice of its own, and this tends to incite
the vocal cords, but it doesn't help you see.
In the realm of Time, no precipice creates
an echo's formal, answering symmetry.

Stifling. Only when lying flat on your back
can you launch, with a sigh, your dry speech toward those mute,

infinite regions above. With a soft sigh.
But the thought of the land's vastness, your own minute
size in comparison, swings you forth and back
from wall to wall, like a cradle's rockabye.

Therefore, sleep well. Sweet dreams. Knit up that sleeve.
Sleep as those only do who have gone pee-pee.
Countries get snared in maps, never shake free
of their net of latitudes. Don't ask who's there
if you think the door is creaking. Never believe
the person who might reply and claim he's there.

XII

The door is creaking. A cod stands at the sill.
He asks for a drink, naturally, for God's sake.
You can't refuse a traveler a nip.
You indicate to him which road to take,
a winding highway, and wish him a good trip.
He takes his leave, but his identical

twin has got a salesman's foot in the door.
(The two fish are as duplicate as glasses.)
All night a school of them come visiting.
But people who make their homes along the shore
know how to sleep, have learned how to ignore
the measured tread of these approaching masses.

Sleep. The land beyond you is not round.
It is merely long, with various dip and mound,
its ups and downs. Far longer is the sea.
At times, like a wrinkled forehead, it displays
a rolling wave. And longer still than these
is the strand of matching beads of countless days;

and nights; and beyond these, the blindfold mist,
angels in paradise, demons down in hell.
And longer a hundredfold than all of this

128

are the thoughts of life, the solitary thought
of death. And ten times that, longer than all,
the queer, vertiginous thought of Nothingness.

But the eye can't see that far. In fact, it must
close down its lid to catch a glimpse of things.
Only this way—in sleep—can the eye adjust
to proper vision. Whatever may be in store,
for good or ill, in the dreams that such sleep brings
depends on the sleeper. A cod stands at the door.

1975

December in Florence

"He has not returned to his old Florence,
even after having died . . ."

—ANNA AKHMATOVA

I

The doors take in air, exhale steam; you, however, won't
be back to the shallowed Arno where, like a new kind
of quadruped, idle couples follow the river bend.
Doors bang, beasts hit the slabs. Indeed,
the atmosphere of this city retains a bit
of the dark forest. It
is a beautiful city where at certain age
one simply raises the collar to disengage
from passing humans and dulls the gaze.

II

Sunk in raw twilight, the pupil blinks but gulps
the memory-numbing pills of opaque streetlamps.
Yards off from where the Signoria looms,
the doorway, centuries later, suggests the best
cause of expulsion: one can't exist
by a volcano and show no fist,
though it won't unclench when its owner dies.
For death is always a second Florence in terms of size
and its architecture of Paradise.

III

Cats check at noon under benches to see if the shadows are
black, while the Old Bridge (new after repair),
where Cellini is peering at the hills' blue glare,
buzzes with heavy trading in bric-a-brac.
Flotsam is combed by the arching brick.
And the passing beauty's loose golden lock,
as she rummages through the hawkers' herd,

flares up suddenly under the arcade
like an angelic vestige in the kingdom of the dark-haired.

IV

A man gets reduced to pen's rustle on paper, to
wedges, ringlets of letters, and also, due
to the slippery surface, to commas and full stops. True,
often, in some common word, the unwitting pen
strays into drawing—while tackling an
"M"—some eyebrows: ink is more honest than
blood. And a face, with moist words inside
out to dry what has just been said,
smirks like the crumpled paper absorbed by shade.

V

Quays resemble stalled trains. The damp
yellow palazzi are sunk in the earth waist-down.
A shape in an overcoat braves the dank
mouth of a gateway, mounts the decrepit, flat,
worn-out molars toward their red, inflamed
palate with its sure-as-fate
number 16. Voiceless, instilling fright,
a little bell in the end prompts a rasping "Wait!"
Two old crones let you in, each looks like the figure 8.

VI

In a dusty café, in the shade of your cap,
eyes pick out frescoes, nymphs, cupids on their way up.
In a cage, making up for the sour terza-rima crop,
a seedy goldfinch juggles his sharp cadenza.
A chance ray of sunlight splattering the palazzo
and the sacristy where lies Lorenzo
pierces thick blinds and titillates the veinous
filthy marble, tubs of snow-white verbena;
and the bird's ablaze within his wire Ravenna.

VII

Taking in air, exhaling steam, the doors
slam shut in Florence. One or two lives one yearns
for (which is up to that faith of yours)—
some night in the first one you learn that love
doesn't move the stars (or the moon) enough.
For it divides things in two, in half.
Like the cash in your dreams. Like your idle fears
of dying. If love were to shift the gears
of the southern stars, they'd run to their virgin spheres.

VIII

The stone nest resounds with a piercing squeal
of brakes. Intersections scare your skull
like crossed bones. In the low December sky
the gigantic egg laid there by Brunelleschi
jerks a tear from an eye experienced in the blessed
domes. A traffic policeman briskly
throws his hand in the air like a letter X.
Loudspeakers bark about rising tax.
Oh, the obstinate leaving that "living" masks!

IX

There are cities one won't see again. The sun
throws its gold at their frozen windows. But all the same
there is no entry, no proper sum.
There are always six bridges spanning the sluggish river.
There are places where lips touched lips for the first time ever,
or pen pressed paper with real fervor.
There are arcades, colonnades, iron idols that blur your lens.
There the streetcar's multitudes, jostling, dense,
speak in the tongue of a man who's departed thence.

1976

132

In England

FOR DIANA AND ALAN MYERS

Brighton Rock

And so you are returning, livid flush of early dusk. The chalk
Sussex rocks fling seaward the smell of dry grass and
a long shadow, like some black useless thing. The rippling
sea hurls landward the roar of the incoming surge and
scraps of ultramarine. From the coupling of the splash of
needless water and needless dark arise, sharply
etched against the sky, spires of churches, sheer
rock faces, these livid summer dusks, the color
of landed fish; and I revive. In the bushes, a careless
linnet cries. The horizon's clean-cut clothesline
has a single cloud pegged out upon it, like a shirt,
and a tanker's masts dip and sway, like an ant
fallen over on its back. Into my mind floats someone's
phone number—the ripped-out mesh
of an empty trawl. A breeze fans my cheek.
The sea swell lulls an anxious splinter,
and a motionless boat lies awash in its reflection.
In the middle of a long or at the end of a short
life, one goes down to the waves not to bathe but for the sake
of that dark-gray, unpeopled, inhuman surface,
as like in color to the eyes, gazing unwinking at it,
as two drops of water. Like silence at a parrot.

East Finchley

Evening. A bulky body moves quietly along a narrow
walk, with brush-cut hedges and rows of fuchsias
and geraniums, like a dreadnought on a country canal.
His right jacket sleeve, heavily chalk-dusted, betrays
the way he makes his living, as does his very voice:
"You can get away with watering roses and gladioli
somewhat less than dahlias or hyacinths—once or
twice a week." And he quotes me figures from

The Amateur Gardener's Handbook
and a line from Virgil. The ground swallows the water
with unexpected haste, and he hides his eyes. In the living room,
sparely furnished, deliberately bare,
his wife—he's been married twice—as befits wives,
lays out, humming, John Galsworthy's favorite patience,
"Spider." On the wall a watercolor: in a river
a bridge is reflected, who knows where.

Anyone living on an island is aware that sooner
or later all this ends: the water in the tap
ceases to be fresh, tastes salty; the foot,
crunching through the gravel and straw, senses
a sudden chill inside the toe end of the boot.
In music there's that place when the record
starts to spin against the moving needle.
On the mantelpiece a stuffed quail looms
that once relied on an infinity of forest,
a vase with a sprig of silver birch,
and a postcard of an Algerian bazaar: heaps
of multicolored stuffs, bronze vessels,
camels somewhere at the back—or is it hills?—
men in turbans. Not like us.

An allegory of memory, embodied in a hard
pencil poised in the air above the crossword.
A house, on a deserted street laid out on a slope,
in whose identical windows the setting sun
reflects as if on those of an express train
heading for an eternity where wheels are not required.
The sweet bedroom (a doll between the pillows)
where she has her "nightmares." The kitchen,
where the gas ring's humming chrysanthemum gives out
the smell of tea. And the outlines of the body
sink into an armchair the way sediment settles in liquid.
Amid the absurdity, horror, ennui of life,
beyond the windows stand the flowers, like tiny

apparel somehow inside out—a rose, symbol
of infinity with its clustered eights,
a dahlia's wheel, spinning between its bamboo bars
like Boccioni's disheveled locomotive,
fuchsia dancers, and, not yet fully open,
irises. Floating in peace, a world
where no one asks, "What's that? What did you say?
Would you repeat that?"—for here the echo
sends the word back unfailingly to the ear
even from as far as the Chinese Wall. Because you
uttered just one word: "Flowers."

Soho
A massive Venetian mirror holds the opaque profile
of a silk-robed beauty with the crimson wound
of a soundless mouth. The listener scans the walls,
whose pattern has altered over eight years to "Scenes
at Epsom Races." Flags. A jockey in scarlet cap
flies to the winning post on a two-year-old
colt. All merge into one great blur. The stands
go berserk. ". . . didn't reply to my
second letter, so I decided . . ." The voice
is, as it were, a struggle between the verb
and the absent tense. The young, thin hand
ripples the locks that are flowing, falling
into nowhere, like many rivers'
waters. Presently straddling oaken
stallions, two who have fallen heroically in foreign
sheets gallop round the table with its unfinished
bottle toward the gate in what's-it
street. Flags droop down, the wind dies, and drops
of moisture gleam on a rider's lips,
and the stands simply vanish . . . A yellow lamp
burns by the gate, slightly gilding the snowdrifts like
the crumbling crust on a Viennese pastry. No matter who
gets here first, though, in this street the bell
doesn't ring and the hoofs of the gray or the bay

in the present past, even reaching the post, leave no
traces, like carousel horses, on real snow.

Three Knights
In the old abbey chancel, in the apse, on the floor,
three knights sleep their last sleep, gleaming
in the chancel's gloom like stone sturgeon,
scales of chain-mail, armor-plate gills. All three
hawk-nosed and hatchet-faced, head-to-heel
knights: in breastplate, helmet, long sword. And sleep
longer than they woke. Dusk in the chancel. Arms
crossed on the chest, like carps.

The flash follows the camera's click—a kind
of shot (anything that hurls us forward
onto the wall of the future's a shot). The three,
frozen still, enact once again within
the camera what has already taken place—at Poitiers,
or the Holy Land: a traveler in a straw hat is,
for those who died for Father, Son,
and Holy Ghost, more fearful than the Saracen.

The abbey sprawled at ease along the riverbank.
Clumps of green trees. White butterflies
flutter over flower beds by the chapter house.
The cool of an English noonday. In England, as nowhere else,
nature, rather than diverting, soothes the eye;
and under the chancel wall, as if before
a theater curtain lowered once and for all,
the hawthorn's applause singles out none of them with its call.

North Kensington
The rustle of an *Irish Times* harried by the wind along
railway tracks to a depot long abandoned,
the crackle of dead wormwood, heralding autumn,
a gray tongue of water close by gums of brick.
How I love these sounds—the sounds of aimless

but continuing life, which for long enough
have been sufficient, aside from the crunch of
my own weighty tread on the gravel. And I fling a bolt skyward.
Only a mouse comprehends the delights of waste ground—
a rusting rail, discarded metal pins,
slack wire, reduced to a husky C-sharp,
the defeat of time in the face of metal.
All beyond repair, no further use.
You can only asphalt it over or blast
it clean off the face of the earth, used by now
to grimacing concrete stadia and their bawling crowds.
Then the mouse will come. Slowly, no rush,
out into the middle of the field, tiny as the soul
is in relation to the flesh, and, raising its
little snout, aghast, will shriek, "What is this place?"

York: In Memoriam W. H. Auden

The butterflies of northern England dance above the goosefoot
below the brick wall of a dead factory. After Wednesday
comes Thursday, and so on. The sky breathes heat;
the fields burn. The towns give off a smell of striped
cloth, long-wrapped and musty; dahlias die of thirst.
And your voice—"I have known three great poets. Each
one a prize son of a bitch"—sounds in my ears
with disturbing clarity. I slow my steps

and turn to look round. Four years soon
since you died in an Austrian hotel. Under the crossing sign
not a soul: tiled roofs, asphalt, limestone,
poplars. Chester died, too—you know that
only too well. Like beads on a dusty abacus,
sparrows sit solemnly on wires. Nothing so much
transforms a familiar entrance into a crowd of columns
as love for a man, especially when

he's dead. The absence of wind compels taut leaves
to tense their muscles and stir against their will.

The white butterflies' dance is like a storm-tossed ship.
A man takes his own blind alley with him wherever he goes
about the world; and a bent knee, with its obtuse angle,
multiplies the captive perspective,
like a wedge of cranes holding their course
for the south. Like all things moving onward.

The emptiness, swallowing sunlight—something in common with
the hawthorn—grows steadily more palpable
in the outstretched hand's direction, and
the world merges into a long street where others live.
In this sense, it is England. England, in this sense,
still an empire and fully capable—if
you believe the music gurgling like water—
of ruling waves. Or any element, for that matter.

Lately, I've been losing my grip a little: snarl
at my shopwindow reflection; while my finger
dials its number, my hand lets the phone fall.
Closing my eyes, I see an empty boat,
motionless, far out in the bay.
Coming out of the phone booth,
I hear a starling's voice—in its cry alarm.
But before it flies away the sound

melts in the air. Whose blue expanse, innocent of objects,
is much like this life here (where things stand out more in the desert),
for you're not here. And vacuum gradually
fills the landscape. Like flecks of foam,
sheep take their ease on bottle-green waves
of Yorkshire heather. The corps de ballet of nimble
butterflies, taking their cue from an unseen bow,
flicker above a grass-grown ditch, giving the eye

no point of rest. And the willow herb's vertical stalk
is longer than the ancient Roman road,
heading north, forgotten by all at Rome.

Subtracting the greater from the lesser—time from man—
you get words, the remainder, standing out against their
white background more clearly than the body
ever manages to while it lives, though it cry "Catch me!"—

thus the source of love turns into the object of love.

Stone Villages
The stone-built villages of England.
A cathedral bottled in a pub window.
Cows dispersed across the fields.
Monuments to kings.

A man in a moth-eaten suit
sees a train off, heading, like everything here, for the sea,
smiles at his daughter, leaving for the East.
A whistle blows.

And the endless sky over the tiles
grows bluer as swelling birdsong fills.
And the clearer the song is heard,
the smaller the bird.

1976

Plato Elaborated

I

I should like, Fortunatus, to live in a city where a riv-
er would jut out from under a bridge like a hand from a sleeve,
    and would flow toward the gulf, spreading its fingers
like Chopin, who never shook a fist at anyone as long as he lived.

There would be an Opera House, in which a slightly overripe
tenor would duly descant Mario's arias, keep-
    ing the Tyrant amused. He'd applaud from his loge, but
I from the back rows would hiss through clenched teeth, "You creep."

That city would not lack a yacht club, would not lack
a soccer club. Noting the absence of smoke from the brick
    factory chimneys, I'd know it was Sunday,
and would lurch in a bus across town, clutching a couple of bucks.

I'd twine my voice into the common animal hoot-
ing on that field where what the head begins is finished by the foot.
    Of the myriad laws laid down by Hammurabi
the most important deal with corner kicks, and penalty kicks to boot.

II

I'd want a Library there, and in its empty halls I'd browse
through books containing precisely the same number of commas as
    the dirty words in daily gutter language—
words which haven't yet broken into literary prose. Much less into verse.

There'd be a large Railroad Station in that city—its façade,
damaged in war, would be much more impressive than the outside
    world. Spotting a palm tree in an airline window,
the ape that dozes within me would open its two eyes wide.

And when winter, Fortunatus, threw its coarse shroud over the square,
I would wander, yawning, through the Gallery, where
every canvas, especially those of David and Ingres,
would seem as familiar as any birthmarks are.

From my window, at dusk, I would watch the horde
of bleating automobiles as they flash back and forth
past shapely nude columns in Doric hairdos,
standing pale and unrebellious on the steps of the City Court.

III

There would be a café in that city with a quite
decent blancmange, where, if I should ask why
we need the twentieth century when we already
have the nineteenth, my colleague would stare fixedly at his fork or his knife.

Surely there is a street in that city with twin rows of trees,
an entranceway flanked by a nymph's torso, and other things equally
recherchés:
and a portrait would hang in the drawing room, giving you an idea
of how the mistress of the house looked in her salad days.

I would hear an unruffled voice calmly treat
of things not related to dinner by candlelight;
the flickering flames on the hearth, Fortunatus,
would splash crimson stains on a green dress. But finally the fire would go
out.

Time, which—unlike water—flows horizontally, threading its way
from Friday to Saturday, say,
would, in the dark of that city, smooth out every wrinkle
and then, in the end, wash its own tracks away.

IV

And there ought to be monuments there. Not only the bronze riders I would
know by name—

men who have thrust their feet into History's stirrups to tame
   History—I would know the names of the stallions also,
considering the stamp which the latter came

to brand the inhabitants with. A cigarette glued
to my lip, walking home well past midnight, I would conjecture aloud—
   like some gypsy parsing an open palm, between hiccups,
reading the cracks in the asphalt—what fate the lifeline of the city showed.

And when they would finally arrest me for espionage,
for subversive activity, vagrancy, for *ménage*
   à trois, and the crowd, boiling around me, would bellow,
poking me with their work-roughened forefingers, "Outsider! We'll settle
                                        your hash!"—

then I would secretly smile, and say to myself, "See,
this is your chance to find out, in Act Three,
   how it looks from the inside—you've stared long enough at the outside—
so take note of every detail as you shout, '*Vive la Patrie!*' "

                                        [February] 1977

Letters from the Ming Dynasty

I

Soon it will be thirteen years since the nightingale
fluttered out of its cage and vanished. And, at nightfall,
the Emperor washes down his medicine with the blood
of another tailor, then, propped on silk pillows, turns on a jeweled bird
that lulls him with its level, identical song.
It's this sort of anniversary, odd-numbered, wrong,
that we celebrate these days in our "Land-under-Heaven."
The special mirror that smooths wrinkles even
costs more every year. Our small garden is choked with weeds.
The sky, too, is pierced by spires like pins in the shoulder blades
of someone so sick that his back is all we're allowed to see,
and whenever I talk about astronomy
to the Emperor's son, he begins to joke . . .
This letter to you, Beloved, from your Wild Duck
is brushed onto scented rice paper given me by the Empress.
Lately there is no rice but the flow of rice paper is endless.

II

"A thousand-li-long road starts with the first step," as
the proverb goes. Pity the road home does
not depend on that same step. It exceeds ten times
a thousand li, especially counting from zeros.
One thousand li, two thousand li—
a thousand means "Thou shalt not ever see
thy native place." And the meaninglessness, like a plague,
spreads from words onto numbers, onto zeros especially.

Wind blows us westward like the yellow tares
from a dried pod, there where the Wall towers.
Against it man's figure is ugly and stiff as a frightening hieroglyph,
as any illegible scripture at which one stares.
This pull in one direction only has made

me something elongated, like a horse's head,
and all the body should do is spent by its shadow
rustling across the wild barley's withered blade.

1977

The Rustle of Acacias

Summertime, the cities empty. Saturdays, holidays
drive people out of town. The evenings weigh
you down. Troops could be marched in at even pace.
And only when you call a girlfriend on the phone,
who's not yet headed south and is still at home,
do you prick up your ears—laughter, an international drone—

and softly lay the phone down: the city and the regime
are fallen; the stoplights more and more often gleam
with the red. Picking up a newspaper, you read it from
where "Doing the Town" spills its microscopic type.
Ibsen is leaden. A. P. Chekhov is trite.
Better go for a stroll, to work up an appetite.

The sun always sets behind the TV tower. The West
is right there—where ladies are frequently in distress,
where gents fire six-shooters and say, "Get lost!"
when they're asked for money. There "Man Oh Man"
climbs from a silver clarinet fluttering in black hands.
The bar is a window opened onto those lands.

A pyramid of full bottles has a New York chic;
that sight alone will give you a kick.
What reveals it's the Orient, though, is the bleak, oblique
cuneiform of your thoughts, a blind alley each—
and the banknotes either with Mohammed or with his mountain peak
and a hissing into your ear of a passionate "Do you speak . . ."

And when, after, you weave homeward, it's the pincer device,
a new Cannae where, voiding his great insides
in the bathroom, at 4 a.m., with his eyes
goggling out at you from the oval mirror

above the washbasin, and gripping his very near
sword, "Cha-cha-cha" utters the new conqueror.

[1974–75]

Elegy: For Robert Lowell

I

In the autumnal blue
of your church-hooded New
England, the porcupine
sharpens its golden needles
against Bostonian bricks
to a point of needless
blinding shine.

White foam kneels and breaks
on the altar. People's
eyes glitter inside
the church like pebbles
splashed by the tide.

What is Salvation, since
a tear magnifies like glass
a future perfect tense?
The choir, time and again,
sings in the key of the Cross
of Our Father's gain,
which is but our loss.

There will be a lot,
a lot of Almighty Lord,
but not so much as a shred
of your flesh. When man dies
the wardrobe gapes instead.
We acquire the idle state
of your jackets and ties.

II

On the Charles's bank
dark, crowding, printed letters
surround their sealed tongue.
A child, commalike, loiters
among dresses and pants
of vowels and consonants

that don't make a word. The lack
of pen spells
their uselessness. And the black

Cadillac sails
through the screaming police sirens
like a new Odysseus keeping silence.

III

Planes at Logan thunder
off from the brown mass
of industrial tundra
with its bureaucratic moss.

Huge autoherds graze
on gray, convoluted, flat
stripes shining with grease
like an updated flag.

Shoals of cod and eel
that discovered this land before
Vikings or Spaniards still
beset the shore.

In the republic of ends
and means that counts each deed
poetry represents
the minority of the dead.

Now you become a part
of the inanimate, plain
terra of disregard
of the common pain.

IV
You knew far more
of death than he ever will
learn about you or
dare to reveal.

It might feel like an old
dark place with no match
to strike, where each word
is trying a latch.

Under this roof
flesh adopts all
the invisibility of
lingering soul.

In the sky with the false
song of the weathercock
your bell tolls
—a ceaseless alarm clock.

1977

149

Strophes

I

Like a glass whose imprint
leaves a circular crown
on the tablecloth of the ocean
which can't be shouted down,
the sun has gone to another
hemisphere where none
but the fish in the water
are ever left alone.

II

In the evening here it's
warm. The silence is
completed literally, dearest,
by a parrot's speechlessness.
Into the shrubs of celandine
the moon pours its milk:
far away, in outline,
a body's inviolable silk.

III

Dearest, what's the point of
arguing over the past
which, in its own turn, is over.
The needle's forever lost
in the human haystack,
not to be found in there.
Feels like hitting a shadow
or—moving your queen on a square.

IV

All that we've got together,
what we've called our own,

time, regarding as extras,
like the tide on pebble and stone,
grinds down, now with nurture,
now with a chisel's haste,
to end with a Cycladean sculpture,
with its featureless face.

V

Ah, the smaller the surface,
the more modest the hope
of faithfulness and unselfish
love for this speck or drop.
It may be that a body's loss,
in general, from view
is the vengeance on farsightedness
the landscape thinks its due.

VI

Only space spots self-interest
in a finger pointing afar,
and light has its swiftness
in an empty atmosphere.
So eyes receive their damage,
from how far one looks.
More than they do from old age
or from reading books.

VII

The impact of darkness's
harm is identical,
for dark's implied flatness
borrows from the vertical.
Man is only the author
of the tightly clenched fist;
thus spoke the aviator
vanishing into the mist.

The bleaker things are, for some reason,
the simpler. No more do you
crave for an intermission
like a fiery youth.
The light on the boards, in the stage wings,
grows dim. You walk out right
into the leaves' soft clapping,
into the U.S. night.

IX

Life's a freewheeling vendor:
occiput, penis, knee.
And geography blended
with time equals destiny.
Its power is learned of faster
if the stick drives it in.
You bow to the Fatal Sister
who simply loves to spin.

X

My forehead's withered forget-me-
not twists my dental set.
Like our thirty-third letter
I jib all my life ahead.
You know, dear, all whom anguish
pleads for, those out of reach,
are prey of the laws of language—
periods, commas, speech.

XI

Dearest, there are no unfortunates,
no living and no dead.
All's just a march of consonants
on crooked legs, instead.
The swineherd exaggerated,
obviously, his role;

his pearl, however unheeded,
will outlast us all.

XII

True, the more the white's covered
with the scatter of black,
the less the species cares
for its past, for its blank
future. And that they neighbor
just increases the speed
the pen picks up on the paper,
promises little good.

XIII

You won't receive an answer
if "Where to?" swells your voice,
since all parts of the world are
joined up in the kingdom of ice.
Language possesses a pole, named
"North," where a voice won't hoist
its flag, where the snow finds holes and
cracks in the Elzevir cast.

XIV

These lines are a doomed endeavor
to save something, to trace,
to turn around. But you never
lie in the same bed twice.
Not even if the chambermaid
forgets to change the sheets;
this isn't Saturn, you won't
land from its ring on your feet.

XV

From the drab carousel that
Hesiod sings and chides
you get off not where you got

on, but where night decides.
No matter how hard you're rubbing
the dark with your pupils, the Lord's
idea of repetition's
confined to the jibing words.

XVI

Thus one skewers a morsel
of lamb, rakes the fire up.
I've done my best to immortal-
ize what I failed to keep.
You've done your best to pardon
all my blunderings.
In general, the satyr's song
echoes the rustle of wings.

XVII

Dearest, we are even.
We are immunized, so to speak,
with each other, as if for
pox in a time of plague.
The object of evil gossip
alone gets a forearm shot
with its consoling chance of
dwindling into a spot.

XVIII

Ah, for the bounty of sibyls,
the blackmail of future years,
as for the lash of our middle
names, memory, no one cares.
To them belongs, like bundles
to storks, the sick-sweetness of lies.
But as long as forgiveness
and print endure, we're alive.

XIX

These things will merge together
in the eyes of the crew
peering from their flying saucer
at the motley scene below.
So whatever their mission
is, I suppose it's best
we're apart and their vision
won't be put to the test.

XX

Well, then, remove the Virgin
from the gold frame; put in
the family snapshot version:
a view of the earth from the moon.
A cousin never came close in
to photograph us two
together, nor did the plainclothesmen.
All had too much to do.

XXI

More out of place than a mammoth
in a symphony den
is the sight of us both smothered
in the present. Good men
of tomorrow will surely wonder
at such a diluted mix:
a dinosaur's passions rendered
here in the Cyrillic marks.

XXII

These rambling phrases feature
an old man's twaddle, spew.
At our age, judges issue
stiffer sentences to
criminals, and, by the same token,
to their own fragile bones and teeth.

But the free word has no one
there to get even with.

XXIII

So we switch lights off in order
to knock over a stool.
All talk about the future
is the same old man's drool.
Better, dearest, to bring
it all to an end, with grace,
helping the darkness along
with the muscles of one's own face.

XXIV

Here our perspective ends. A pity
that it's so. What extends
is just the winding plenty
of time, of redundant days;
gallops in blinkers of cities,
etc., to the finish in view;
piling up needless words of which
none is about you.

XXV

Down near the ocean,
a summer night. I feel
the heat like a strange hand's motion
on my skull. Orange peel
stripped from its content withers,
grows hard. And the flies flit
like the priests of Eleusis,
performing their rites over it.

XXVI

I hear the lime tree whisper,
leaning my head on my hand.
This is worse than the whimper

156

and the famous bang.
This is worse than the word said
to soothe children after a fall,
because after this there follows
nothing at all.

1978

San Pietro

Three weeks now and the fog still clings to the white
bell tower of this dull brown quarter
stuck in a deaf-and-dumb corner
of the northern Adriatic. Electric
lights go on burning in the tavern at noon.
Deep-fried yellow tints the pavement
flagstone. Cars at a standstill
fade out of view without starting their engines.
And the end of a sign's not quite legible. Now
it isn't dampness that seeps through the ocher and terra-cotta
but terra-cotta and ocher that seep through the dampness.

Shadow draws sustenance from the light
and responds with Christian rejoicing
as a coat is taken down
from its nail. Shutters have spread their wings
like angels plunged headfirst
into someone else's squabbles. Here and there
scab-encrusted stucco peels off,
exposing inflamed red bricks, and skivvies,
drying for three weeks, have gotten
so attached to the open air and their line
that if someone goes outdoors it's with
nothing on under his jacket, barefooted in his slippers.

Two in the afternoon. A postman's silhouette
takes on sharp definition in a hallway only
to become an instant later a silhouette again.
A bell, as it tolls in the fog,
merely repeats the procedure.
So you automatically glance around

in your own direction—like a random stroller
trying for a better look at a pretty girl's ankles
as she rustles past—but you can't see a thing
except scraps of fog. No wind; only stillness.
Indirection. Around a bend
streetlamps trail off like white ellipses,
followed by nothing but a smell of seaweed
and the outline of a pier. No wind.
And stillness like the whinny of Victor
Emmanuel's never faltering cast-iron mare.

II

In winter, dusk, as a rule, comes too early—
somewhere external, out there, up above.
Tightly swaddled in tattered gauze,
the hands of the town clock
lag behind the scattered daylight
fading in the distance.
A lodger out for some cigarettes
ten minutes later returns to his room
via the tunnel his own body has
burrowed through the fog.
The continuous drone of an unseen airplane
conjures up the hum of a vacuum
at the far end of a hotel corridor,
then dies away, blotting up the light.
"*Nebbia*," yawns the weatherman;
momentarily, eyelids close
like a clam when a fish swims by
(with the pupil briefly descending
into its mother-of-pearl darkness).
A lightbulb framed by an archway looks like
a youngster absorbed in his reading
under the covers; the covers are gathered,
like the toga of a saint in a niche. The present,
our time, bounces off the rusty brick

of the old basilica with a thump, as if
a white leather ball had been slammed against it
by schoolboys after school.

Shabby façades, chipped and pitted,
with no option of standing in profile.
Only the bare calves of curved balusters
animating the tightly shuttered balconies
on which no one—neither heiress nor governess—
has emerged in two hundred years.
Cornices chosen by monsters wedded
in embrace or simply bored to death.
Columns guttering like stearin,
and the blind, agate splendor
of impenetrable glass behind which lurk
a couch and an upright piano:
ancient secrets that are in fact
best kept dark by daylight.

When the weather's cold, normal sound would rather
bask in the warmth of a throat than risk echo's whimsy.
A fish is tight-lipped; deep inland
a turtledove sings its song. But you can't hear
either one. A canal bridge spanning fresh water
keeps the hazy bank on the other side
from breaking away and drifting seaward.
So then, on breath-coated glass, one can trace the initials
of those whose absence is hard to swallow;
and a cherished monogram trickles down
as the tail of a sea horse. Apply that red
sponge of your lungs and soak up the thick milky
mist—the breath of Amphitrite and her Nereids!
Stretch out a hand—and your fingertips
will touch a torso that's flecked with tiny
bubbles and scented with the iodine of childhood.

III

A swish of ruffles on the washed and ironed
sheet of the bay and, for a moment, colorless air
condenses into a pigeon or a sea gull,
but quickly dissipates. Dinghies, longboats,
gondolas, flatbottoms, hauled from the water,
lie scattered like odd shoes on the sand
creaking underfoot. Remember:
any movement is basically
a shift of body weight from one location
to another. Remember: the past won't fit
into memory without something left over;
it must have a future. And remember carefully:
only water, and it alone,
everywhere and always stays true to it-
self, unsusceptible to metamorphoses, level,
present wherever dry land
is gone. And the inflation of living—
with its beginning, middle, thinning calendar,
end, et cetera—shrinks before
colorless, shallow, eternal ripples.

The rigid, lifeless wire of a grapevine
quivers imperceptibly with its own tension.
Trees in the garden blackness,
indistinguishable from a fence resembling
someone without anything or, more important,
anyone left to confess to.
Twilight. No wind. The stillness.
The crunch of coquina, the rustle of crushed,
moldering reeds. A tin can launched skyward
by the tip of a shoe goes sailing
out of sight, and a minute later
there is still no sound of it falling on
wet sand. Or, for that matter, a splash.

[1977]
Venice

GORBUNOV

AND

GORCHAKOV

.

Gorbunov and Gorchakov

"So, what'd you dream of this time, Gorbunov?"
"Oh, mushrooms mostly." "Mushrooms? Curious.
Again?" "Again." "You really make me laugh."
"And why is that? It's pretty serious.
Regularity in sleep's the stuff
the doctors seem to think is curing us."
"No offense—but you've not had enough
of all this fungus?" "Well, up here I guess
it's all I've got." "In Leningrad we have
so many dreams, but 'mushroom' clearly is

the one you're wedded to." "And what
are all you Leningraders dreaming, then?"
"Well, it depends. Of concerts forested
with bows. Of avenues and alleys. Men—
just faces. (All in all, they're fragmented.)
The Neva, bridges. Or a page I can
discern—although the nurse collects, come bed-
time, all our specs—without my glasses on!"
"That dream's too much for these dull eyes to read!"
"And then I dream myself back here again."

"Who needs real life? Just take a look around.
Now there's a dream. The day's gratuitous.
The dawn dims dreams like that. And how you groan
with rage when you're awakened.—Mickiewicz!
Try and keep it down, okay?—For one
of those I'd gladly slumber through to dusk,
miss supper, too . . ." "Sometimes my dreams are prone
to birds, to bullfinches, a kid who is
leaping puddles—and it's me . . ." "What's wrong?
Go on!" "I think I've got the flu. Do these

things interest you at all? What for?" "Beats me.
Just do." "I dream of childhood: sneaking through
an attic with my pals, just two or three
of us. And of old age—nowhere to go
to shake off *that* unholy mess, I see.
Old man, young brat . . ." "Bleak apposition, no?"
"Oh, Gorbunov, that's pure stupidity.
These dreams are only manufactured so
as to give our nights variety,
to give day's heritage a jolt or two."

"Now there's a conundrum, this 'heritage.'
A question, though, you can't ignore:
what *of* old age? You hardly act your age,
or even have gray hairs." "Or ever snore
quite like Babanov on the window ledge?
Or ever, like Mickiewicz does, resort
to bustling and garbled badinage?
What'd we get imagination for
if not to use it pump-like to discharge
old age into our dreams." "Forgive me, Gor-

chakov, but in that case it can't be true
it's you you're dreaming of." "The Crosses was
constructed for stone-headed fools like you.
And there they'll keep you living under glass!
So tell me who I'm dreaming of . . . yoo hoo!"
"Gor-kiewicz . . . or Gor-banov, no?" "You ass!
You're crazy, Gorbunov." "The face I knew—
as yours—with their gray hair. My friend, for us
there's daily self-deceit aplenty to
disgust." "Next they'll sew your pocket closed."

"I sport pajamas with no underwear
on as it is." "At times I see a ring
of burning logs, and stoves . . ." "A real one there!
Streets, conversations. Simply things. The string

and woodwind sections playing as a pair.
And women. And, perhaps, a spicy fling."
"Just yesterday I dreamt of silverware
for six." "Do they amount to anything—
your dreams—or whirl like chaos everywhere?"
"Some seem coherent, some just menacing."

"Herr Freud says we're imprisoned by our dreams."
"I've always heard that we are slaves to habit.
Apparently you're stumped by what this means."
"No, I can see the page on which I read it."
"Freud was a liar." "Liars come in reams . . .
Now let's suppose you're in the mood to have it—"
"You mean the thing in pants?" "Or out, it seems
—but dream your face with titmice gnawing at it.
No gossip's more explicit than your dreams."
"And so this brings us to your mushrooms, *ibid.*"

"They're just like islands. (Mushrooms even sprout
like little islands.) And the same can stand
for streets and alleys, dead ends, words. Throughout
our lives we speak in spurts, or tend to. And
between the spurts, like silence, all about
is grass. But you can touch them with your hand!
And so they have unbounded rights, and what
sustains the solid ground on which I stand
seems as unsteady as a rocking float
the Neva's currents bear away from land."

"Then you're just like those fishermen who face
the water, watching where their bobbins go,
for hour after hour lodged in place?
I've got it right?" "So far, exactly so."
"And, during supper, fashioning new shapes
of lures, lighthearted, in the evening's glow?"
"And hiding mealworms in my tackle case!"
"You'll be locked in here forever." "No!

Why are you aggravating me?" "Because
my name is Gorchakov, as well you know."

Gorbunov and Gorchakov

"Had supper?" "Yeah, some vegetables, a dish
of Jell-O." "Things keep looking up, I see.
And what's outside?" "The starry fields." "What's this?
Another Galileo, doubtlessly!"
"With the departure of Aquarius
around the twentieth of February, we
see Pisces in ascendancy, the fish-
sign pledging rivers will again run free."
"And what about the earth?" "The earth?" "Well, yes.
What's down below?" "That alley edged with trees."

"You know what, Gorbunov? Your case is sad:
a neo-Newton-*cum*-analysand.
There's this guy Khomutov, who says amid
the lockups' retching, histrionics, and
the noise, 'Name's Hamilton, and I'm not mad.'
And yet he snores just like a khariton."
"The seaport boom that Peter made
brought all assorted Teutons on.
The names were harder than the work they did.
Our Khomutov may be a Hamilton."

"The heater's on, and yet I feel a chill."
"Don't lean against the window, then." "Why not?
You think your shiny pets above us will . . . ?"
"Are you convinced?" "Oh no, I'm full of doubt:
I see the snowdrifts and the lane. That's all."
"Look over there: Aquarius is out,

he's bending with the Dipper." "We'd do well
to have a telescope. You wouldn't shout
so much." "A telescope! In here? Like hell!"
"What *are* you getting so worked up about?"

"You've put your filthy feet up on my cot.
At least you could have taken off those mold-
y slippers first." "I'm cold. You know, the thought
devoted to your chanterelles has told
on me. I'm chilled down to my bones without
my slippers on. And so you shouldn't scold."
"Did Freud dream up such progress? That I doubt.
And progress is a thing we should uphold:
the activist, he dreams a rainy wood;
the passivist contracts a nasty cold."

"Your chanterelles are hazards to the sane.
Beware, they're far from harmless, Gorbunov.
How much importance do you give to them?"
"As much as I give love." "And what is love?"
"The end to loneliness." "The very end?"
"It's being able, once, to stand above
the bed and, by just bending over in
the silence, with your hands, brow, breath, touch life."
"What are you staring at? The stars? The lane?"
"The opposite of empty narrative."

"Toss me an apple." "Catch." "Just tell me this:
what are your mushrooms, if you know at all?"
"Whenever I see toadstools in the grass
or forest floor, I find that I recall,
well, love. It's in the mind, or blood perhaps,
for always like an echo, dim but real,
I feel it." "That's just habit and, alas,
the mind's penchant for going general."
"The hands do that. Upstairs what's striking is
a total dearth of the habitual."

"So in the darkness of your sleep you dream
of chanterelles?" "Yes, constantly." "And so
you dream of love?" "It's all the same . . . You seem
to think that's strange." "Not strange. It's sinful, though.
Yes, sinful, and, to tell the truth, I deem
the whole thing utterly disgraceful." "No!"
"What's got you smirking now?" "You're such a scream."
"Toss me an apple, won't you?" "Sure, although
you'll never catch all that the mushrooms mean."
" 'Mushrooms'? That's polygamy, you know.

There now! I planted that one on your chin!
The bitterness I feel is manifest
in my reproach." "You tell me it's a sin,
but sin is something punished in the flesh,
and how can Gorbunov be punished when
life's agonies lie focused in his breast
as in a prism? Is the future clear
of obstacles?" "Apparently we're guests
at someone's wake." "Apparently my grin
makes me, today at least, an optimist."

"And the Last Judgment?" "That's just memory
in flashback, like a film. Why magnify
Apocalypse? Come on, what's it to me?
Five months spent in a wasteland. Merely five.
Well, I've blown half my life and I would be
content to sleep with mushrooms till I die.
I know, however, when and where I'll flee
before the Fiery Angel of the Sky . . ."
"Pain crushes pride." "No, not a bit. The tree
of pride sucks up our suffering to thrive."

"You're saying you don't fear the dark?" "It has
its landmarks, and with some of them I am
acquainted rather well." "You swear it does?"
"Plenty. Just give a whistle and they'll come."

"Vanity's mother is inventiveness."
"I doubt the wisdom of that apothegm.
A man's soul never feels the loss of space."
"And of dead creatures would you say the same?"
"I think the soul, while living in this place,
assumes the features of its mortal frame."

CANTO III

Gorbunov in the Night

"It's night. The hospital. The hostile ground . . .
This hardly qualifies for tragedy . . .
Besides, the tougher life a mortal's found,
the smoother things will seem on Judgment Day
for this soul, when the sentences resound.
I feel, when life is really wretched, I
could tolerate with ease a second round.
That's why inside the man—a child, and why
the mushrooms got me here, though all they meant
to me is out there somewhere, far away.

I dream of chanterelles, but never dream
now of my wife . . . It seems that's as it ought
to be. As fabric tears where thinnest. Some
truth in—got her pregnant, guess I thought
I'd make her stay. The reasoning of a bum.
Apparently I finally bottomed out.
Don't know about my soul, although I am
about my eardrums' health in little doubt:
I hear Babanov now—he's humming, comb
in mouth; a sheet is rustling on a cot.

I hear a voice amid these nighttime sounds—
not auricular hallucination, for

171

the ear's outfitted even with defense
against the pressure at the ocean's floor.
Besides, I'm contradicted by its sense,
that voice—consistent, hollow, sure.
Whose voice is it? Can't be my wife's. And since
persistently the supernatural world
stays silent as my wife, it can't be saints.
Oh, how I wish I had my muffler here!

It's night. The hospital. The lane, the drifts
of snow. An alder hums, contesting heaven.
Kike-wise the night nurse in the hallway lifts
his Jewish telescope and peers in, laughing.
My pupil's shrinking, shrinking—it resists
the bed contracting on me like a coffin.
And my blood bubbles like bicarbonates.
My ankle freezes as it comes uncovered.
My mind divides the way a microbe splits
and in the silence multiplies forever.

Yes, two of us, before the altar. Inasmuch . . .
She left, and somewhat irritated, maimed,
I crave an interlocutor to match.
Yes, there were two. Indeed, so two remained.
Relieving February, enter March:
that's how the altar, in its turn remind-
ing one of guardsmen, like the still night-watch,
because of how the calendar's designed,
obstructs the silence, my assault on which
creates another force field here inside.

She left. I am possessed by, I possess
myself. Myself? Well, maybe I should call
for Gorchakov? . . . Hey, Gorchakov! . . . I guess
the bed-bell's rung. But is it, after all,
so senseless for one pair of vying lips,

especially without a music hall,
to sing as two? I watch them as they press
together, syllable by syllable.
I am—a circle cleaved. Thus, more or less,
we're magnets, horseshoe-shaped, identical.

Night. Night. My lips performing a duet.
You think that it's too good for you? I say
that there's a special coziness in it.
It is a contradiction, yes, but they
are close. Almost a family when bit.
And all the more so in a brief display.
The upper lip is like a groom, to wit:
The lower lip is like his fiancée.
But that which splits in two will surely split
into two hundred just as easily.

And everything that's been twofold is then
accountable, is then no longer moot.
The solitude dilemma's answered when
it's split. Despair divides my soul like wood—
in two—and yet it's not that I remain
beside it *tête-à-tête.* Two-souledness would
seem atheistic, but it's not the flame
that logs require: the inverse makes it hot.

O God in heaven, if you're so designed
that you can listen to two voices blast
at once from but one set of lips and find
in them not noise but strife between the past
and future, raise to you my coughing mind
and plant its microbes where your light is cast.
Divide among them with your mighty hand
the sum of these convulsive thoughts and days.
And leave the fraction of me left behind
to triumph over silence then, at least.

But if I really need a listener, send,
O Lord, without delay, a denizen
of heaven down to me. I won't pretend
to be superior to him in sin
or sarcasm. He wouldn't comprehend
them anyway. But if that's out, well then,
let cherubs and not Gorchakov ascend
above the filthy hole they keep me in,
and, like your blessing, circle to the end
above the sobbing and surveillant men."

Gorchakov and the Doctors

"Well, Gorchakov, make your report." "You mean
on Gorbunov?" "Of course, on Gorbunov."
"His mental operation is, when seen
in toto, dialectical, but half
of all his statements clearly contravene
the Party's views, and several, as to both
events and things, are new to us." "A sign
his blood is not nitrogenous enough,
and thus we see disintegration in
the patient's self-controlling operative."

"His chin is puffy, asymmetrical.
His brows close-knit and thick. His nose is mapped
with intersecting veins that twist and swell."
"Bad kidneys, I should say." "His forehead, wrapped
in compresses and asymmetrical as well,
is like a knot of arteries that snapped.
His weakness and his god's the chanterelle.
With women, you might say he's handicapped.

'The inner world is made majestical;
the outer, correspondingly, is scrapped'—

now there's your standard Gorbunov-ish line.
In regular pronouncements more or less
like this one, one can easily divine
all his wrongheaded—his non-Partyness."
"A leftward shift. He's out to undermine
our trusted Marxist principles." "There is
too little evidence." "Well, does he whine
at atmospheric changes?" "Does he miss
the fairer sex a lot?" "No, there he's fine,
his manner, really, the antithesis,

in fact, of a . . . oh, what's it called? I say . . ."
"Composure, Gorchakov." "A paramour."
"And how's he down below? . . . *Déshabillé*,
his privates . . ." "Strictly business. Out the door,
the can, and back again three times a day.
If you'll forgive my crudeness." "Say no more.
And have a glass of water." "Water?" "Hey!
You were expecting cognac?" "No! I'm sure
I never touch the stuff!" "Then tell us why
you licked your lips when I began to pour."

"I'm not sure why . . . Some memory of water."
"Water? What?" "I can't remember what.
I'm sorry . . ." "Supper, did you drink a lot, or—"
"No . . . you've tied my mind up in a knot . . .
But wait! A man . . . a well . . . and sands like Tartar
hordes a-whirling round . . . He hasn't got
a drop to drink; he's thin; it's hotter, hotter . . .
Sun is at . . . what do you call it . . . at
the zenith. Hostile ground. It's getting harder
now to see. Then, boom, a well . . ." "Proceed!"

"Then everything again is empty, dead!
The well, well, disappeared with all the rest . . ."
"Gorchakov? What's wrong?" "I've lost my head.
I'm sorry. I admit I was impressed
when with such majesty today he made
his full idealism manifest."
"Who? Gorbunov?" "Of course! Who else? He said . . .
I . . . er . . . oh, please forgive me, I digress."
"No, no. Don't worry. Please, do go ahead."
"I'm too involved with Gorbunov, I guess.

Non-Party! *That's* what's wrong with him!
Indeed! And when the temperature approaches
zero, he moves to that end of the room . . .
well . . . toward the heater . . . to the left." "Prodigious!"
"Is he at all religious?" "Is a hymn?
He is exceedingly relig-religious!
Sometimes I am afraid the day will come
he'll kneel and summon God from heaven's reaches
down to bless the sanitorium."
"Well, being so non-Party, sure he's anxious."

"So: 'deviations to the left.' " "Ha-ha!"
"Dear colleague, what's so funny?" "Just the plain
stupidity of what you said just now.
Observe: the heater, as we ascertain,
is left of Gorchakov, it surely . . ." "Ah,
is right of Gorbunov! Like king and queen
in chess. Well, to be safe we won't withdraw
the other option but instead maintain
the presence of the two phenomena."
"What good's a song without a good refrain?"

"Well, Doctors, do we have our diagnosis?
Staple this; now, Gorchakov, please sign
here, at the bottom." "Haven't got my glasses."
"Won't mine do?" "They might. Let's see: 'We find

some deviations to the left at places' . . .
That's for sure! . . . 'and to the right' . . . That's fine!
They're both correct. We'll fix these lordly asses.
Either we'll exterminate their kind,
or—" "Thank you, Comrade Gorchakov. It pleases
us to let you off at Eastertime."

"I thank you, friends. Mere thanks don't say enough
to thank in full . . . What now? Should I salaam?
Where's Gorbunov? I've got to open up
his eyes! My God, not one true word . . . I am—
but who am I so self-reproaching of?
To hell with woodsy paranoiacs! Damn!
The warp's gone crazy under which the woof
has lost its thread while sliding home.
It's so peculiar now that Gorchakov
speaks Gorbunov's maniac idiom."

A Song in the Third Person

"He said to him." "And then he said to him."
"And then he said." "He answered." "And he said."
"Then he." "And he then said into the wind."
"He gazed into the dark and said." "He said
again to him." "But, so to speak, to say
he said is not the same as saying what
he said." "And then he said, 'Don't lose your way
in details; all is clear. That's that.' "
"The one he-said flows on into the next."
"Until he-saids of sin and penance flow
together." "Silent on the table rests
he-said." "And in the end they form a row,
like Tartar yokes." "And then he said to him."

"And he connected his he-said, in line
with that he-said, whose echo echoed thin."
"And then he said to him, and filled the time."

"And then he said." "It is as when a stone
is thrown into a pond. The rings—one, two,
six . . ." "And he said." "The rings are really one,
although the radius is stretched, it's true."
"He-said—a ring." "He-said—another ring."
"And his he-said collided with the ground."
"His own he-said came like a boomerang
back to slap him." "No more new worlds around."
"He said." "He said." "He said." "He said." "He said."
"A train!" "And on a line without an end."
"And starting at the station of He-said."
"And who would want to make the tracks his bed?"
"And then he said." "But in response he said."
"He said, then vanished." "On the platform see
he-said." "He said." "But if he-said's a dead
object, should not the same be true of he?"

"And he to him." "And he." "And he to him."
"All right, let's say the evening has begun."
"And he to him." "And it's no idle whim
to think the two together are but one."
"A question—'he.' " "Whose answer is—'to him.' "
"And vice versa." "Yes, they are the same."
"Though there's a strip of light dividing them."
"Only so that each can have a different name."
"Is he related, then, to him?" "Does not
the world of senseless objects boast of some
relations closed to analytic thought?"
"If not a relative, a sort of chum?"
"What won't the judge's chamber analyze!
The judge sits down; his glasses have no glass."
"Then what is he to him?" "A thin disguise
for the he-said." "That beats in-laws, I guess."

"A massive building. Featureless façade.
Two faces pallid from the stench they breathe."
"They are not here." "And where could they have gone?"
"To the he-said-to-him or to the he."
"A massive building. Through the window peer
two silhouettes." "And pandemonium,
as in a station." "Never silence here?"
"Just in the gaps between he-said-to-him."
"A 'said,' you know, requires she."
"But we've been talking of the said of he."
"But, all in all, the silence pleases me."
"Anathema resounds less threateningly."
"So in this place they're scared of silence?" "No,
they are united by he-said, the way
they are by time and place. It is as though
some grand instinct to incest were at play."

"And that's a form of action, isn't it?"
"Oh yes, for they are full of interplay."
"And will they never quit?" "They'll never quit."
"No doubt it's like a proper noun that way."
"That's right. A proper noun is concentrate.
Substitutions, alterations, slight
omissions—such things cannot enter it."
"And that's the vehicle of questions, right?"
"That's it precisely! Indirect discourse
is in reality the most direct."
"And this is something anyone ignores
at peril of his happiness." "Detect-
ing all pronouncements that He-said recites,
like children by the church doors waiting, one
appears almost to enter in the heights
achieved *before* the dialogue's begun."

"Well, what'd you dream about, He-said-to-him?"
"The doctors are too near." "So what? Go on."
"I dreamed of waves. I dreamed that I could swim

179

far out to sea." "Unrealistic! Un—"
"Already he's forgotten all about
his mushrooms." "That's impossible!" "Could be."
"He's simply speaking for them both, no doubt."
"That sort of thing absorbs infinity."
"I saw a host of waves pass in review
as clearly as could be. And as they passed
I saw the sky, and just as clearly, too . . ."
"That's something like a double-barreled blast."
". . . the crests, like manes of horses when
they drag a sinking cart, their only thought
is breaking loose." "And weren't there drowning men
or shipwrecks?" "Aivazovsky I am not!
I saw the spuming breakers. And the shore,
a giant horseshoe . . . And, a distance off,
the He-said moved upon the clouds. It wore
the smile of Gorbunov, of Gorchakov."

CANTO VI

Gorbunov and Gorchakov

"Well, what'd you dream of this time, Gorbunov?"
"But I've already told you all about
my meeting with the doctors." "Knock it off.
I overheard it all myself just out
there in the hall." "I'm saying, Gorchakov—"
"That you dream only of the sea, no doubt."
"That's right, the sea." "You are beyond belief."
"I don't insist on your belief. It's not
important." "What a tangled web you weave
with all your lies. It's easy to pick out

a bad egg by its putrid odor! Phew!"
"Just shut your mouth!" "Why should I shut my mouth?"

"Oh, Gorchakov, I know you through and through . . ."
"X-ray technician now?" "Your 'funny' stuff
is out of place, you know. You might live to
regret it." "Oh, imagine that!" "Don't laugh . . .
Why is it the commission always knew
what we'd discussed as soon as you'd gone off?
You played the stoolie for them, didn't you?
So quit your bride-like blushing, Gorchakov."

"You're angry." "I'm not angry." "Don't torment
me, Gorbunov." "I you? That's funny!" "See,
you're angry." "No, I'm not. And if you want,
I'll even swear to God." "But that would be
unpleasant for you." "I'm not hesitant."
"You seemed to say that with sincerity."
"Now you're starting that again? I can't
believe you think it's worth it watching me."
"So then you'll swear to it." "I bet you won't
believe me if I do." "Well, probably."

"And *I* don't follow what you mean by that."
"I'm mixing up the chaff and wheat." "You are
unable to believe in anything! No, not
in words, or even holy signs." "There's war
in the Crimea—smoke is all about.
That's something, isn't it? I quote from our
grandfather Krylov . . . Prison's what you've got
ahead, you know." "You ought to go before
they send you." "Hey, what are you gaping at?"
"Orlova and Ulanova, two stars."

"I think I'll wander down the hall." "Why?" "Oh,
no reason, just a headache. It's a crime
the way you're always asking questions." "Go
to hell." "What are you after, pal, sublime
illumination?" "Maybe. How 'bout you?"
"You shit! I'm sure you play the stoolie, slime."

181

"I'm just extending my horizons." "Though
without beliefs." "A skeptic in my prime!
Denunciations, conversations—so
it goes. All helps to brighten up the time."

"And somehow time helps brighten up the days."
"I think my head is better." "So you won't
reveal your dream? Come on, no more delays."
"Oh, all that's sad and ugly. I just want
to watch the lights reflecting on the glass."
"Well, shadows from the boardwalk, friend . . ."
"Ulanova! Orlova, too, who stays
in darkened background!" "Coffee's cold." "They meant
a lot, you know. We were at war, and they
were symbols, of a kind, for our home front."

"The second half of February. Look
at what the hands are pointing to." "It's just
zero's radius." "The numbers?" "Like
the border of a plate . . . I somewhere crossed
this service, *à la* Meissen—" "I relate
to counterfeits." "—*King's Workshop* was embossed
on it, and under that a sun like light
that's beaming from a gasolier." "A glass
of gin right now . . ." "A water bottle I'd
not turn away tonight, if it were passed.

Look there! The shadows stream across the lane!"
"Excuse me, I would rather like to see
us turn the conversation back again . . .
to clocks." "What for?" "You judge more cruelly
than I deserve." "Your own lips are to blame."
"So, is it really zero?" "Yes." "But why?"
"Because outside is emptiness." "But then
inside it's warmer than outside can be."
"But one can simply call a heated room
a product of the freezing earth and sky."

"And what about the woodpiles?" "Well, I guess
they're links between outdoors and in—" "Oh, Lord,
the wind is whistling through the crevices!
I'm freezing cold, and hungry as a bear."
"Physicians aren't as big as sicknesses."
"An inner sanctum's greater than a door."
"It is, you know, a shelter nonetheless."
"Don't be a hypocrite. And furthermore,
remember, Gorchakov; the utterness
of uttered words surpasses disbelief by far."

"Yes, as cold is larger than the heat."
"So, too, the clock hands are inferior
to time." "The hollow in the tree can't beat
the tree." "Though hollows are superior
to squirrels." "Who are certainly more sweet
than eagles." "And the fish . . . that thing . . . so pure . . ."
"I want my body naked, head to feet!"
"Where there's a radius, there's, as it were,
a fork and plate." "And burnt wood—" "Can't compete
with my hot-water bottle, that's for sure."

Gorbunov and Gorchakov

"Had supper?" "Yeah, a plate of day-old greens.
It's always greens." "We've got the right to eat
bird food here. Still, it's no use making scenes."
"But why do they refuse to give us meat?"
"Look, there's new firewood stacked up between—"
"I have a perfect right to be upset!"
"No, the administration's right. I mean,
it's right within the radius it's set."
"But neither gut nor cranium's too keen
to squeeze inside it." "Let us not repeat

a conversation we've already had . . .
Besides, my kidney's acting up." "But I—
I am outside the radius." "You're mad!
Then who's this standing here?" "A shell, you see."
"When I was young, the soul's infinitude
was something on which one had much to say."
"But me, I'm *married*. Don't you understand?
My wife—and daughter—both outside the ra-
dius." "You need a bracing shower, friend."
"You know one in the neighborhood?" "Well, try

Opochka Station." "Some place you dreamed?" "Like hell!
More likely you dreamed me." "But it's a day
by train out in the provinces!" "You real-
ly get around." "I should escape this." "Why
waste the time and effort? I can tell
you've really put down roots here, anyway."
"You've put down roots here, too." "In general,
I've gotten lazy, though I am, they say,
swift as the wind. It's really not my style
to walk around in hiking boots." "Okay,

calm down." "I'm calm." "How much'd you make?" "A few
hundred, old currency." "Where at?" "A place in . . ."
"Are you thinking I'll report on you?"
"Who would deny himself the fine sensation?"
"*My* silence ain't enough to save you." "True.
Yes, well, you know, on reconsideration . . ."
"You'd rather think me traitor through and through
than try to speculate on a location."
"Alas, my genealogy is too
ignoble to perform such speculation."

"So why attack the menu?" "It's the rut
of eating . . . Well, I'm not a veteran
in here, and this unvaried menu—" "But
you're using restaurants as comparison."

"I'm stretching out the radius somewhat
to get my family in." "They slaughter one
fat lamb a night at home, no doubt." "Well, what
I'm getting at is that it's still too soon
for me to sacrifice the past." "Oh, cut
the crap." "Why call it crap?" "It's overdone."

"I've stretched the radius's distance way
out to my home." "So much the worse, my friend."
"I'm only one leg of the compass. They,
the stationary leg, support me." "And
somehow this helps to brighten up the day,
this wider radius that you command?"
"The narrower. Down here that's just the way
things are: some move as strangers, others stand
still." "Though a stationary lamppost, say,
reflected in a puddle, will expand."

"I'm moving! Look!" "I don't know where the start
is, but I know the end's in Leningrad
snowdrifts." "I move, therefore I am. Descartes
would envy me." "Of course! It makes me glad
to see enthusiasm from the heart."
"As for me, this slumming in your head
is simply boring." "What about your chart:
the Dipper and the skyline, and all that?"
"Aries: it ascends, curating March."
"A telescope's the thing I wish we had."

"Precisely! Then the both of us could see
those fixèd stellar feet." "Progenitors
of motion." "Making the stability
of both Opochka and Kamchatka ours."
"Born late in March, it is my destiny
to wander. I've been fingerprinted . . . stars
are such unstable points of gravity
they set us all to trembling . . ." "Of course,

as one born under Aries, you should be
beneath a cap of Karakulan furs."

"You think I'm trembling from cold?" "That's why
your toes are turning blue." "And you? What is
your sign?" "Well, I belong to Gemini.
Born under Gemini, in May." "I guess
that makes you warm." "I guess." "Come on. Don't try
to play the genius with non-geniuses!"
"Compared to you it's clear enough that I
am scarcely cold at all." "Enough of this!"
"But, Gorchakov, what's wrong?" "It's all a lie!"
"Oh no, it's true—the months and all." "Alas,

we can't afford a telescope. And thus
we'll never see our distant sponsors." "You're
forgetting that, although the radius
is scorned in life, the compass will endure
forever, Gorchakov." "It's hideous—
the possibility of dying here,
believing it's the end." "Ridiculous!
You won't die." "No? You think not?" "Yes." "You're sure?"
"Of course. We cannot carry on into the next
the burden we, in this life, have to bear."

Gorchakov in the Night

"Your line assures me immortality!
My brain, like convolutions in the bed-
clothes—flooded by the glimmer (towering
above my tiny flame) your words have shed.
Colitis is a curse! . . . thoughts clamoring
inside my head like demons in a brood.

Your torch can't seem to set aglow my wick!
Oh, Gorbunov, your words have set my blood
to seething through my cranium, the way
a spark ignites the chips of bone-dry wood.

He's gone . . . He's left me only monologue.
And the night dial's radius . . . He's stored
some apples as security and lobbed
off like Pilate! In the corner curled,
I will inspect the folding of my robe.
I have a salad bowl—I can discard
its dried remains and doff it like a rogue
in a veritable bowler. Where's this starred
empyrean? The ceiling and the rug.
The window—the reflection of the ward.

Night. Windows swirl the ward and double it.
The bulwarks of infinity. They're all
encased in shutters, though, and don't permit
their own reflections farther than the wall.
In that space—rear end forward—one's a bit
uncertain just whose bed is whose. I'd fall
asleep now if I could, though I admit
I'd like to kill myself in general.
And thus—since here a thing's its opposite—
risk delving deeper still into my soul.

I'd like to fall asleep . . . The orderlies
are still on duty . . . Is the room's reflection
helping them? It merely multiplies
the mess . . . Infinity's multiplication.
I watch myself expand before my eyes;
the panes, encouraging imagination,
press a mile into the space that lies
between the bunks. The fiery sensation
gazing at that distant star implies
that gravity is just degeneration.

Regularity in sleep's the core—
indeed, what helps us to recuperate.
So what do I need Gorbunov, then, for?
Whatever for? . . . Shall we abbreviate
our speech by Gorbunov? No gossip's more
explicit than a dream. No eye as great
as dreams. Herr Freud of course has written we're
imprisoned by them . . . Strange to meditate
on this again . . . When there's no other cure,
the grave, of course, will make a hunchback straight . . .

But these disordered musings are the state
that follows from the silence of the near-
by beds. I feel my very self's at stake
when I don't have an interlocutor.
It is in words alone that I partake
of life. They need a witness and an heir!
And, Gorbunov, you are, make no mistake,
my judge. While I am but an agent here,
connecting sleep and sleeplessness, to make
appraisals of front teeth beyond repair.

It's night. The window vent. Oh, if the guard
would only open it! But it's no use.
My face and shoulders are securely barred
in its reflected surface. If the nurse
would open it, a leak would surely start
in the reflection, and, in turn, induce
a wayward patient who was so inspired—
especially since it isn't far—to loose
his face at least en route to Leningrad.

Oh, Gorbunov! Like any simpleton,
I feel I'm nothing but the radius
a clock hand makes! To wait for me—beyond
the bordered plate or here—I'd have to guess
pitifully, there isn't anyone.

For these dimensions are, for you, alas
too circumscribed. Ahead your martyrdom
is waiting: it's been fitted to your size.
The horror there's a variation on
a ladder's rung, a little door, the pass

where you're expected for too long. My sin
is only that my call won't get to you.
You, Gorbunov! As long as I am in
this world, I know I must surrender to
your power! To you I raise my prayers. I can
go nowhere that your words do not pursue
me. Come to me, I beg you, speak again!
I have to hear your words resounding through
the air. If I've denounced them, it has only been
because I cannot part with them, I know.

Forgive me when you leave me here at last.
It isn't that I fear our parting when,
with walking papers crumpled in my fist,
I finally stretch to you my parting hand.
Like all one has to bear—the catalyst
of boredom and indifference—my friend,
do not resent me, crave revenge. At best
I'm like an echo which continues sound
to save it, in the end, from being lost:
I love you and betray you, too, to pain."

Gorbunov and the Doctors

"Well, Gorbunov, we've brought you here to tell
us everything." "About?" "Your dreams." "About
the compass." "And your daughter." "And the shell."

"And give us names, details." "Let's see. I doubt
my daughter figures in my dreams at all.
In fact, I'm sure of it." "Oh, cut it out!"
"Come on!" "I dreamed about the sea." "Oh hell!"
"Let's do without the wet stuff." "And without
'anchors aweigh' and 'o'er the seas' as well."
"About Opochka . . ." "Can't imagine what

you're after that one for." "For your own good."
"A line that smacks—" "It's necessary. We—"
"—that smacks of questions that Red Riding Hood
asked Granny. You'll recall, I'm sure, that she
inquired about the ears . . . 'Don't be afraid . . .'
She answers, 'Oh, I am afraid . . .' 'Tee-hee—
the better, pet, to hear you with.' " "Who would
have figured that he would turn out to be
a coward." "Anyway, the girl is saved."
"There is a plus in everything, you see."

"Say something, Gorbunov." "You realize
that we'll get angry if you make us wait
too long." "What are you waiting for?" "For lies
unmet by protests to evaporate."
"And then?" "Well, then I think it would be nice
to speak on equal terms, don't you?" "I hate
his whimpering, his stupid shrugs and sighs.
Nurse, an injection will facilitate . . ."
"He's trembling." "Naturally. The needle's size
has caused his thinking to accelerate."

"Well, Gorbunov, recalled your dream?" "It was
the sea. Just that." "No chanterelles?" "In short,
alas, there are no more of them." "Alas?"
"A habit. I got used to their support."
"It often happens, when their women pass
away or go away, that men resort
to words of grief like that." " 'Alas'—a man's

word, when it's said in quotes." "But it's the sort
of word one's likely to hear widows use."
"We'll put that down as well in the report."

"Dreams bare the secret canvas of a man,
of what takes place inside." "And what the eyes
observe is of less interest to us than
what's hidden, for the reason that—" "What lies
outside is Gorchakov. I know." "Well then,
the point is not the mischievous disguise
he has assumed; it's what your dreams make plain:
you gravitate to darker depths." "I guess
I'm dreaming like the Neva flows, you mean.
But mouths of rivers speak not of demise,

but just the opposite: of procreation."
"It's scarcely bearable that any freak
or bum should dump descendants on the nation."
"A pity. For the river, as the Greek
philosopher remarked, though flowing, stays in
one place." "Which is the problem all men seek
to solve." "And Newton's moral." "There! He's raising
Newton!" "And Lomonosov." "Outside?" "A week
in February. Time of hibernation,
denunciations, snowstorms." "It's unique

among the months, in terms of days." "A kind
of cripple." "Don't you think it easier
to live through?" "Shamefully. In fact, I find
it easier than easy to endure."
"And rivers?" "What about them?" "Don't they bind
themselves in ice?" "But it was man we were—"
"Know what awaits you?" "I suspect a signed
certificate committing me." "Yes, sir.
Considering the things you have in mind,
We'll have to keep you on forever here."

"What for? . . . However, well, it's obvious
one must control oneself to be let go."
"And call for Gorchakov." "One can discuss
the stars with him." "Of course." "Which goes to show
that there's a plus in most things." "Yes, a plus!"
"And he, like God, is omnipresent, though
he's in the habit of denouncing us."
"It's nails that hold a horseshoe up, you know."
"How strange that Gorbunov, nailed to the cross,
must look for help from Gorchakov below."

"But why exaggerate like this? Why mumble
these Golgothan thoughts?" "But can't you see
that this is a catastrophe." "You bundle
eternity up with catastrophe."
"Eternity's the bung that plugs the bunghole.
That's why he doesn't want eternity."
"Yes, this is all too hard for him to follow."
"Hey, Gorbunov, you want a cup of tea?"
"Oh, why have you forsaken me?" "Dear fellow,
whom are you calling now?" "He seems to be

lamenting Gorchakov again." "Why not
his daughter or his wife? Why Gorchakov?"
"The whole thing's egotism." "You sure we've got
it right? It's really Gor—" "Hey, Gorbunov!
Look here, your fate has been decided." "What
of Gorchakov's?" "Well, live with the rebuff:
we're freeing him. You're on your own. I'd not
waste sighs on such a creep." "From this day forth,
as usual, my friend, when life is shot,
eternity begins." "Speech signing off."

A Conversation on the Porch

"A massive city in its twilight shroud."
"The streets, like lines in ledgers, parallel."
"A massive madhouse stands." "Looks like a void
existing at the center of the well-
planned universe." "The gate obscures from view
an icy courtyard filled with snow and cords
of wood." "Which is a conversation, too,
since all these things have been described in words."
"Out here are men, and there, the lunatics
who know internal and eternal pain."
"Not 'men' themselves?" "But can one ever fix
the title to one's neighbor?" "They're not men?
The expressions in the eyes, the stance, the frame:
head, sturdy shoulders, legs, and arms that reach . . ."
"The moment that we give a thing a name,
that thing's transformed into a part of speech."
"But what about the body?" "It obeys
the rule." "And what about this place?" "It's called
a madhouse." "And the days?" "Their names are days."
"Oh, everything's transformed again to old

Sodom, built of greedy words. But how
do they come by the right?" "—A word that rings
a nasty bell." "My head's already so
besotted with these words devouring things."
"No question that it causes heads to spin."
"As seas make Gorbunov's; it's for the birds."
"And so it's not the sea that surges in-
to shore, but words are overlapping words."
"And words are sort of holy relics." "Yes,
though once things hung . . . Names are defense
against the very things that they express."

"Against the sense of life?" "Well, in a sense."
"Do they defend against the Passion, too?"
"Against all passions." "God forbid!" "For He
designed His lips for words . . . But then He drew
forth words in His defense." "Well, basically,
that's why His life is so prophetic. It's
insurance that we won't go down, but swim."
"And thus His life's the one thing that admits
two meanings." "It's, therefore, a synonym."

"But what about eternity? Does it
resemble He-said in a Cossack coat?"
"It is the only word that hasn't yet
devoured its earthly object in its throat."
"A hardy word-shield!" "Hardly." "Yet the man
protected by the cross is saved, at least."
"Not fully so." "You mean the synonym
can give no greater guarantee than this?"
"That's true." "But what of love? Can love not stem
the tide of aimless chatter?" "Either you've
descended from the sphere of seraphim
or you're confusing potency with love."
"No word is so devoid of telltale signs."
"And there's no cover that has so devoured
its object, obfuscating its designs.
And nothing is so rending as a word."
"But try regarding this objectively;
to wit: the general observation seems
to be that words are also things, so we
are saved at last!" "It's then the silence comes.

Silence is the future of the days
that roll toward speech, with all we emphasize
in it, as, in our greetings, silence pays
respect to unavoidable goodbyes.
Silence is the future of the words

whose vowels have gobbled up internally
the stuff of things, things with a terror towards
their corners; a wave that cloaks eternity.
Silence is the future of our love;
a space, not an impediment, a space
depriving love's blood-throbbed falsetto of
its echo, of its natural response.
Silence is the present for the men
who lived before us. And, procuress-like,
silence gathers all together in
itself, admitted by the speech-filled present. Life
is but a conversation in the face
of silence." "Gestures, quarrels, men incensed."
"A twilight talking to a murky close."
"With walls that stand like arguments against."

"A massive city in its twilight shroud."
"A speech by chaos, rendered plain as hell."
"Here stands the massive madhouse, like a void
existing at the center of the well-
planned universe." "Goddamn this draft!" "Your curse
won't hurt my ears. My friend, it isn't life
before me but a victory of words."
"And verily the nouns are verbalized!"
"A bird flies upward from its nest when food
is what the little bird is looking for."
"Indeed, a star that climbs above the field
seeks out a brighter interlocutor."
"And all night long, as far as one can view,
with postal slowness, in its turn, the plain
keeps up the conversation." "How can it, too?"
"By means of jaggedness in the terrain."
"But can one, at such distance, hear enough
to know which blabbermouth he bothers with?"
"The higher pitch belongs to Gorbunov,
to Gorchakov, the low." "For what it's worth."

Gorbunov and Gorchakov

"So, what'd you dream of this time?" "Nothing new."
"Then I won't ask." "What's this? You feeling racked
by shame or something suddenly?" "No, view
it simply as a sense of measure, tact."
"How very generous." "What can I do?
This place has gotten to me. And the fact—"
"What fact?" "That I have landed here." "Oh, you
are capable of causing cardiac
arrest. Just take your facts and go to . . . to . . ."
"Come off it now. We've got to interact."

"And who am I to you?" "I wouldn't know."
"No matter . . . So I guess you're leaving. When?"
"Right after Easter." "And from here you'll go . . . ?"
"Home." "They won't hesitate to take you in?"
"They won't." "Where do you live?" "The address? Oh,
I never give that out to anyone."
"That strikes me as a lie." "If you say so."
"Don't tell me fairy tales." "But then again
you won't be coming by to visit." "No?
And why is that?" "Because the outcome's been

decided." "Then you're right." "I think I am."
"You *think* so?" "Oh, I'm sorry! That popped out
by accident. I've no right to dream
of doubt." "So tell me, when you're home, about
the house, how d'you think you'll pass the time?"
"That's my concern." "You're the one who thought
that we should 'interact.' And yet your tone
is hardly conversational. It's odd."
"It's just my nature." "Well, an apple, then,
to change your mood?" "Okay, a nibble, but
I promise I won't take the goods and run . . .

'Hoist-or-heave'—that's my kind of work. Believe
me, pal, all others are superfluous."
"My eyes are being shrouded! Hoist-or-heave,
hoist-or-heave—oh, that's synonymous
with all that happens to me now." "Be brave.
We promise not to drop you." " '*We?*' What does
'we' mean?" "Don't be afraid. Before I leave
I'll teach you palmistry." "If that's the case
I turn my back on you." "You mean that we've
no friendship left? There's no more to discuss?

You could be kinder." "Evidently this
is what my genes designed." "Existence, though,
determines—" "Tea?" "Okay . . . deter—" "I guess
it's cold. You want it warmed a bit?" "Uh, no . . .
cold's fine . . . determines consciousness."
"I'd take that sentence left to right." "Ah, so
you think I am a Jew?" "This apple was
plucked from the tree of knowledge by a Jew."
"No, it was Eve who did the plucking, ass."
"Eve may have, but it seems he did it, too."

"But still, he was a genius in his way.
He founded science, and he's got a name
that's sonorous, in any case." "Let's try
to skip the names. That palindrome
would set them chopping off my hands today."
"You know, he, too, consigned himself to pain.
And now he has whole peoples in his sway."
"Panmongolism! There's a loaded term."
"He was condemned as well." "You mean to say
he was condemned to parting?" "Just condemned."

"But what is parting?" "Must we linger on
this word?" "It's for my files. Elucidate
the ways of parting." "They depend upon
from whom one parts. That's what's at stake.

Where you remain. Can you remain as one,
named So-and-so, in such a place and state?
And if from someone close, to whom he's gone
and for how long." "And if forever?" "Wait . . .
You stand and gape into the dark, alone—
the sort of dark that lowered lids create

for sleeping in. And so you shudder now
and then from grief. The darkness, being real,
is clearly visible. Though now, you know,
there isn't any sea or chanterelle."
"And even in the spring you think it's so?
The springtime makes it easier, I feel."
"I doubt it." "—doubt it gazing at the snow."
"You're like a thing extracted from a field."
"Unlike a gum, the earth's not bleeding, though."
"This evidently is as God has willed.

And what does parting mean to you?" "Decay . . .
Doors closed behind you as you disappear.
And, if it's day, the brilliance of the day."
"And if it's night?" "At night the atmosphere
comes into play—perhaps a single stray
light or a bench in some deserted square."
"And does the memory of a loved one stay
with you for long?" "You'd better be more clear."
"Well, after losing me what will you say?"
"In general, loss isn't hard to bear."

"If that's the way you feel about it, why
go on about our 'friendship'?" "In this instance
we're the better for the fact that we
live here together at this little distance:
the reason being that to really be—"
" 'Really to be'! Or, better yet, 'existence'. . ."
"—to really cease to be . . . Nonentity
will make my absence give, for one who listens

to the plain, it's plain monotony."
"You mean, therefore, that you will be my silence."

Gorbunov and Gorchakov

"Have you had supper?" "Have indeed. And you?"
"Uh-huh." "How'd you like the cabbage mush?"
"In texture, cabbage mush gives little to
the palate; and it didn't fill me much."
"It's watery and empty as a rule—
to quote the proverb." "Sad." "Could use a dash
of vinegar, for pungency, it's true."
"Well, all is empty." "But one emptiness
tastes different from another one." "I do
yearn for a thing to sink my teeth in, yes."

"In this hell-hole into which we're cast,
there's nothing left to do but to begin
a month before the start of Lent to fast."
"I guess you're speaking of the madhouse, then."
"Our geography is small, at best."
"And afterwards?" "You're always asking! When
is afterwards?" "When crucifixion's past."
"And what's that mean?" "It's just an idiom."
"You'd think they'd use some basil leaves at least."
"As usual they'd mix the bromide in."

"Yeah, none of this will turn out well, I fear.
This bromide is unhealthy, nasty stuff."
"It's dispossessing all of us of hair.
Just look at any pillow: daily fluff
is sacrificed by our Babanov there,
Mickiewicz sheds his eyebrows, and I have

now lost the battle on my crown. I swear
the dope makes you anemic." "Cools you off
between the devil and the rib—that's where
it sits, so we don't wreck our brains with love."

"I took it in the army." "You alone?"
"No, everyone. We called it 'Unmanalov' or
'Antihardon,' 'cause with just a dram
we all forgot Ulanova-Orlova."
"Mine was dark, but now it's gone so blond!
The warp is gone on which this rug was woven.
It won't make the gray it would have gone . . ."
"But don't forget the basic circumstances given."
"And what, dear sir, is that supposed to mean?"
"That you won't need it at the rate you're going."

"You're right." "Don't shake." "I'm cold." "Here, put your hands
beneath the blanket." "Thank you. Tell me, what
is love?" "I told you . . ." "But I know that sounds
each bear their various boundaries; they've got
many different levels." "Love still stands
for parting's preface." "No!" "I'm willing that
I be a monument to lies, who sends
his children and their progeny to fart
upon his head!" "Come on, don't be a dunce.
I said that 'cause, as usual, I'm bored."

"Damn the draft in here! It chills the blood!"
"They've puttied shut the cracks." "Now there's a joke.
The radiator's cold as well." "It's cold
and dirty in this place around the clock."
"There's a star above that tree I could
discern without a telescope." "You look
at one; no star ascends without a brood."
"It's just occurred to me, just as a lark:
what if they chopped the cross for firewood—
would its image rise again in smoke?"

"You're nuts." "I'm only showing some concern
for your affairs." "Praiseworthy charity!
What are you really after, though?" "The churn
of warmth back in a cold extremity."
"You said it. Mine are all about to turn
to ice." "I'm right." "There's inhumanity
in that." "Let's lay the logs star-shaped to burn."
"You're right. Stars bring to mind eternity—
unlike the cross, I am ashamed to own."
"I'd rather say a bad infinity."

"What time is it?" "Apparently it's night."
"Oh, please, don't start in on the zodiac."
"I know my wife and daughter are outside."
"Well, what I said of love is as exact
for marriage." "For myself, I wouldn't mind
it someday. But for you it's a mistake."
"My marriage irritates you, I've divined."
"You should have wed the darkness." "I can't hack
monotony. Indeed, I take delight
in each domestic jam and cul-de-sac."

"What time is it? It's almost zero." "Oh.
That late." "Since I have no mathematic prowess,
I'll tell you I consider every 0
a forerunner of plus." "My lips, empowered
by yawning and by biting, quickly go
to circle." "What's achieved, then, when you throw it
all into a single heap?" "The snow-
capped pinnacles where unscaled Elbrus towered."
"Did earth create concavity that's so
immense?" "It showed itself to be a coward."

"If mountains are to be your leitmotif,
then think about Golgotha; March 15,
the Ides of March, is almost here, and I've
made up my mind to jump in some ravine."

"Or you could hide behind a cloud as if
behind an Oriental veil, a scene
you'd play the spirit in." "You measure with
a yardstick of your own. However, mine
won't measure that two-headed summit. It
just presses all the courtyard snowdrifts down."

Conversations about the Sea

"One is immortal, goes your argument.
But to the sorrow of your prophecy,
I am already half an invalid.
Your light cannot drive off the dark from me—
not any more than night-lights by the bed
drive off my dreams. I don't reproach you. We
must stop reproach. Isn't that the point?
Before my open or my shutting eye
something mighty always seethes ahead
as if it were the sea. I think it is the sea.

It's night. The hospital. On hostile ground.
I cannot bear to listen to you lest
I tremble from the cold and shame about
that torch. Because the sea will never best
its own concavity. I won't go down
into it, though. Though truth is dearer . . . Trust
I won't allow you into any harm!
Enough of that! It seems you hardly rest
in certainty that it's the sea around
us and not simply . . . woe. Oh, *why* this test?"

"Perhaps it is indeed the sea . . . the cries
of gulls above a woman tossing crumbs

of bread from off a pier. And like the waves
her flounce flaps in the wind; her ragged hem
is slapping at her shoes. So, in a blaze
of screeching battle, there she stands alone:
she tosses bread and stares into the haze . . .
As if, become farsighted for a time,
she holds a bee in Turkey in her gaze."

"Yeah, that's the sea. Precisely that. The deep
of life from which, like knights in chain-mail coats,
so very long ago we all sprang up
that if you hadn't struck this distant note
again just now, I would have let it sleep,
forgetting that, in fact, the world has got
a bottom and horizon and a type
of space besides this one where it's our fate
to stare at painted walls, a lilac stripe.
But 'he that hath ears to hear, let him be mute.' "

"There's something bigger in the world than us,
a thing that warms us, though it doesn't warm
itself; that, with the help of Boreas,
stuffs hollows up with hills, collecting them
around to be of one another's use.
I feel as though I'm striding through a dream:
upstairs to light, downstairs to the abyss,
up to the threshold of Elysium,
all by myself, amid the blooming crests
where Nereus' escalators hum."

"But ocean's a too-foreign element
to buy the story of some 'Tally ho'
across it. Ice of course is different.
No, Gorbunov, the end of all your woe
is not in sight. It seems that you are meant
to measure out your grief in years—you know,
just like they did in Exodus. I can't

say where each year your wanderings will go,
where water's woven into sky . . . this tent
of sky's so broad, for whom can one man howl?"

"My soul's too weak for calling. From now on,
wherever fate sees fit for me to be,
from Paradise to squatting in the john,
not painted walls but waves are what I'll see.
And that's not bragging, Gorchakov. A man
like me, in such celestial disarray,
well, what would he be pleading for? For one
who hath the ears to hear, artillery
repeat of waves is far more pleasant than
a tearful prayer that this cup pass from me."

"But that's a sin! . . . What's wrong with me? Today
I, cursing you, forgot that woodpile scene's
details: you asked about (as I replay
it in my head) my dreams. And in response
I tried to speak my mind, that dreams employ
the heritage of day. And then it seems
you called my mushrooms islands. I reply:
How hard it is beneath our craniums!
And now you see the sea—to that I say,
Absurd! Though yours has greater rights, the dreams

are both the same." "And sleep?" "The doctors' cure:
the core of cores." "And like in streams, we sink
in it." "We sink into the darkness. Your
imagination sucks. What cripple-think!"
"Sleep's an exit from the blackness." "Gor-
bunov forgets the age we're trapped within.
I tell you that your dream's not new!" "But nor
is man." "Why speak of man?" " 'Cause man's a thing
that dreams alone can take the credit for."
"And what about a man is most distinct?"

"The eyelids. Close them, you see darkness, right?"
"But in the light?" "In light, too, as a rule . . .
And suddenly you see, your eyes shut tight,
a feature. One, a second . . . third . . . You feel
your ears hum; your mouth's cold. The height
of sky. And children running down the quay. A gull
is catching bread crumbs midway through its flight."
"Am I not there? On that embankment?" "All
I see, that moment, everything in sight
is real—more real than you there on your stool."

Conversation in a Conversation

"But that's delirium! You hear? So look,
we need a witness . . . Here, Babanov, you.
Now, in a robe without a belt or hook,
I'll perch upon this stool in public view.
Well, Gorbunov, you see me, right?" "I took
no notice." "Even of my long johns' hue?"
"No." "I'll obliterate your portrait! Look
here, Gorbunov! The sea becomes a stew
now that the wind is kicking up! You snake,
you hear?" "I have already answered no."

"So that's the way it is! Well then, let's use
our fists! Taught! Blockheads must be taught a lesson!
Take that! Well now, can you conjecture whose
hand hit you—mine? Babanov's?" "In that session?
um, well, was it . . . Gor-banov's?" "You refuse
to blame me! You'd forgive my sins! Your ocean
will burst the faucets soon, and you'll know whose!"
"He-he." "What are you laughing at, you crashing

idiot! You fool!" "Hey, what's the noise?"
"Get out of here, Mickiewicz!" "I'm the boss in

here, and if a pal has closed his eyes,
the more so as it's night already, those
around him should, I think, shut up." "You flies!
I slugged him, well, because . . . he didn't close
his eyes from pain." "I really do advise
you to shut up." "Mickiewicz, your brain loose
or what? What's wrong with you? It isn't wise,
you know, opposing me." "I'll bust your nose!"
"Ouch, ouch, my corns!" "What's going on, you guys?"
"Damned if I know." "Someone got his toes

stepped on." "Watch it, I hear the doctors!" "Jeez-
us Christ! Get in the sack, quick!" "I'm in bed."
"And, Gorbunov, don't you so much as sneeze.
Just cover up and . . ." "But he's really dead
asleep already." "What?" "I hear the keys!"
"Asleep? Impossible! You're cracked!" "I said
shut up, you fool!" "Babanov, stash it, please."
"Leave him alone." "I only want a bit . . ."
"Just you try squealing, Gorbunov." "But he's
asleep." "Oh no. We're really in for it."

"How should you greet your doctors?" "Showing some
respect . . . Get up, you crippled lunatics!"
"You got a gripe about the grub, you scum?"
"There was a fight in here. I heard it." "Nix,
my friend, there wasn't." "Don't be quarrelsome.
The night clerk said he heard a fight." "I'll fix
that liar!" "Save your tricks. We're not so dumb."
"Whose piss is that?" "Some dick's." "Who mentioned dicks?
I asked you whose it is, not where it's from."
"Yes, whose? An eagle's?" "No. A Kuban Cossack's."

"Mickiewicz!" "Yeah?" "Well, wipe it up, you creep!"
"We keep the peace here. Better learn your place."
"What's wrong with Gorbunov?" "Uh . . . he's asleep."
"So get to sleep and don't disturb the peace."
"We're on our way." "That's right. Bad little sheep."
"We're going." "We'll hear houseflies buzz
you'll be so quiet. Got it? Not a peep!"
"Excuse me, fellows, but I've got to piss."
"Tomorrow." "Gorchakov, they're in your keep."
"Here's news for you: a sputnik is in space."

"They've gone." "Hey, Gorchakov! What's that? Your piss?"
"Go f——." "All right, let's close our little eyes."
"I'd love to have a cake for Easter." "Yes,
to break the fast. Some butter, some good-size
salami . . ." "You should have asked the doctor." "Guess
you could've—he was asking, doctor-wise."
"In the confusion I forgot." "I wish
you'd shut . . ." "Hey, look at Gorchakov, you guys!
He's whispering to Gorbunov, his lips
pressed close." "He's trying to apologize."

"You're really sleeping? Far as I can tell,
you're really sleeping . . . how the strands are wound
in knots! I cannot understand myself . . .
For God's sake, please forgive, forgive me, friend.
Here, let me fluff this battered pillow full.
How's that? . . . my self and self are out of tune.
Forgive me . . . This is more than I can well
perform. Now, sleep . . . to speak of glances, one
could not find much to pause on here, where all
is obstacle. On obstacles alone.

Sleep, Gorbunov. Until they sound
retreat. I only want to guard your rest.
To hell with it! with the alarum's round!

207

Though obstacles are new to you, I'm used
to them. Forgive me for my bragging, friend.
Forgive me my disharmony, at best.
Sleep, sleep, and I will wait beside your bed.
Not over you, not under, but here next
to you . . . Don't care how many years they send
you up! I'll wait to meet your opened eyes.

What do you see? The sea? Two seas or more?
You wander wave-filled hallways . . . Fishes stare
with dumb expressions out of every door.
I'm right behind you . . . But from God knows where
ten thousand bubbles bubble up before
my eyes . . . And I can't follow, I can't bear
the pressure . . . What? What's that? My mind's gone . . . or
hallucinating conversation . . . Look there!
Down from the north the wind's begun to roar!
The pillow's squashed, the part has left your hair."

19

TO

URANIA

.

May 24, 1980

I have braved, for want of wild beasts, steel cages,
carved my term and nickname on bunks and rafters,
lived by the sea, flashed aces in an oasis,
dined with the-devil-knows-whom, in tails, on truffles.
From the height of a glacier I beheld half a world, the earthly
width. Twice have drowned, thrice let knives rake my nitty-gritty.
Quit the country that bore and nursed me.
Those who forgot me would make a city.
I have waded the steppes that saw yelling Huns in saddles,
worn the clothes nowadays back in fashion in every quarter,
planted rye, tarred the roofs of pigsties and stables,
guzzled everything save dry water.
I've admitted the sentries' third eye into my wet and foul
dreams. Munched the bread of exile: it's stale and warty.
Granted my lungs all sounds except the howl;
switched to a whisper. Now I am forty.
What should I say about life? That it's long and abhors transparence.
Broken eggs make me grieve; the omelette, though, makes me vomit.
Yet until brown clay has been crammed down my larynx,
only gratitude will be gushing from it.

1980

To a Friend: In Memoriam

It's for you whose name's better omitted—since for them it's no arduous task
to produce you from under the slab—from one more *inconnu*: me, well, partly
for the same earthly reasons, since they'll scrub you as well off the cask,
and because I'm up here and, frankly, apart from this paltry
talk of slabs, am too distant for you to distinguish a voice,
an Aesopian chant, in that homeland of bottle-struck livers,
where you fingered your course to the pole in the moist universe
of mean, blabbering squinchers and whispering, innocent beavers;
it's for you, name omitted, the offspring of a widowed conductress, begot
by the Holy Ghost or by brick courtyard's soot circling all over,
an abductor of books, the sharp pen of the most smashing ode
on the fall of the bard at the feet of the laced Goncharova,
a word-plyer, a liar, a gulper of bright, measly tears,
an adorer of Ingres, of clangoring streetcars, of asphodels' slumbers,
a white-fanged little snake in the tarpaulin-boot colonnade of gendarmes in
full gear,
a monogamous heart and a torso of countless bedchambers—
may you lie, as though wrapped in an Orenburg shawl, in our dry, brownish
mud,
you, a tramper through hell and high water and the meaningless sentence,
who took life like a bumblebee touching a sun-heated bud
but instead froze to death in the Third Rome's cold-piss-reeking entrance.
Maybe Nothing has no better gateway indeed than this smelly shortcut.
Man of sidewalks, you'd say, "This will do," adding, "for the duration,"
as you drifted along the dark river in your ancient gray, drab overcoat
whose few buttons alone were what kept you from disintegration.
Gloomy Charon in vain seeks the coin in your tightly shut shell,
someone's pipe blows in vain its small tune far above heavy, cumulous curtains.
With a bow, I bid you this anonymous, muted farewell
from the shores—who knows which? Though for you now it has no
importance.

1973

212

October Tune

A stuffed quail
on the mantelpiece minds its tail.
The regular chirr of the old clock's healing
in the twilight the rumpled helix.
Through the window, birch candles fail.

For the fourth day the sea hits the dike with its hard horizon.
Put aside the book, take your sewing kit;
patch my clothes without turning the light on:
golden hair
keeps the corner lit.

1968

213

A Polar Explorer

All the huskies are eaten. There is no space
left in the diary. And the beads of quick
words scatter over his spouse's sepia-shaded face
adding the date in question like a mole to her lovely cheek.
Next, the snapshot of his sister. He doesn't spare his kin:
what's been reached is the highest possible latitude!
And, like the silk stocking of a burlesque half-nude
queen, it climbs up his thigh: gangrene.

[July 22] 1977

Lithuanian Nocturne

TO TOMAS VENCLOVA

I

Having roughed up the waters,
wind explodes like loud curses from fist-ravaged lips
in the cold superpower's
innards, squeezing trite wobbles
of the do-re-mi from sooted trumpets that lisp.
Nonprincesses and porous
nonfrogs hug the terrain,
and a star shines its mite clouds don't bother to tamper
with. A semblance of face
blots the dark windowpane
like the slap of a downpour.

II

Greetings, Tomas. That's my
specter—having abandoned its frame in a fleabag somewhere
overseas, rowing through
whipped-up thick northern cumulus, thereby
tearing from the New World—which wings homeward,
and this thoroughfare
duly brings him to you.

III

Late Lithuanian dusk.
Folk are scuffling from churches protecting the commas
of their candle flames in trembling brackets of hands;
in the freezing courtyards
chickens peck in the sodden sawdust,
over stubbled Zhemaitija's contours
snow's aswirl like the ashes from burnt-out celestial wards.
From the doors flung askew,
fish soup's odor is oozing. A youngster, half naked,
and a kerchiefed old hag chase a pig to the sty.

215

And a cart-riding Jew,
late for home, drums the village's cobblestone, trying to make it,
yanks the reins hard
and bellows "Gerai!"

IV
Sorry for the invasion.
Take this apparition for, let's
say, an early return of the quote back to its Manifesto's
text: a notch more, say, slurred, and a pitch more alluring
for being away.
Thus don't cross yourself, etc.,
and don't torture gauze curtains: I'll vanish as fast as
roosters herald the day.
Sorry for the intrusion.
Don't reel into a bedroom in fright:
it's just frailty that widens its reach at the cost of state borders.
Like a stone that avenges a well
with its multiple rings,
I buzz over the Baltic, like that ill-fated flight
of Girenas and Darius, the immortals!—
but on less brittle wings.

V
Evening in the Empire,
in a destitute province. A conifer force
wades the Neman and, bristling with darkening lances,
takes old three-storied Kaunas; a blush of remorse
sweeps the stucco as darkness advances,
and the cobblestones glisten like bream in a net.
At the opera, up soars a patterned
curtain, while in an archway the object of passion
gets divided by three, with, I bet,
no leftovers. The dark thrills the calm
tulle. A star, shining in a backwater,
does so all the more brightly: like a card played in suit.
And your delta-like palm

drums the pane, flowing into the outer
dark—a cheerless pursuit.

VI
Every speech after midnight
develops a blind man's technique.
Even "homeland," by touch, feels like Lady Godiva.
Cobweb-shaded, the mikes
of the secret police in a bard's quarters pick
up the mattress's sighs, and the dripping saliva
of the national anthem: the tune that dislikes
using words. Here reticence reigns. Trembling leaves
torn between their reverse and their surface
irritate a lamppost. Spurning loudspeakers, a man
here declares to the world that he lives
by unwittingly crushing an ant,
by faint Morse's
dots of pulse, by the screech of his pen.

VII
That's whence that mealy grain
of your cheeks, your quite addressless, senseless
stare, your lisping, your hair
with its shade of weak colorless tea down the drain;
that's whence, too, one's whole life's honest, hesitant sentence:
a comma-bound affair.
It is thence also its
upward spinoffs: my washed-out appearance
in your windows; uprisings—with threats to invade—
of sharp willow twigs, etc.;
ocean's pages, one's leafings through them in the quest for a period,
a horizon, a fate.

VIII
Our cuneiform, Tomas! With my margin-prone
predicates! with your subjects, hearthbound and luckless!
Our inkpot alliance! Its splurge!

Doodling lace, herringbone,
Roman writ *cum* Cyrillic, harking to Magnavox's
ends-*cum*-means demiurge!
Our imprints! In damp twisted sheets
—in that flabby brainlike common cotton—
in our loved ones' soft clay, in our children without us, or
as a bruise that still sits
on the firmament, brought on-
to its cheek by a youngster whose sore
eye was trying to fathom the distance from that
famed Lithuanian inn,
to the multieyed face gazing sideways
like some old squinting Mongol beyond our spiked earthly fence,
poised to put fingers in-
to his mouth—that old wound of your namesake!—to find its
tongue and alter, like seraphs and silence
do, his verbs or their tense.

IX
Tomas, we are alike;
we are, frankly, a double:
your breath
dims the same windowpane that my features befuddle.
We're each other's remote
amalgam underneath,
in a lackluster puddle,
a simultaneous nod.
Twist your lips—I'll reply with the similar grimace of dread.
I'll respond to your yawn with my mouth's gaping mollusc.
I'll cry rivers to your
hundred-watt swollen tear overhead.
We're a mutual threat,
Castor looming through Pollux,
we're a stalemate, no-score,
draw, long shadows' distress
brought to walls by a match that will die in a minute,
echoes tracing in vain the original cry

as small change does its note.
The more life has been ruined, the less
is the chance to distinguish us in it
with an indolent eye.

X

What do specters live by?
By the refuse of dreams,
borders' dross, the chaff of mute odd numbers or even,
for addresses are what makes reality hark
back. A lane gnashes, gumlike, its porches agleam;
like a simpleton's cheese, alleys' yellow is eaten
by the fox of the dark
hours. Avenging its permanence, a
place stuffs time with a tenant, a lodger—
with a life-form, and throws up the latch.
And an epoch away
I still find you in this dog-eared kingdom of cudgel
forests, plains, well-preserving one's features, one's thinking and such,
but above all, the pose:
in her many-miled, damp
hemp nightgown, in her high-voltage curlers,
dormant Mother Lithuania's taking her rest
by the shore, as you're gluing your plump
lips to her bare and colorless
glassy half-liter breast.

XI

There are places in which
things don't change. These are a substitute
for one's memory. These are the acid
triumphs of fixative. There each mile
puts striped bars into focus; one's suit
gravitates to a silhouette, added
to one's thinking. Meanwhile,
soldiers keep growing younger. The past
peers ahead with a wary

eye, well matching the khaki attire of youth,
and one's fate, like a border trespasser, reels fast
into brittle old age with its spittle, its aching, its weary
shuffling down the infinity-reeking night pavements. In truth,
night's the border where reality, like
Tartars, threatens the kingdom
of what has been lived through with a raid, or perhaps vice versa;
where logs
join their trees and split back into logs, where daylight
grabs what night's left unhidden
under tight eyelids' locks.

XII

Midnight. Cries of a jay
sound human and charge Mother Nature
with the crime of thermometers: with zerocide.
His bleak shield thrown away
and sword ditched, Prince Vytautas is ready to venture
our flatulent Baltic, with the Swedes out of sight
but in mind. However, the land
overtakes him, assuming the shape of a lengthy
pier, to catch up with freedom long fled
climbing over flat ladderlike waves. In the end,
the best-built beaver dam in the woods cries a-plenty:
tears gleam silver and lead.

XIII

Midnight in a deciduous region,
in a province the shade
of topcoats. Belfries' wedges. A swatch of a cloud
to enshroud a contiguous nation. Below,
haystacks, pastures, a glade
of roof tiles, colonnades, brick, cast-iron; and—proud
in his boots—a by-blow
of the state. Midnight's oxygen gets
flooded with interference, with weather reports, news, and prayers,
with the Vizier of Woes

and his rounded numbers, with anthems, sextets,
jigs, decrees, with anathema-sayers,
banning things no one knows.

XIV

A specter wanders in Kaunas. It enters, by chance,
a cathedral. Runs out. Drifts along Laisves Boulevard. Enters
empty "Tulpe," slumps down on a chair.
Yet the waiter who'd glance
in this corner will spot just white napkins, or embers
of the cabs outside, snowflakes circling—and stare
at the street. You would envy, I think,
me: for invisibility comes into fashion
with the passage of years—as the body's concession to its
soul, as a well-taken hint
of the future, as Paradise's fathom-
like attire, as a drawn-out minus that fits
everyone. For all profit from absence, from stark
nonextension: a mountain, a valley,
a brass pendulum plate with two glimmers to serve,
the Almighty that gazes from stars
downward, mirrors, a squealer,
corridors, you yourself.

XV

A specter loiters about in Kaunas. It is
but your thoughts of me added
to the air, but a vacuum rampant, and not
that tempestuous sermon of social bliss.
So don't envy me at it,
simply note
in this faint apparition a kin
or an aspect of air—like these words, with their fear of the morning,
scattered thinly at midnight by some slurring voice—
a sound more like houseflies
bravely clicking a tin,
and which won't satiate

the new Clio adorning
checkpoint gowns, but in which
ever-naked Urania is to rejoice!
Only she, our Muse
of the point lost in space, our Muse of forgotten
outlines can assess, and in full,
like a miser, the use
of small change, immobility's token
paid for flights of the soul.

XVI
That's whence, Tomas, the pen's
troth to letters. That's what must explain gravitation,
don't you think?
With the roosters' "Time's up,"
that light-entity rends
its light self from its verbs and their tense,
from its hair-shirted nation.
from—let's loosen the trap—
you: from letters, from pages, from sound's
love for sense, from incorporeality's passion
toward mass, and from freedom's, alas,
love for slavery's haunts—
for the bone, for the flesh, and
for the heart—having thus
liberated itself, that light-entity soars up to ink-
like dark heavenly reaches,
past blind cherubs in niches,
past the bats that won't wink.

XVII
Muse of dots lost in space! Muse of things one makes out
through a telescope only! Muse of subtraction
but without remainders! Of zeros, in short.
You who order the throat
to avoid lamentation,
not to go overboard,

that is, higher than "la"!
Muse, accept this effect's
little aria sung to the gentle
cause's sensitive ear,
and regard it and its do-re-me-ing tercets
in your rarefied rental
from the viewpoint
of air,
of pure air! Air indeed is the epilogue
for one's retina: nobody stands to inhabit
air! It is our "homeward"! That town
which all syllables long
to return to. No matter how often you grab it,
light or darkness soon darn with their rapid
needles air's eiderdown.

XVIII
Every thing has a limit: the horizon that splits
a round eye; for despair, it is memory; often
it's the hand's fabled reach.
Only sound, Tomas, slips,
specter-like, from the body. An orphan
sound, Tomas, is speech.
Push the lampshade aside, and by staring
straight ahead
you'll see air *en face*:
swarms of those
who have stained it
with their lips before us.

XIX
In the kingdom of air!
In its equality of
gulps of oxygen to our syllables! In the transparent
lumped-like-clouds exhalations of ours! In that
world where, like our dreams haunt the ceiling,
our O's

shape the vault of the palate,
where a star gets its shine from the vat
of the throat! That's how the universe
breathes. And that's what a rooster's sharp yokel
meant by sparing the larynx the draught's dry assaults.
Air, the tongue's running course!
And the firmament's a chorus of highly pitched vocal
atoms, alias souls.

XX
That is why it is pure!
In this world, there is nothing that bleaches
pages better (except
for one's dying) than air.
And the whiter, the emptier, which is
homelike. Muse, may I set
out homeward? To that out-loud
realm where witless Boreas
tramples over the trophies of lips in his flight,
to your grammar without
punctuation, to your Paradise of our alphabets
and tracheas,
to your blackboard in white.

XXI
In the sky
far above the Lithuanian hills
something sounding like a prayer
for the whole of mankind, droning cheerlessly, drifts
toward Kurshskaia Point. This is St. Casimir's
and St. Nicholas's mumbling in their unattainable lair
where, minding the passage of darkness, they sift
hours. Muse! from the heights where you
dwell, beyond any creed's stratosphere, from your rarefied ether,
look, I pray you, together
with those two,

after these pacified sunken plains' sullen bard.
Do not let handmade darkness envelop his rafter.
Post your sentinels in his back yard.
Look, Urania, after
both his home and his heart.

1974

Twenty Sonnets to Mary Queen of Scots

I

Mary, I call them pigs, not Picts, those Scots.
What generation of what clan in tartan
could have foreseen you'd step down from the screen
a statue, and bring life to city gardens—
the Luxembourg, to be precise? I came
here to digest a Paris lunch and stare
with the dull eyes of a decrepit ram
at the new gates and into ponds. And here
I met Your Highness. And to mark that meeting
and since "all the dead past now lives anew
in my cold heart," by way of greeting,
I'll stuff the old gun full of classic grape-
shot, squandering what remains of Russian speech
on your pale shoulders and your paler nape.

II

The war to end all wars produced ground zero.
The frying pan missed fat that missed pork chops.
Mary, I was a boy then, and saw Zarah
Leander approach the scaffold, clippety-clop.
Whatever you may say, the axman's blade
equates the ditches to the lofty reaches
(cf. our luminary rising late).
We all came to the surface from the pictures,
but something calls us, at the hour of gloom,
back to the Spartacus, whose plushy womb
is cozier than a European evening.
There the stars hang, the grandest a brunette;
there are two features, everybody queuing,
and not an empty seat, I bet.

III

I, who have traveled half my earthly road,
make my appearance in the Luxembourg
and contemplate the petrified gray curls
of thinkers and of scribblers. Gents and broads
are strolling to and fro; a whiskered
blue copper glistens from the thicket;
the fountain purrs, the children laugh,
and not a soul to greet with "Bugger off."
And you, untiring, Mary, stand and stand,
in the stone garland of your girl friends—stunned
French queens of once-upon-has-been,
in silence, with a sparrow in your hair.
You'd think the garden was a cross between
the Pantheon and *Déjeuner sur l'herbe.*

IV

The beauty whom I later loved—quite likely
more tenderly than you loved Bothwell—had
some features similar to yours ("My God,"
I automatically whisper, lately
recalling them). Moreover, we,
like you, did not make a happy pair.
Wearing a mackintosh, she went off somewhere.
To sidestep the straight line of destiny,

I cut across another line—whose edge
is sharper than a knife blade: the horizon,
Mary. With neck above that thing outstretched—
not for the oxygen but the breathtaking poison
that bursts my Adam's apple with a squeal—
the larynx's sort of grateful for the deal.

V

The number of your lovers, Mary, went
beyond the figure three, four, twenty, twent-
y-five. A crown, alas, gets dented, bent,

or lost between the sheets with some odd gent.
That's why a monarchy comes to an end
while a republic may be permanent
(see ancient pillars or a monument).
And your Scots barons neither couldn't, nor can't
think otherwise. They wouldn't relent
in pressing their quite sordid argument—
that is, that they, your Scottish lords, can't see
what makes a throne so different from a cot.
O *rara avis* of your century!
To your compatriots you were a slut.

VI

I loved you. And my love of you (it seems,
it's only pain) still stabs me through the brain.
The whole thing's shattered into smithereens.
I tried to shoot myself—using a gun
is not so simple. And the temples: which one,
the right or left? Reflection, not the twitching,
kept me from acting. Jesus, what a mess!
I loved you with such strength, such hopelessness!
May God send you in others—not a chance!
He, capable of many things at once,
won't—citing Parmenides—reinspire
the bloodstream fire, the bone-crushing creeps,
which melt the lead in fillings with desire
to touch—"your hips," I must delete—your lips.

VII

Paris is still the same. The Place des Vosges
is still, as once it was (don't worry), square.
The Seine has not run backward to its source.
The Boulevard Raspail is still as fair.
As for the new, there's music now for free,
a tower to make you feel you're just a fly,
no lack of people whom it's nice to see,
provided you're the first to blurt "How's life?"

Paris by night, a restaurant . . . What chic
in words like these—a treat for vocal cords.
And in comes *eine kleine nachtmuzhik*,
an ugly cretin in a Russian shirt.
Café. Boulevard. The girlfriend in a swoon.
The General-Secretary's-coma moon.

VIII

In my decline, in a land beyond the seas
(discovered in Your Highness's time, methinks),
splitting my animated frame between
a stove and a divan with busted springs,
I muse how just a few words would have been
enough for us, if fate had crossed our paths:
you would have simply called me "dear Ivan,"
and I'd have answered with one word, "Alas."

Scotland would have been our mattress then.
I'd have displayed you to the haughty Slavs.
Port Glasgow would have seen a caravan
of satins, Russian cakes, and shoes of bast
come sailing in. And we'd have met our fate
together. Severed by a wooden blade.

IX

A plain. Alarum. Enter two. The clash
of battle. "Who are you?" "And you yourself?"
"Us? we are Protestants, we don't observe . . ."
"And we are Catholics." "Ah, bloody Papists!" Crash!
And then the corpses lie about like trash,
the endless din of crows' first-come-first-served.
And later—winter, sleigh rides through the slush.
A shawl from Persia. "Persia! Ah! what nerve!"
"A land where peacocks make their peahens blush."
"Yet even there a queen at night can shush
her shah." "Or mate him, playing chess up north
in a cute Hollywood-style modest castle." Slash:

a plain again. Time: midnight. Enter two.
And drown you with their wolfish who-is-who.

X

An autumn evening. All but with the Muse.
Alas, not heeding the relentless lyre.
That's nothing new. On evenings such as these
you'd play for kicks even the army choir.
Becoming yesterday, today won't use
new sheets of paper, pen, or oatmeal's mire
and let the crippled Hamburg cooper cruise
night skies at length. About the secondhand,
soiled, scratched, or badly dented items:
time seems a teeny bit more confident
than fresh tomatoes, and at least won't bite them.
The door may creak: death, having failed to knock,
will stand before you in her moth-holed frock.

XI

A clang of shears, a momentary chill.
Fate, envying the sheepfolk for their wool,
knocks off our crowns and bridal wreaths at will—
quite indiscriminately. And the heads as well.
Farewell, young dudes, their proud dads, their ill-
kept promises, divorces, all to hell.
The brain's like a skyscraper in whose still
tight shell each cell ignores another cell.
That's how the twins in distant Siam swill
their booze: one does it, but they both feel swell.
No one has shouted to you, "Watch out!"
Nor did you, Mary, know enough to shout,
"I am alone"—while boring God and pew
with Latin pleas—"There are a lot of you!"

XII

What is it that makes History? Well, bodies.
And Art?—a body that has lost its head.

Take Schiller, say. Young Friedrich served his notice
to History. You never dreamt, I bet,
a Jerry'd get, out of the blue, so hot as
to resurrect the ancient case, long dead.
It's not his business to discuss your quotas:
who had you or who didn't in a bed.

But then, perhaps, like every other Hans,
our Fritz was simply frightened of the ax.
And secondly, dear Mary, let me stress:
there's nothing, barring Art, sublunar creatures
can use to comprehend your gorgeous features.
Leave History to Good Queen Bess.

XIII

A ram shakes out his ringlets, alias fleece,
inhaling lazily the scent of hay.
All round are standing Glencorns, Douglases,
et al. These were the words they spoke that day:
"They have cut off her head." "They have, alas."
"Just think what those in gay Paree will say."
"The French? About the head of some poor lass?
Now, were it aimed above the knee, they may . . ."
"She's not a man, though. Came out in her shift."
"That's not enough to rest one's case upon . . ."
"You could see through it. Shameless!" "What of it?
Could be she's got no gown for putting on."
"Yeah, she's no Russian. 'Ivanov,' I mean,
suggests a wench whichever case it's in."

XIV

Love is more powerful than separation, but
the latter is more lasting. Plus, the greater
the statue, the more palpably it ain't her.
Her voice, her wits, smell, finally, are cut
off. While one blames it on the granite that
you won't kick up your legs to starry heights, for

so many fingers' failure to decipher
your petticoats, one has to punish but

one's awkward self. It's not 'cause so much blood
and so much water—equally blue—
have flowed under the bridge, but since the brass
bed screams at night under a lonely lad,
I'd have erected, too, a stone for you,
but I would cut it in transparent glass.

XV
Your ruin, Mary, wasn't the grooms who'd got
no carpenters to raise the roofbeams higher
in that small chamber where they bravely fought;
nor was it that smart ink, which only fire
makes visible (and you were never caught);
nor that Elizabeth loved England's plot
indeed more than you did your Scottish shire
(which is the truth, though some will cry it's not);
nor those good tunes the Spaniard would admire,
especially coming from a royal throat;
no, what they killed you for—let's clear the mire—
was something to which they, in those old days,
could see no end: the beauty of your face.

XVI
As corners vanish, softened by the dark,
a square, too, gradually becomes a sphere.
The crimson wood, like a doused fire,
peers into night with all its pores of bark,
in silence, listening to cranes up there.
Triggered by swishing leaves, a setter's bark
flies to the seven stars that mutely stare
on withered winter crops, forlorn and stark.

How few among those things that once could cause
a tear of pleasure have survived the passage

into the humus shade, how little stays.
The fountain pen now has to stick to those
that failed to heed another season's message,
to squeak and echo "Melancholy Days."

XVII

The thing that dragged from English mouths a shout
of wonderment, that still impels
my own two lips—keen for a lipsticked pout—
to use foul epithets, that rang the bells
for Philip, sending his great painter out
and ordering the great Armada sail;
it was—it seems I can't complete the big
buildup of phrases—well, your wig,
red, lying fallen from your fallen (wow,
that's rich!) head, was your one and only bow
to any audience (with no free seat),
and though it didn't cause a major fight
among spectators, it was such a sight
it brought your enemies to their cold feet.

XVIII

To one whose mouth has said farewell to you,
not just to anyone, isn't it all the same,
whatever tasteless crusts he has to chew
in years to come? I'll wager you became
accustomed to the lack of do-re-mi.
And if you didn't, don't be cross with me:
ratlike the tongue goes scurrying through a mound
of rubbish, seeking treasure left behind.

Forgive me then, fair idol on the lawn.
Yes, separation is no fool, to own
them measly peanuts. For between us lie
eternity and ocean. Literally.
Plus Russian censorship, in case you ask.
They could have done the job without an ax.

XIX

The Scots have wool now, Mary (and it all
looks spick-and-span like from the cleaners, great).
At six o'clock life judders to a stall,
leaving no mark upon the sunset's plate.
The lakes—unnumbered as in days gone by—
have spawned strange monsters (serpentine and frisky),
and soon they'll have their private oil supply,
Scotch oil, to go in bottles meant for whisky.
It looks like Scotland got along just fine
without you, and England, too, one hears.
And you in this *jardin* of French design
don't look the madcap of those yesteryears.
And there are dames through whose silk folds I'd rummage—
but the comparison would do you damage.

XX

With simple pen (rebellious, not true!)
I've sung this meeting under foreign eaves
with her who taught me from the screen a few
facts of the heart on '48's cold eves.

Now judge, ye of all races and beliefs:
(a) if he learned his lessons (one or two),
(b) the new setting where a Russian lives,
(c) moments of grammatical voodoo.

Nepal's far capital is Katmandu.

Being absolute, the arbitrary gives
a helping hand to everything we do.

Leading the life I lead, I am grateful to
the sheaf of previously snow-white leaves
of paper, rolled for simply blowing through.

1974

234

North Baltic

TO C.H.

When a blizzard powders the harbor, when the creaking pine
leaves in the air an imprint deeper than a sled's steel runner,
what degree of blueness can be gained by an eye? What sign
language can sprout from a chary manner?
Falling out of sight, the outside world
makes a face its hostage: pale, plain, snowbound.
Thus a mollusc stays phosphorescent at the ocean's floor
and thus silence absorbs all speeds of sound.
Thus a match is enough to set a stove aglow;
thus a grandfather clock, a heartbeat's brother,
having stopped this side of the sea, still tick-tocks to show
time at the other.

1975

The Berlin Wall Tune

TO PETER VIERECK

This is the house destroyed by Jack.
This is the spot where the rumpled buck
stops, and where Hans gets killed.
This is the wall that Ivan built.

This is the wall that Ivan built.
Yet trying to quell his sense of guilt,
he built it with modest gray concrete,
and the booby traps look discreet.

Under this wall that (a) bores, (b) scares,
barbed-wire meshes lie flat like skeins
of your granny's darnings (her chair still rocks!).
But the voltage's too high for socks.

Beyond this wall throbs a local flag
against whose yellow, red, and black
Compass and Hammer proclaim the true
Masonic dream's breakthrough.

The border guards patiently in their nest
through binoculars scan the West
and the East; and they like both views
devoid, as it were, of Jews.

Those who are seen here, thought of, felt,
are kept on a leash by the sense of Geld
or by a stronger Marxist urge.
The wall won't let them merge.

Come to this wall if you hate your place
and face a sample of cosmic space

where no life forms can exist at all
    and objects may only fall.

Come to this scornful of peace and war,
    petrified version of either/or
meandering through these bleak parts which act
    like your mirror, cracked.

Dull is the day here. In the night
    searchlights illuminate the blight
making sure that if someone screams,
    it's not due to bad dreams.

For dreams here aren't bad: just wet with blood
    of one of your like who's left his pad
to ramble at will; and in his head
    dreams are replaced with lead.

Given that, it's only time
    who has guts enough to commit the crime
of passing this place back and forth on foot:
    at pendulums they don't shoot.

That's why this site will see many moons
    while couples lie in their beds like spoons,
while the rich are wondering what they wish
    and single girls eat quiche.

Come to this wall that beats other walls:
    Roman, Chinese, whose worn-down, false
molars envy steel fangs that flash,
    scrubbed of thy neighbor's flesh.

A bird may twitter a better song.
    But should you consider abortion wrong

or that the quacks ask too high a fee,
come to this wall, and see.

1980

Dutch Mistress

A hotel in whose ledgers departures are more prominent than arrivals.
With wet Koh-i-noors the October rain
strokes what's left of the naked brain.
In this country laid flat for the sake of rivers,
beer smells of Germany and seagulls are
in the air like a page's soiled corners.
Morning enters the premises with a coroner's
punctuality, puts its ear
to the ribs of a cold radiator, detects sub-zero:
the afterlife has to start somewhere.
Correspondingly, the angelic curls
grow more blond, the skin gains its distant, lordly
white, while the bedding already coils
desperately in the basement laundry.

1981

Allenby Road

At sunset, when the paralyzed street gives up
hope of hearing an ambulance, finally settling for
strolling Chinamen, while the elms imitate a map
of a khaki-clad country that lulls its foe,
life is gradually getting myopic, spliced,
aquiline, geometrical, free of gloss
or detail—be it cornices, doorknobs, Christ—
stressing silhouettes: chimneys, rooftops, a cross.
And your closing the shutters unleashes the domino
theory; for no matter what size a lump
melts in your throat, the future snowballs each "no"
to coin a profile by the burning lamp.
Neither because there is a lot of guilt
nor because local prices are somewhat steep,
nobody picks this brick pocket filled
with change that barely buys some sleep.

1981

The Fifth Anniversary

JUNE 4, 1977

A falling star, or worse, a planet (true or bogus)
might thrill your idle eye with its quick hocus-pocus.
Look, look then at that locus that's better out of focus.

———

There frowning forests stand decked out in rags and tatters.
Departing from point A, a train there bravely scatters
its wheels toward point B. Which station hardly matters.

There causes and effects are drowned in murky waters.
One's corpse there lies unseen; so does, of course, one's foetus.
It's different with birds; but eggs don't beg for photos.

At dusk a Steinway grand twangs out a thin B-minor.
There musty jackets hang, the moth their redesigner.
On rocks, enchanted oaks nod to a passing liner.

———

There a puddle in the yard is neither round nor square.
There single mothers pot their daughters in day care.
A boisterous mountain stream strives for the third shore there.

A kid stares down his dad there all the way to breeches.
There rockets carry up crafts filled with barking bitches
plus officers whose pay suggests the upper reaches.

There weeds submit to green: a sort of common harness.
A principle of sound owes to a bee that's harmless.
A copy, sparing its original, stays armless.

———

241

In winter, Arctic winds shake parks to herald foul days,
and radiators which absorb the dust in hallways
possess more ribs than girls. A freezing man, though, always

prefers the former, which, in turn, appear more eager.
At tea, a candy hurts a tooth that's scarcely bigger.
A sleeping guard enjoys wet dreams and pulls the trigger.

There on a rainy day a sulphur match looks shocking.
They say, "It's only us," with rotten smirks while knocking.
There fish scales shine with tin, in lakes where fish are soaking.

———

There having voted yes, they sob in toilet corners.
There icons in the church turn black from incense burners.
The army shows who's who to folks across the borders.

There orchards burst in view, thus aping epic horsemen.
The liquor store's long queue needs only you to worsen.
Behind you and in front, you find the same stiff person.

There snatches of old tunes hang in the air they brighten.
Wheat left the zeal of state: it's a collector's item.
There martens quit the woods, whose branches fail to hide them.

———

There even when you lie flat on a sheet of cotton,
your shadow dwarfs a palm in Palestine, begotten
most likely in a dream. There deserts lie well-trodden

by sugar bowls' houseflies, which trek on foot, old-style.
There under rakish roofs small windows squint hostile.
The world map is replaced there by a large Holstein

a-mooing on a hill, awash in sunset's slobber.
There steel mills far away belch heavy smoke and clobber,
though no one needs all that; no matter drunk or sober.

There owls hoot late at night on matters vain and ashen.
No leader seems quite fit to stop green leaves' ovation.
There brain folds spurn straight thought for being out of fashion.

The hammer-hugging sickle there adorns the banner.
But nails are not struck home and weeds submerge the planner:
into the Great Machine someone has lobbed a spanner.

Apart from these, there are no enigmas, signs in heavens.
The landscape's dull, and its horizon's notched with cave-ins.
There gray is all the rage—the tint of time and cabins.

———

I grew up in those parts. I used to share a cigarette
with their most gifted bard. Was kept, a guilty secret,
in cells. Admired lead skies, as well as windswept liquid.

There I thought I would die. From boredom or from terror.
If not in friendly arms, then at their hands. But there or
somewhere nearby. Today I see my error.

I see that I was wrong. For on a stage the actor
means less than backdrops do. Space is a greater factor
than horsemen. Space won't tell the front legs from the back two.

———

Well, I'm no longer there. The sense of loss, as much as
this was indeed a loss, is best displayed by statues
in galleries, or by their vases' mute "Don't touch us."

The place sustained this loss. Some moss combined with lichen,
encountering the hole I've made, will quickly stitch it.
A connoisseur of hues won't tell you later which one

is missing. This feels odd but constitutes a variant.
It would be odder still to lie there low and ironed
or play a warrior valiant and nudge an aging tyrant.

———————

So I'm no longer there. All things have rules to reckon.
I never liked fat cats, and never kissed an icon.
And on a certain bridge, a black cast-iron Gorgon

seemed in those parts to me the truth's most honest version.
So later having met her in gigantic person,
I haven't turned to stone and let my lumpy portion

of savage screams go stale. I hear the Muse's prattle.
I sense the thread within strained by the Parcae's shuttle:
the spheres still tolerate my CO_2 life rattle,

———————

as my free-flapping tongue, a glutton for clear lyric
sends its Cyrillic thanks into the blue acrylic
to fate—since fate can grasp the meaning in Cyrillic

as well. I face pure space, which tolerates no columns
nor torsos of Apollos, nor pyramids, nor chorus.
There, it appears, I need no guide; at least, it follows.

Scratch on, my clawlike pen, my pilgrim staff, my salvage!
Don't rush our shuffling words: the age wheel-deep in garbage
won't overtake us and won't grab you, barefoot savage.

———————

This won't be heard up North, nor where hot sands hug cactus.
I don't know anymore what earth will nurse my carcass.
Scratch on, my pen: let's mark the white the way it marks us.

1977

Polonaise: A Variation

TO Z.K.

I

Autumn in your hemisphere whoops cranes and owls.
A lean nation's frontier slips off like a loosened harness.
And though windows aren't sealed yet, your camisole's
cleavage adds to the shadows the parlor harvests.
As the lamps flare up, one may well denounce
one's own curves as jarring the jigsaw puzzle
of the rooms whose air savors every ounce
pecked by Frederyk's keyboard-bedeviled nozzle.
In the full moon, the stubble gets lavished with
nobody's silver by sloughy waters.
Roll on your side, and the dreams will blitz
out of the wall like those fabled warriors
heading east, through your yard, to dislodge the siege
of tall hemp. Still, their hauberks won't hide their tatters.
Yet, since they look alike, you, by getting hitched
only once, let an army across your mattress.

II

Reddish tiles of the homestead, and the yellow shade
of its stuccoed dwellings, beset with shingles.
Either cartwheels are craving an oval shape
or the mare's hoof, hitting the cow-moon, shimmies,
and slumped haystacks flash by. Alders, nothing-clad,
in their basket carry away the river.
And the leaden plow in the furrowed clouds
bodes no good to gray winter crops racked with fever.
To your woolen stockings and linen hem
burdocks cling like nobody's child that loses
in the end its grip. And space is stitched firm
with the threadbare rain, and Copernicus turns out useless.
Still, the iris gleams, and the milky tint,
with those scattered birthmarks, your dress effaces.

Long a silhouette to yourself, you won't
fall into anyone's fond embraces.

III

I admit that one's love should be greater, more
pure. That one could, like the son of Cronus,
size up the darkness, perfect its lore,
and drop, unnoticed, within your contours.
That one could reconstruct, pore by pore, your true
looks, with idle atoms and mental power;
or just peer at the mirror and state that you
are me: for whom do we love but our-
selves? Yet chalk one up for Fate: your watch
may be running behind, for in our future
already that bomb has exploded which
leaves intact only the furniture.
Does it really matter who's run away from whom?
Neither time nor space is matchmaking for us
who took full advantage of sampling some
of those ages to come, and whatever follows.

1981

The New Jules Verne

TO LEV AND NINA LOSEFF

I

A perfect line of horizon. Without a blot. A swanky
clipper, whose Franz Liszt profile keeps stabbing
the waves. Tight cables are creaking. A naked monkey
with a scream leaps out of the naturalist's hot cabin.

Dolphins bounce along. As someone remarked somewhere,
only bottles in bars experience no seasickness.
A squall tears off the punch line of a joke, and the captain's bare
fists in a flurry challenge the mizzen's stiffness.

At times, the piano tinklings waft from the lounge: pure, guileless.
The navigator ponders the course, scratching behind his ear.
And the blueness of space straight ahead blends inside the spyglass
with the blueness of space withering at the rear.

II

You can tell a passenger from a sailor
by the swishing silk of his underwear,
by the quality of what he eats and where,
by the repetition of some meaningless question and a general air of failure.

You can tell a sailor from a lieutenant
by the absence of an epaulette,
by the age that he's at,
by the nerves wrung tight like cables, or, say, a pennant.

You can tell a lieutenant from a captain
by the stripes, his hazel eyes' razzmatazz,
by the snapshot of Blanche or of Françoise,
by his reading of Kant, Maupassant, Karl Marx, and his buying smokes by
the carton.

You can tell a captain from the Admiralty
by the lonely thinking, by the profound disgust
toward anything that is blue and vast,
by the memory of his in-laws, which loses, he thinks, its accuracy.

And only a ship acts always as though she could
be another ship. Combing the waves that hold her,
a ship resembles at once an albatross and an alder
from under whose feet the ground has slipped for good.

III

Exchanges in the Lounge
"Of course the Archduke is a monster! And of course it matters!
But he's trying his best, whereas his subjects, they . . ."
"Masters resent their slaves, slaves resent their masters.
Feels like a vicious circle!" "Like a sort of ring buoy, I'd say."

"What a splendid sherry!" "Gosh, you know, I couldn't sleep a wink.
It's this frightful sun: it burns your skin through the bodice."
". . . but what if we've sprung a leak!? I've read leaks are hard to notice.
Imagine, we've sprung a leak! And we are—to sink!

Has this ever happened to you, Lieutenant?" "No, but I have had a sour
experience with a shark." "Yeah? But I mean, a leak. What if . . ."
"Well, then you'll finally meet the passenger from 8-F."
"Who is that?" "She's the governor's daughter, sailing to Curaçao."

IV

Exchanges on the Deck
"I, Professor, too, as a kid, wanted, and badly so,
to discover some insect, or, better still, a virus . . ."
"Right. And what happened?" "Well, science involves new values . . .
Plus, the usual tsuris . . ." "Sorry?" "You know: the dough."

"What is man, anyway? I tell you: he is a gnat!"
"But back there, in Russia, monsieur, do you also have rubber, as in . . ."
"Valdemar! I said stop it! You bit my lip, you rat.
Don't forget, Valdemar, that I am . . ." "I am sorry, cousin."

"Listen, buddy." "Well, what?" "What is that thing far off?"
"Where?" "On the right." "I see nothing." "At two o'clock, out there."
"Oh, that . . . maybe a whale. Got any smokes?" "Nope. Zero . . .
but—it's rising! It's rising so fast! And it is, by Jove . . ."

V

The sea is more various than the terra
firma. It's harder for you to grapple
with, not to mention stare at.
A fish is more intricate than an apple.

The land means four solid walls, a ceiling.
We are scared of wolves or of bears. Although some are ready
to detect in the latter a human feeling
and address one as "Teddy."

The sea has no room for these sorts of worries.
A whale, in its primordial splendor,
won't respond to a name like Boris;
Dick is a better tender.

The sea is filled with surprises; some are unpleasant.
Many a maritime upheaval
can't be ascribed to the evil crescent
of the moon or the human eye's lesser evil.

Ah, sea dwellers' blood is colder than ours. Their goggle
mesmerizes even fishmongers. The late Charles Darwin
would have quit legislating his gentle jungle
had he tried some limited scuba diving.

VI

Exchange on the Bridge
"Captain! We're passing the fathoms where *The Black Prince*
went down. For reasons unknown." "Navigator Benz!
Return to your cabin and sober up!"
". . . the fathoms where the Russian *Tsarina*, too, took the rap
and was lost . . ." "Navigator Benz! I'll banish you to the can!
Do you hear me?!" ". . . for reasons un . . ."
The clipper's unswerving on its blue track.
Africa, Asia, the New and the Old World lag
behind. Taut sails look like question marks in profile.
Space's answer is in the back.

VII

Exchange in a Cabin
"Irina!" "Ah, what?" "Take a look at that thing, Irina."
"But I am asleep." "All the same. Look!" "Where?" "In the porthole.
What is that?" "Looks like somebo . . . like samba . . . like submarine . . .

Huh?
What did you say?" "But it coils!" "So what. In the water, all
things coil." "Irina!" "What? Where are you dragging me? I am completely

naked."
"Yes, but just look!" "Oh, stop pushing me!" "You see?" "Well, I
look. Yes, it coils. But I think—I take it—
But it's a gigantic octopus! And it's climbing in! Nikolai!!!"

VIII
The sea is ostensibly lifeless, yet
it's full of monstrous life-forms which your mind-set
won't grasp until you hit the king-size sea-bed.

At times, this gets proven by what's been angled
or by shimmering waves whose rather languid
mirror reflects things happening under the blanket.

While on the surface, a man wants to sail fast and be there first.
Submerged, he gets this wish reversed;
suddenly he feels a thirst.

There, underneath, man feels dry within.
Life appears to him short and green.
Submerged, man can be only a submarine.

From the mouth, bubbles are bursting free.
In the eyes, an equivalent of sunrise replaces glee.
In the ears, a colorless baritone keeps uttering: "One. Two. Three."

IX

"Dear Blanche, I write this to you sitting inside a gigantic octopus.
A miracle, but the stationery and your picture survived. This jelly
is hard to inhale. Yet in a sense it's populous:
there are a couple of savages, both playing the ukulele.
Main thing: it's dark. I strain my eyes and listen.
Sometimes I make out some arches and vaults. When I write, it also
                                                     becomes less black.
I resolve to examine the metabolic system.
That's the only railroad to freedom. Kisses. Your faithful Jacques."

"It's like being back in the womb . . . Still, one should be grateful
for the octopus. Sharks are worse. So is water as such—for yours truly.
Am still searching. The savages brought a grapefruit.
But when I ask for directions, all I hear is 'Hoolie-hoolie.'
All I see are infinite, slippery, coiling tunnels.
Some peculiar, tangled system that's hard to memo-
rize. And unless I'm delirious, yesterday in these trammels
I bumped into somebody who calls himself Captain Nemo."

"Nemo again. Invited me to his rooms. I went.
He says he has reared this octopus as a protest
against society. Well, earlier, I understand,
he was married, with kids. But his wife—the hottest
pants in town . . . and so forth. And he had no choice. He says

the world drowns in Evil. The octopus ('opus' for some) avenges
hubris and heartlessness, alias earthly ways.
Promised me immortality if I don't leave the trenches."

"Tuesday. Supper at Nemo's. Caviar, cognac, *fromage*—from, I
guess, both *Prince* and *Tsarina*. The savages served: good manners.
We discussed the matter raised yesterday, that is, my
immortality; Pascal's *Pensées*; recent La Scala tenors.
Just think: evening, candles. The octopus all around.
Nemo with his goatee and baby-blue, nay, prenatal
eyes. If I think of his loneliness, my heart starts to pound . . ."

That's the last Mlle Blanche Delarue heard from Jacques Benz, navigator.

X

When the ship doesn't arrive at the port of call
on time, or later on, the Business
Manager says in his office, "Hell!"
The Admiralty says, "Jesus."

Both are quite wrong. But how could they know what had
transpired? You can't interrogate a seagull
or a shark with its streamlined head.
Nor is sending an eager

doggie down the track of much help. And anyway, what sort
of tracks are there at sea? All this is valiant
bunk. One more triumph—via the absurd—
for waves contesting dry land.

Oceanic events are, as a rule, abrupt.
Still, long afterward, the waves toss the remnants of their brief sally:
life vests, splinters of masts, a rat—
none with fingerprints, sadly.

And then comes autumn. And later on, winter cuts
in. The sirocco tatters awnings that summer fancied.

Silent waves can drive the best attorney nuts
with their show of a sunset.

And what gets crystal-clear is that it's dumb to grill
(turning your vocal cords into a shortwave's risen
pitch) the blue ripples perfecting their sharp-as-steel
line of the horizon.

Something bobs up in the papers, burying under their slants
the facts, driblets really. Who can crack it . . .
A woman wearing brown clutches the drapes and slumps
slowly onto the carpet.

The horizon's improving. The air's filled with iodine and salt.
Far away, breakers pummel with great abandon
some inanimate object. And the bell of old
keeps tolling grimly at Lloyd's of London.

[1976]

Lines on the Winter Campaign, 1980

The scorching noon, the vale in Dagestan . . .

—MIKHAIL LERMONTOV

I

A bullet's velocity in low temperatures
greatly depends on its target's virtues,
on its urge to warm up in the plaited muscles
of the torso, in the neck's webbed sinews.
Stones lie flat like a second army.
The shade hugs the loam to itself willy-nilly.
The sky resembles peeling stucco.
An aircraft dissolves in it like a clothes moth,
and like a spring from a ripped-up mattress
an explosion sprouts up. Outside the crater,
the blood, like boiled milk, powerless to seep into
the ground, is seized by a film's hard ripples.

II

Shepherd and sower, the North is driving
herds to the sea, spreading cold to the South.
A bright, frosty noon in a Wogistan valley.
A mechanical elephant, trunk wildly waving
at the horrid sight of the small black rodent
of a snow-covered mine, spews out throat-clogging
lumps, possessed of that old desire
of Mahomet's, to move a mountain.
Summits loom white; the celestial warehouse
lends them at noontime its flaking surplus.
The mountains lack any motion, passing
their immobility to the scattered bodies.

III

The doleful, echoing Slavic singing
at evening in Asia. Dank and freezing,
sprawling piles of human pig meat

cover the caravansary's mud bottom.
The fuel dung smolders, legs stiffen in numbness.
It smells of old socks, of forgotten bath days.
The dreams are identical, as are the greatcoats.
Plenty of cartridges, few recollections,
and the tang in the mouth of too many "hurrahs."
Glory to those who, their glances lowered,
marched in the sixties to abortion tables,
sparing the homeland its present stigma.

IV

What is contained in the drone's dull buzzing?
And what in the sound of the aero-engine?
Living is getting as complicated
as building a house with grapes' green marbles
or little lean-tos with spades and diamonds.
Nothing is stable (one puff and it's over):
families, private thoughts, clay shanties.
Night over ruins of a mountain village.
Armor, wetting its metal sheets with oil slick,
freezes in thorn scrub. Afraid of drowning
in a discarded jackboot, the moon
hides in a cloud as in Allah's turban.

V

Idle, inhaled now by no one, air.
Imported, carelessly piled-up silence.
Rising like dough that's leavened,
emptiness. If the stars had life-forms,
space would erupt with a brisk ovation;
a gunner, blinking, runs to the footlights.
Murder's a blatant way of dying,
a tautology, the art form of parrots,
a manual matter, the knack for catching
life's fly in the hairs of the gunsight
by youngsters acquainted with blood through either
hearsay or violating virgins.

VI

Pull up the blanket, dig a hole in the palliasse.
Flop down and give ear to the *oo* of the siren.
The Ice Age is coming—slavery's ice age is coming,
oozing over the atlas. Its moraines force under
nations, fond memories, muslin blouses.
Muttering, rolling our eyeballs upward,
we are becoming a new kind of bivalve,
our voice goes unheard, as though we were trilobites.
There's a draft from the corridor, draft from the square windows.
Turn off the light, wrap up in a bundle.
The vertebra craves eternity. Unlike a ringlet.
In the morning the limbs are past all uncoiling.

VII

Up in the stratosphere, thought of by no one,
the little bitch barks as she peers through the porthole:
"Beach Ball! Beach Ball! Over. It's Rover."
The beach ball's below. With the equator on it
like a dog collar. Slopes, fields, and gullies
repeat in their whiteness cheekbones
(the color of shame has all gone to the banners).
And the hens in their snowed-in hen coops,
also a-shake from the shock of reveille,
lay their eggs of immaculate color.
If anything blackens, it's just the letters,
like the tracks of some rabbit, preserved by a wonder.

1980

Café Trieste: San Francisco

TO L.G.

To this corner of Grant and Vallejo
I've returned like an echo
to the lips that preferred
then a kiss to a word.

Nothing has changed here. Neither
the furniture nor the weather.
Things, in one's absence, gain
permanence, stain by stain.

Cold, through the large steamed windows
I watch the gesturing weirdos,
the bloated breams that warm
up their aquarium.

Evolving backward, a river
becomes a tear, the real
becomes memory which
can, like fingertips, pinch

just the tail of a lizard
vanishing in the desert
which was eager to fix
a traveler with a sphinx.

Your golden mane! Your riddle!
The lilac skirt, the brittle
ankles! The perfect ear
rendering "read" as "dear."

Under what cloud's pallor
now throbs the tricolor

of your future, your past
and present, swaying the mast?

Upon what linen waters
do you drift bravely toward
new shores, clutching your beads
to meet the savage needs?

Still, if sins are forgiven,
that is, if souls break even
with flesh elsewhere, this joint,
too, must be enjoyed

as afterlife's sweet parlor
where, in the clouded squalor,
saints and the aint's take five,
where I was first to arrive.

1980

The Hawk's Cry in Autumn

Wind from the northwestern quarter is lifting him high above
the dove-gray, crimson, umber, brown
Connecticut Valley. Far beneath,
chickens daintily pause and move
unseen in the yard of the tumbledown
farmstead, chipmunks blend with the heath.

Now adrift on the airflow, unfurled, alone,
all that he glimpses—the hills' lofty, ragged
ridges, the silver stream that threads
quivering like a living bone
of steel, badly notched with rapids,
the townships like strings of beads

strewn across New England. Having slid down to nil
thermometers—those household gods in niches—
freeze, inhibiting thus the fire
of leaves and churches' spires. Still,
no churches for him. In the windy reaches,
undreamt of by the most righteous choir,

he soars in a cobalt-blue ocean, his beak clamped shut,
his talons clutched tight into his belly
—claws balled up like a sunken fist—
sensing in each wisp of down the thrust
from below, glinting back the berry
of his eyeball, heading south-southeast

to the Rio Grande, the Delta, the beech groves and farther still:
to a nest hidden in the mighty groundswell
of grass whose edges no fingers trust,
sunk amid forest's odors, filled

with splinters of red-speckled eggshell,
with a brother or a sister's ghost.

The heart overgrown with flesh, down, feather, wing,
pulsing at feverish rate, nonstopping,
propelled by internal heat and sense,
the bird goes slashing and scissoring
the autumnal blue, yet by the same swift token,
enlarging it at the expense

of its brownish speck, barely registering on the eye,
a dot, sliding far above the lofty
pine tree; at the expense of the empty look
of that child, arching up at the sky,
that couple that left the car and lifted
their heads, that woman on the stoop.

But the uprush of air is still lifting him
higher and higher. His belly feathers
feel the nibbling cold. Casting a downward gaze,
he sees the horizon growing dim,
he sees, as it were, the features
of the first thirteen colonies whose

chimneys all puff out smoke. Yet it's their total within his sight
that tells the bird of his elevation,
of what altitude he's reached this trip.
What am I doing at such a height?
He senses a mixture of trepidation
and pride. Heeling over a tip

of wing, he plummets down. But the resilient air
bounces him back, winging up to glory,
to the colorless icy plane.
His yellow pupil darts a sudden glare
of rage, that is, a mix of fury
and terror. So once again

he turns and plunges down. But as walls return
rubber balls, as sins send a sinner to faith, or near,
he's driven upward this time as well!
He! whose innards are still so warm!
Still higher! Into some blasted ionosphere!
That astronomically objective hell

of birds that lacks oxygen, and where the milling stars
play millet served from a plate or a crescent.
What, for the bipeds, has always meant
height, for the feathered is the reverse.
Not with his puny brain but with shriveled air sacs
he guesses the truth of it: it's the end.

And at this point he screams. From the hooklike beak
there tears free of him and flies *ad luminem*
the sound Erinyes make to rend
souls: a mechanical, intolerable shriek,
the shriek of steel that devours aluminum;
"mechanical," for it's meant

for nobody, for no living ears:
not man's, not yelping foxes',
not squirrels' hurrying to the ground
from branches; not for tiny field mice whose tears
can't be avenged this way, which forces
them into their burrows. And only hounds

lift up their muzzles. A piercing, high-pitched squeal,
more nightmarish than the D-sharp grinding
of the diamond cutting glass,
slashes the whole sky across. And the world seems to reel
for an instant, shuddering from this rending.
For the warmth burns space in the highest as

badly as some iron fence down here
brands incautious gloveless fingers.

We, standing where we are, exclaim
"There!" and see far above the tear
that is a hawk, and hear the sound that lingers
in wavelets, a spider skein

swelling notes in ripples across the blue vault of space
whose lack of echo spells, especially in October,
an apotheosis of pure sound.
And caught in this heavenly patterned lace,
starlike, spangled with hoarfrost powder,
silver-clad, crystal-bound,

the bird sails to the zenith, to the dark-blue high
of azure. Through binoculars we foretoken
him, a glittering dot, a pearl.
We hear something ring out in the sky,
like some family crockery being broken,
slowly falling aswirl,

yet its shards, as they reach our palms, don't hurt
but melt when handled. And in a twinkling
once more one makes out curls, eyelets, strings,
rainbowlike, multicolored, blurred
commas, ellipses, spirals, linking
heads of barley, concentric rings—

the bright doodling pattern the feather once possessed,
a map, now a mere heap of flying
pale flakes that make a green slope appear
white. And the children, laughing and brightly dressed,
swarm out of doors to catch them, crying
with a loud shout in English, "Winter's here!"

1975

Sextet

TO MARK STRAND

I

An eyelid is twitching. From the open mouth
gushes silence. The cities of Europe mount
each other at railroad stations. A pleasant odor
of soap tells the jungle dweller of the approaching foe.
Wherever you set your sole or toe,
the world map develops blank spots, grows balder.

A palate goes dry. The traveler's seized by thirst.
Children, to whom the worst
should be done, fill the air with their shrieks. An eyelid twitches
all the time. As for columns, from
the thick of them someone always emerges. Even in your sweet dream,
even with your eyes shut, you see human features.

And it wells up in your throat like barf:
"Give me ink and paper and, as for yourself,
scram!" And an eyelid is twitching. Odd, funereal
whinings—as though someone's praying upstairs—poison the daily grind.
The monstrosity of what's happening in your mind
makes unfamiliar premises look familiar.

II

Sometimes in the desert you hear a voice. You fetch
a camera in order to catch the face.
But—too dark. Sit down, then, release your hearing
to the Southern lilt of a small monkey who
left her palm tree but, having no leisure to
become a human, went straight to whoring.

Better sail by steamer, horizon's ant,
taking part in geography, in blueness, and
not in history, this dry land's scabies.

Better trek across Greenland on skis and camp
among the icebergs, among the plump
walruses as they bathe their babies.

The alphabet won't allow your trip's goal to be
ever forgotten, that famed point B.
There a crow caws hard, trying to play the raven;
there a black sheep bleats, rye is choked with weeds;
there the top brass, like furriers, shear out bits
of the map's faded pelt, so that they look even.

III

For thirty-six years I've stared at fire.
An eyelid is twitching. Both palms perspire:
the cop leaves the room with your papers. Angst. Built to calm it,
an obelisk, against its will, recedes
in a cloud, amidst bright seeds,
like an immobile comet.

Night. With your hair quite gone, you still dine alone,
being your own grand master, your own black pawn.
The kipper's soiling a headline about striking rickshaws
or a berserk volcano's burps—
God knows where, in other words—
flitting its tail over "The New Restrictions."

I comprehend only the buzz of flies
in the Eastern bazaars! On the sidewalk, flat
on his back, the traveler strains his sinews,
catching the air with his busted gills.
In the afterlife, the pain that kills
here no doubt continues.

IV

"Where's that?" asks the nephew, toying with his stray locks.
And, fingering brown mountain folds, "Here," pokes
the niece. In the depths of the garden, yellow

swings creak softly. The table dwarfs a bouquet
of violets. The sun's splattering the parquet
floor. From the drawing room float twangs of a cello.

At night, a plateau absorbs moonshine.
A boulder shepherds its elephantine
shadow. A brook's silver change is spending
itself in a gully. Clutched sheets in a room elude
their milky/swarthy/abandoned nude—
an anonymous painful painting.

In spring, labor ants build their muddy coops;
rooks show up; so do creatures with other groups
of blood; a fresh leaf shelters
the verging shame of two branches. In autumn, a sky hawk keeps
counting villages' chicklets; and the sahib's
white jacket is dangling from the servant's shoulders.

V

Was the word ever uttered? And then—if yes—
in what language? And where? And how much ice
should be thrown into a glass to halt a *Titanic*
of thought? Does the whole recall the neat shapes of parts?
Would a botanist, suddenly facing birds
in an aquarium, panic?

Now let us imagine an absolute emptiness.
A place without time. The air *per se*. In this,
in that, and in the third direction—pure, simple, pallid
air. A Mecca of it: oxygen, nitrogen. In which
there's really nothing except for the rapid twitch-
ing of a lonely eyelid.

These are the notes of a naturalist. The naughts
on nature's own list. Stained with flowerpots.
A tear falls in a vacuum without acceleration.
The last of hotbed neu-roses, hearing the

faint buzzing of time's tsetse,
I smell increasingly of isolation.

VI

And I dread my petals' joining the crowned knot
of fire! Most resolutely not!
Oh, but to know the place for the first, the second,
and the umpteenth time! When everything comes to light,
when you hear or utter the jewels like
"When I was in the army" or "Change the record!"

Petulant is the soul begging mercy from
an invisible or dilated frame.
Still, if it comes to the point where the blue acrylic
dappled with cirrus suggests the Lord,
say, "Give me strength to sustain the hurt,"
and learn it by heart like a decent lyric.

When you are no more, unlike the rest,
the latter may think of themselves as blessed
with the place so much safer thanks to the big withdrawal
of what your conscience indeed amassed.
And a fish that prophetically shines with rust
will splash in a pond and repeat your oval.

1976

Minefield Revisited

You, guitar-shaped affair with tousled squalor
of chords, who keep looming brown in an empty parlor,
or snow-white against laundered expanses, or
dark—at dusk especially—in the corridor,
strum me a tune of how drapery makes its cloudy
rustle, how a flipped-up switch ravages half a body
with shadow, how a fly prowls the atlas, how in the garden
outside, the sunset echoes a steaming squadron
of which there survived only a middy blouse
in the nursery, how hidden in the satin trousers
the comb of a Turkish dog trainer, when played, elevates his poodle
beyond Kovalevska, beyond its idol
to a happy occasion: that is, to yelping forty
times at some birthday, while wet and frothy
firework stars fizz and fade in the foggy trembling
glass, and carafes on a tablecloth feign the Kremlin.

[July 22] 1978

Near Alexandria

TO CARL PROFFER

The concrete needle is shooting its
heroin into cumulous wintry muscle.
From a trash can, a spy plucks the crumpled morsel—
a blueprint of ruins—and glances east.

Ubiquitous figures on horseback: all
four hooves glued to their marble bracket.
The warriors apparently kicked the bucket,
crushing bedbugs on the linen sprawl.

In the twilight, chandeliers gleam, akin
to bonfires; sylphides weave their sweet pattern:
a finger, eight hours poised by the button,
relaxes fondling its hooded twin.

Windowpanes quiver with tulle's soft ply;
the besom of naked shrubs is bothered
by the evergreen rustle of money, by the
seemingly nonstop July.

A cross between a blade and a raw
throat uttering no sound whatever,
the sharp bend of a level river
glistens, covered with icy straw.

Victim of lungs though friend to words,
the air is transparent, severely punctured
by beaks that treat it as pens treat parchment,
by visible-only-in-profile birds.

This is a flattened colossus veiled
by the gauze thickening on the horizon,

edged with the lacework of wheels gone frozen
after six by the curb's gray welt.

Like the mouse creeping out of the scarlet crack,
the sunset gnaws hungrily the electric
cheese of the outskirts, erected
by those who clearly trust their knack

for surviving everything: by termites.
Warehouses, surgeries. Having measured
there the proximity of the desert,
the cinnamon-tinted earth waylays its

horizontality in the fake
pyramids, porticoes, rooftops' ripple,

as the train creeps knowingly, like a snake,
to the capital's only nipple.

1982

Tsushima Screen

The perilous yellow sun follows with its slant eyes
masts of the shuddered grove steaming up to capsize
in the frozen straits of Epiphany. February has fewer
days than the other months; therefore, it's more cruel
than the rest. Dearest, it's more sound
to wrap up our sailing round
the globe with habitual naval grace,
moving your cot to the fireplace
where our dreadnought is going under
in great smoke. Only fire can grasp a winter!
Golden unharnessed stallions in the chimney
dye their manes to more corvine shades as they near the finish,
and the dark room fills with the plaintive, incessant chirring
of a naked, lounging grasshopper one cannot cup in fingers.

1978

A Martial Law Carol

TO WIKTOR WOROSZYLSKI AND ANDRZEJ DRAWICZ

One more Christmas ends
soaking stripes and stars.
All my Polish friends
are behind steel bars,
locked like zeros in
some graph sheet of wrath:
as a discipline
slavery beats math.

Nations learn the rules
like a naughty boy
as the tyrant drools
manacles in joy.
One pen stroke apiece,
minus edits plus
helping the police
to subtract a class.

From a stubborn brow
something scarlet drops
on the Christmas snow.
As it turns, the globe's
face gets uglier,
pores becoming cells,
while the planets glare
coldly, like ourselves.

Hungry faces. Grime.
Squalor. Unabashed
courts distribute time
to the people crushed
not so much by tanks
or by submachine

guns as by the banks
we deposit in.

Deeper than the depth
of your thoughts or mine
is the sleep of death
in the Wujek mine;
higher than your rent
is that hand whose craft
keeps the others bent—
as though photographed.

Powerless is speech.
Still, it bests a tear
in attempts to reach,
crossing the frontier,
for the heavy hearts
of my Polish friends.
One more trial starts.
One more Christmas ends.

[1981]

Folk Tune

It's not that the Muse feels like clamming up,
it's more like high time for the lad's last nap.
And the scarf-waving lass who wished him the best
drives a steamroller across his chest.

And the words won't rise either like that rod
or like logs to rejoin their old grove's sweet rot,
and, like eggs in the frying pan, the face
spills its eyes all over the pillowcase.

Are you warm tonight under those six veils
in that basin of yours whose strung bottom wails;
where like fish that gasp at the foreign blue
my raw lip was catching what then meant you?

I would have hare's ears sewn to my bald head,
in thick woods for your sake I'd gulp drops of lead,
and from black gnarled snags in the oil-smooth pond
I'd bob up to your face as some *Tirpitz* won't.

But it's not on the cards or the waiter's tray,
and it pains to say where one's hair turns gray.
There are more blue veins than the blood to swell
their dried web, let alone some remote brain cell.

We are parting for good, little friend, that's that.
Draw an empty circle on your yellow pad.
This will be me: no insides in thrall.
Stare at it a while, then erase the scrawl.

1980

273

Roman Elegies

TO BENEDETTA CRAVERI

I

The captive mahogany of a private Roman
flat. In the ceiling, a dust-covered crystal island.
At sunset, the windowpanes pan a common
ground for the nebulous and the ironed.
Setting a naked foot on the rosy marble,
the body steps toward its future: to its attire.
If somebody shouted "Freeze!" I'd perform that marvel
as this city happily did in its childhood hour.
The world's made of nakedness and of foldings.
Still, the latter's richer with love than a face, that's certain.
Thus an opera tenor's so sweet to follow
since he yields invariably to a curtain.
By nightfall, a blue eye employs a tear,
cleansing, to a needless shine, the iris;
and the moon overhead apes an emptied square
with no fountain in it. But of rock as porous.

II

The month of stalled pendulums. Only a fly in August
in a dry carafe's throat is droning its busy hymn.
The numerals on the clock face crisscross like earnest
antiaircraft searchlights probing for seraphim.
The month of drawn blinds, of furniture wrapped in cotton
shrouds, of the sweating double in the mirror above the cupboard,
of bees that forget the topography of their hives and, coated
with suntan honey, keep staggering seaward.
Get busy then, faucet, over the snow-white, sagging
muscle, tousle the tufts of thin gray singes!
To a homeless torso and its idle, grabby
mitts, there's nothing as dear as the sight of ruins.
And they, in their turn, see themselves in the broken Jewish

r no less gladly: for the pieces fallen
so apart, saliva's the only solution they wish
for, as time's barbarous corneas scan the Forum.

III

The tiled, iron-hot, glowing hills: midsummer.
Clouds feel like angels, thanks to their cooling shadows.
Thus the bold cobblestone eyes, like a happy sinner,
the blue underthings of your leggy blond friend. A bard of
trash, extra thoughts, broken lines, unmanly,
I hide in the bowels of the Eternal City
from the luminary that rolled back so many
marble pupils with rays bright enough for setting
up yet another universe. A yellow square. Noontime's
stupor. A Vespa's owner tortures the screaming gears.
Clutching my chest with my hand, at a distance
I reckon the change from the well-spent years.
And, like a book at once opened to all its pages,
the laurels scratch the scorched white of a balustrade.
And the Colosseum looms, the skull of Argus,
through whose sockets clouds drift like a thought of the vanished herd.

IV

Two young brunettes in the library of the husband
of the more stunning one. Two youthful, tender
ovals hunch over pages: a Muse telling Fate the substance
of several things she tried to render.
The swish of old paper, of red crepe de Chine. A humming
fan mixes violets, lavender, and carnations.
Braiding of hair: an elbow thrusts up its summit
accustomed to cumulus-thick formations,
Oh, a dark eye is obviously more fluent
in brown furniture, pomegranates, oak shutters.
It's more keen, it's more cordial than a blue one;
to the blue one, though, nothing matters!
The blue one can always tell the owner

from the goods, especially before closing—
that is, time from living—and turn the latter over,
as tails strain to look at heads in tossing.

V

Jig, little candle tongue, over the empty paper,
bow to the rotten breath as though you were courted,
follow—but don't get too close!—the pauper
letters standing in line to obtain the content.
You animate the walls, wardrobe, the sill's sweetbriar:
more than handwriting is ever after;
even your soot, it appears, soars higher
than the holiest wish of these musings' author.
Still, in their midst you earn yourself a decent
name, as my fountain pen, in memory of your tender
commas, in Rome, at the millennium's end, produces
a lantern, a cresset, a torch, a taper,
never a period—and the premises look their ancient
selves, from the severed head down to a yellow toenail.
For an ink pot glows bright whenever someone mentions
light, especially in a tunnel.

VI

Clicking of a piano at the siesta hour.
Stillness of sleepy mews acquires
C-flats, as scales coat a fish which narrows
round the corner. Exhaling quarrels,
inhaling a fusty noon's air, the stucco
flaps its brown gills, and a sultry, porous
cavity of a mouth scatters
around cold pearls of Horace.
I've never built that cloud-thrusting stony
object that could explain clouds' pallor.
I've learned about my own, and any
fate, from a letter, from its black color.
Thus some fall asleep while hugging

a Leica, in order to take a picture
of the dream, to make themselves out, having
awakened in a developed future.

VII

Eggshells of cupolas, vertebrae of bell towers.
Colonnades' limbs sprawled wide in their blissful, heathen
leisure. The square root of a skylark scours
the bottomless, as though prior to prayers, heaven.
Light reaps much more than it has sown: an awkward
body hides in a crack while its shadow shutters
walls. In these parts, all windows are looking northward,
where the more one boozes the less one matters.
North! A white iceberg's frozen-in piano;
smallpoxed with quartz, vases' granite figures;
a plain unable to stop field-glass scanning;
sweet Ashkenazy's ten running fingers.
Never again are the legions to thread those contours:
to a creaking pen, even its words won't hearken.
And the golden eyebrow—as, at sunset, a cornice—
rises up, and the eyes of the darling darken.

VIII

In these squinting alleyways, where even a thought about
one's self is too cumbersome, in this furrowed clutter
of the brain which has long since refused to cloud
the universe, where now keyed up, now scattered,
you trundle your boots on the cobbled, checkered
squares, from a fountain and back to a Caesar—
thus a needle shuffles across the record
skipping its grooves—it is altogether
proper to settle now for a measly fraction
of remaining life, for the past life craving
completeness, for its attempts to fashion
an integer. The sound the heels are scraping
from the ground is the aria of their union,

a serenade that what-has-been-longer
hums to what's-to-be-shorter. This is a genuine
Caruso for a gramophone-dodging mongrel.

IX

Lesbia, Julia, Cynthia, Livia, Michelina.
Bosoms, ringlets of fleece: for effects, and for causes also.
Heaven-baked clay, fingertips' brave arena.
Flesh that renders eternity an anonymous torso.
You breed immortals: those who have seen you bare,
they, too, turned Catulluses, statues, heavy
Neros, et cetera. Short-term goddesses! you are
much more a joy to believe in than a permanent bevy.
Hail the smooth abdomen, thighs as their hamstrings tighten.
White upon white, as Kazimir's dream image,
one summer evening, I, the most mortal item
in the midst of this wreckage resembling the whole world's rib cage,
sip with feverish lips wine from a tender collar-
bone; the sky is as pale as a cheek with a mole that trembles;
and the cupolas bulge like the tits of the she-wolf, fallen
asleep after having fed her Romulus and her Remus.

X

Mimicking local pines, embrace the ether!
The fingertips won't cull much more than the pane's tulle quiver.
Still, a little black bird won't return from the sky blue, either.
And we, too, aren't gods in miniature, that's clear.
That's precisely why we are happy: because we are nothings; speckled
pores are spurned by summits or sharp horizons;
the body is space's reversal, no matter how hard you pedal.
And when we are unhappy, it's perhaps for the same small reasons.
Better lean on a portico, loose the white shirt that billows,
stone cools the spinal column, gray pigeons mutter,
and watch how the sun is sinking into gardens and distant villas,
how the water—the tutor
of eloquence—pours from the rusted lips, repeating

278

not a thing, save a nymph with her marble truants,
save that it's cold and fresh, save that it's splitting
the face into rippling ruins.

XI

Private life. Fears, shredded thoughts, the jagged
blanket renders the contours of Europe meager.
By means of a blue shirt and a rumpled jacket
something still gets reflected in the wardrobe mirror.
Let's have some tea, face, so that the teeth may winnow
lips. Yoked by a ceiling, the air grows flatter.
Cast inadvertently through the window,
a glance makes a bunch of blue jays flutter
from their pine tops. A room in Rome, white paper,
the tail of a freshly drawn letter: a darting rodent.
Thus, thanks to the perfect perspective, some objects peter
out; thus, still others shuffle across the frozen
Tanaïs, dropping from the picture, limping,
occiputs covered with wilted laurels and blizzards' powder—
toward Time, lying beyond the limits
of every spraddling superpower.

XII

Lean over. I'll whisper something to you: I am
grateful for everything: for the chicken cartilage
and for the chirr of scissors already cutting
out the void for me—for it is your hem.
Doesn't matter if it's pitch-black, doesn't matter if
it holds nothing: no ovals, no limbs to count.
The more invisible something is,
the more certain it's been around,
and the more obviously it's everywhere. You
were the first to whom all this happened, were you?
For a nail holding something one would divide by two—
were it not for remainders—there is no gentler quarry.
I was in Rome. I was flooded by light. The way

a splinter can only dream about.
Golden coins on the retina are to stay—
enough to last one through the whole blackout.

1981

To Urania

TO I.K.

Everything has its limit, including sorrow.
A windowpane stalls a stare. Nor does a grille abandon
a leaf. One may rattle the keys, gurgle down a swallow.
Loneliness cubes a man at random.
A camel sniffs at the rail with a resentful nostril;
a perspective cuts emptiness deep and even.
And what is space anyway if not the
body's absence at every given
point? That's why Urania's older than sister Clio!
In daylight or with the soot-rich lantern,
you see the globe's pate free of any bio,
you see she hides nothing, unlike the latter.
There they are, blueberry-laden forests,
rivers where the folk with bare hands catch sturgeon
or the towns in whose soggy phone books
you are starring no longer; farther eastward surge on
brown mountain ranges; wild mares carousing
in tall sedge; the cheekbones get yellower
as they turn numerous. And still farther east, steam dreadnoughts or

cruisers,

and the expanse grows blue like lace underwear.

1981

The Bust of Tiberius

All hail to you, two thousand years too late.
I, too, once took a whore in marriage.
We have some things in common. Plus,
all round, your city. Bustle, shrieking traffic.
Damp alleyways with hypodermic youths.
Also, the ruins. I, a standard stranger,
salute your grimy bust in some
dank chamber storing echoes. Ah, Tiberius!
Here you're not thirty yet. The face displays
a greater confidence in trusted sinews
than in the future of their sum. A head
the sculptor severs in one's lifetime surely
sounds like a prophecy of power. All
that lies below the massive jawbone—Rome:
the provinces, the latifundists, the cohorts,
plus swarms of infants bubbling at your ripe
stiff sausage. A delight in tune
with nourishment by the she-wolf of tiny
Remus and Romulus—the mouths of babes indeed!
that sweetly incoherent mumbling
inside the toga! So we have a bust
that stands for the essential independence
of brain from body: (a) one's own, (b) one
that is Imperial. Should you be carving your
own likeness, you'd produce gray twisted matter.

You haven't reached thirty yet, thus far. Not one
arresting feature to detain observers.
Nor, in its turn, does your observant eye
appear to rest on anything before it:
neither on someone's face nor on
some classic landscape. Ah, Tiberius!

What does it matter what Suetonius
cum Tacitus still mutter, seeking causes
for your great cruelty? There are no causes in
this world—effects alone. And people
are victims of their own effects,
the more so in those steamy dungeons
where everyone confesses. Though confessions
dragged out by torture, like the ones in childhood,
are of a muchness. Far the best of fates
is really to have no part of truth.
It never elevates us. None,
Caesars especially. And at any rate
you seem a man more capable of drowning
in your piscina than in some deep thought.
Plus, shouldn't cruelty be termed a form
of speeding matters up, accelerating
the common fate of things? of a simple body's
free fall in vacuum?—in which, alas,
one always finds oneself when one is falling.

New year. A January pile of clouds
above the wintry town, like extra marble.
The brown, reality-escaping Tiber
and fountains spouting up to where no one
peers down—through lowered eyelids or
through fingers splayed. Another era!
And no one's up to holding by the ears
the wolves consumed with frenzy. Ah, Tiberius!
And such as we presume to judge you? You
were surely a monster, though perhaps more monstrous
was your indifference. But isn't it monsters
—not victims, no—that nature generates
in her own likeness? Ah, how much more soothing
(that is to say, if one should get the choice)
to be wiped off the earth by hell-bound fiends
than by neurotics. Still in your twenties,

with stony looks hewn out of stone, you look
a durable organic engine
of pure annihilation: not some dope,
a slave of passion, channel of ideas,
et cetera. And to defend you from
harsh tongues is like defending oak trees
from leaves, wrapped in their meaningless but clearly
insistent clamor of majority.

An empty gallery. A murky noontime
soiling tall windows with the distant drone
of life. A piece of marble in no fashion
responding to the quality of space . . .
It cannot be that you don't hear me speaking!
I, too, have often made that headlong dash
from rank reality. I, too, became an island
replete with ruins, ostriches. I, too,
struck off a profile with the aid of lamplight.
As for the things I've either coined or said,
it must be said that what I've said is useless,
and not eventually, but already: now.
Can't that be also that acceleration
of history? A bold attempt, alas,
by consequence to overtake causation?
And also in a total vacuum, which
gives no assurance of impressive splashdown.
Should one recant, then? rearrange the dice?
cut yet another deck of cards or atlas?
Who gives a damn: the radioactive rain
will scour us much the same as your historian.
Who'll come around to curse us, then? a star?
the moon? some wandering termite, driven
mad with its multiple mutations, fat
and yolklike? Probably. But having hit
something that's hard in us, it too, I reckon,
will shudder and give up its digging.

"Bust," it will utter in the tongue of ruins
and of contracting muscles. "Bust. Bust. Bust."

1981

Seven Strophes

I was but what you'd brush
with your palm, what your leaning
brow would hunch to in evening's
raven-black hush.

I was but what your gaze
in that dark could distinguish:
a dim shape to begin with,
later—features, a face.

It was you, on my right,
on my left, with your heated
sighs, who molded my helix,
whispering at my side.

It was you by that black
window's trembling tulle pattern
who laid in my raw cavern
a voice calling you back.

I was practically blind.
You, appearing, then hiding,
gave me my sight and heightened
it. Thus some leave behind

a trace. Thus they make worlds.
Thus, having done so, at random
wastefully they abandon
their work to its whirls.

Thus, prey to speeds
of light, heat, cold, or darkness,

a sphere in space without markers
spins and spins.

1981

The Residence

An attractive mansion on the avenue of Sardanapalus.
A pair of cast-iron lions with their hind legs complex.
In the hall, like a grinning footman, the black Steinway lets
the owner's fat-fingered, myopic, porous
grandniece poke its molars in broad daylight.
Lavender smells. Everywhere, including the kitchen,
outnumbering dishes, hang oils and etchings
depicting the Teacher, whose kinfolk might
still be living somewhere in Europe. Hence, sets of Goethe, plus
some Balzacs, chandeliers, capitals, gay putti,
and the very columns whose supple body
houses a battery of the "ground-to-ground" class.

But it feels the coziest in the eastern, i.e., his wing.
Bedroom windows hug poplars, or else it's alders.
And the cricket's chirr's softer than all those idle
bird feeders with their sensitive relay wink.
Here in the evening you may snap the lock, undress
to the lilac sweat shirt, to the matching long johns, whatever.
A far-off crow's nest in the branches suggests the beaver
of a Jewess he knew in his salad days,
but thank heaven they've split. And what really makes you crawl
to the bed are those eight-digit budget figures routinely hoarded
by the staff, or the last mortal screams of his confessed-it-all
son, apparently tape-recorded.

1983

Eclogue IV: Winter

TO DEREK WALCOTT

Ultima Cumaei venit iam carminis aetas;
magnus ab integro saeclorum nascitur ordo.
—VIRGIL, *ECLOGUE IV*

I

In winter it darkens the moment lunch is over.
It's hard then to tell starving men from sated.
A yawn keeps a phrase from leaving its cozy lair.
The dry, instant version of light, the opal
snow, dooms tall alders—by having freighted
them—to insomnia, to your glare,

well after midnight. Forget-me-nots and roses
crop up less frequently in dialogues. Dogs with languid
fervor pick up the trail, for they, too, leave traces.
Night, having entered the city, pauses
as in a nursery, finds a baby under the blanket.
And the pen creaks like steps that are someone else's.

II

My life has dragged on. In the recitative of a blizzard
a keen ear picks up the tune of the Ice Age.
Every "Down in the Valley" is, for sure,
a chilled boogie-woogie. A bitter, brittle
cold represents, as it were, a message
to the body of its final temperature

or—the earth itself, sighing out of habit
for its galactic past, its sub-zero horrors.
Cheeks burn crimson like radishes even here.
Cosmic space is always shot through with matte agate,
and the beeping Morse, returning homeward,
finds no ham operator's ear.

289

III

In February, lilac retreats to osiers.
Imperative to a snowman's profile,
carrots get more expensive. Limited by a brow,
a glance at cold, metallic objects
is fiercer than the metal itself. This, while
you peel eyes from objects, still may allow

no shedding of blood. The Lord, some reckon,
was reviewing His world in this very fashion
on the eighth day and after. In winter, we're
not berry pickers: we stuff the cracks with oakum,
praise the common good with a greater passion,
and things grow older by, say, a year.

IV

In great cold, pavements glaze like a sugar candy,
steam from the mouth suggests a dragon,
if you dream of a door, you tend to slam it.
My life has dragged on. The signs are plenty.
They'd make yet another life, just as dragging.
From these signs alone one would compose a climate

or a landscape. Preferably with no people,
with virgin white through a lacework shroud,
—a world where nobody heard of Parises, Londons; where
weekdays are spun by diffusive, feeble
light; where, too, in the end you shudder
spotting the ski tracks . . . Well, just a pair.

V

Time equals cold. Each body, sooner
or later, falls prey to a telescope. With the years,
it moves away from the luminary, grows colder.
Hoarfrost jungles the windowpane with sumac,
ferns, or horsetail, with what appears
to be nursed on this glass and deprived of color

by loneliness. But, as with a marble hero,
one's eye rolls up rather than runs in winter.
Where sight fails, yielding to dreams' swarmed forces,
time, fallen sharply beneath the zero,
burns your brain like the index finger
of a scamp from popular Russian verses.

VI

My life has dragged on. One cold resembles another
cold. Time looks like time. What sets them apart is only
a warm body. Mule-like, stubborn creature,
it stands firmly between them, rather
like a border guard: stiffened, sternly
preventing the wandering of the future

into the past. In winter, to put it bleakly,
Tuesday is Saturday. The daytime is a deceiver:
Are the lights out already? Or not yet on? It's chilly.
Dailies might as well be printed weekly.
Time stares at a looking glass like a diva
who's forgotten what's on tonight: *Tosca*? Oh no, *Lucia*?

VII

Dreams in the frozen season are longer, keener.
The patchwork quilt and the parquet deal,
on their mutual squares, in chessboard warriors.
The hoarser the blizzard rules the chimney,
the hotter the quest for a pure ideal
of naked flesh in a cotton vortex,

and you dream nasturtiums' stubborn odor,
a tuft of cobwebs shading a corner nightly,
in a narrow ravine torrid Terek's splashes,
a feast of fingertips caught in shoulder
straps. And then all goes quiet. Idly
an ember smolders in dawn's gray ashes.

VIII

Cold values space. Baring no rattling sabers,
it takes hill and dale, townships and hamlets
(the populace cedes without trying
tricks), mostly cities, whose great ensembles,
whose arches and colonnades, in hundreds,
stand like prophets of cold's white triumph,

looming wanly. Cold is gliding
from the sky on a parachute. Each and every column
looks like a fifth, desires an overthrow.
Only the crow doesn't take snow gladly.
And you often hear the angry, solemn,
patriotic gutturals speaking crow.

IX

In February, the later it is, the lower
the mercury. More time means more cold. Stars, scattered
like a smashed thermometer, turn remotest
regions of night into a strep marvel.
In daytime, when sky is akin to stucco,
Malevich himself wouldn't have noticed

them, white on white. That's why angels
are invisible. To their legions
cold is of benefit. We would make them
out, the winged ones, had our eyes' angle
been indeed on high, where they are linking
in white camouflage like Finnish marksmen.

X

For me, other latitudes have no usage.
I am skewered by cold like a grilled-goose portion.
Glory to naked birches, to the fir-tree needle,
to the yellow bulb in an empty passage—
glory to everything set by the wind in motion:
at a ripe age, it can replace the cradle.

The North is the honest thing. For it keeps repeating
all your life the same stuff—whispering, in full volume,
in the life dragged on, in all kinds of voices;
and toes freeze numb in your deerskin creepers,
reminding you, as you complete your polar
conquest, of love, of shivering under clock faces.

XI

In great cold, distance won't sing like sirens.
In space, the deepest inhaling hardly
ensures exhaling, nor does departure
a return. Time is the flesh of the silent
cosmos. Where nothing ticks. Even being hurtled
out of the spacecraft, one wouldn't capture

any sounds on the radio—neither fox-trots nor maidens
wailing from a hometown station.
What kills you out there, in orbit, isn't
the lack of oxygen but the abundance
of time in its purest (with no addition
of your life) form. It's hard to breathe it.

XII

Winter! I cherish your bitter flavor
of cranberries, tangerine crescents on faience saucers,
the tea, sugar-frosted almonds (at best, two ounces).
You were opening our small beaks in favor
of names like Marina or Olga—morsels
of tenderness at that age that fancies

cousins. I sing a snowpile's blue contours
at dusk, rustling foil, clicking B-flat somewhere,
as though "Chopsticks" were tried by the Lord's own finger.
And the logs, which rattled in stony courtyards
of the gray, dank city that freezes bare
by the sea, are still warming my every fiber.

At a certain age, the time of year, the season
coincides with fate. Theirs is a brief affair.
But on days like this you sense you are right. Your worries
about things that haven't come your way are ceasing,
and a simple botanist may take care
of commenting upon daily life and mores.

In this period, eyes lose their green of nettles,
the triangle drops its geometric ardor:
all the angles drawn with cobwebs are fuzzy.
In exchanges on death, place matters
more and more than time. The cold gets harder.
And saliva suddenly burns its cozy

XIV

tongue, like that coin. Still, all the rivers
are ice-locked. You can put on long johns and trousers,
strap steel runners to boots with ropes and a piece of timber.
Teeth, worn out by the tap dance of shivers,
won't rattle because of fear. And the Muse's
voice gains a reticent, private timbre.

That's the birth of an eclogue. Instead of the shepherd's signal,
a lamp's flaring up. Cyrillic, while running witless
on the pad as though to escape the captor,
knows more of the future than the famous sibyl:
of how to darken against the whiteness,
as long as the whiteness lasts. And after.

1977 [1980]

Eclogue V: Summer

TO MARGO PICKEN

I

I hear you again, mosquito hymn of summer!
In the dogwood tepee, ants sweat in slumber.
A botfly slides off the burdock's crumpled
epaulet, showing us that it always
ranked just a private. And caterpillars show us
the meaning of "lower than grass." The rosebays'

overgrown derricks—knee-deep or ankle-
deep in the couch-grass and bindweed jungle—
shine blue from their proximity and their angle
to the zenith. The praying mantis's little
rakes shutter the hemlock's brittle,
colorless fireworks. The scruffy, whittled

thistle's heart looks like a land mine which is
only half exploding its ruddy riches.
The cowbane resembles a hand that reaches
for a carafe. And, like a fisherman's wife, a spider
patches its trawl, strung out between the bitter
wormwood and the hedge mustard's golden miter.

Life is the sum of trifling motions. The silver
twilight of sedge's sheathed blades, the quiver
of many a shepherd's purse, the ever-
shifting tableau of horse sorrel, gentle
alfalfa's ditherings—these engender
our grasp of the rules of a stage whose center

cannot be found. At noonday both wheat and shabby
darnel cast northward their common shadow
because they are sown and shuffled

by the same windy sower about whose humors
the place is still rife with all sorts of rumors.
Give ear to the swishing murmurs

of cock-and-hen brushes! To what a daisy's
odd-or-even whispers! To how a drowsy
coltsfoot dubs these findings crazy.
To how a soft, wild-mint Leda, flattened
by a powerful swanweed, goes raving mad and
mumbles. Small grassplots of summer, flooded

with sunlight! Their homeless moths! Their nettle
pyramids! Their heat! Their total
stupor! Their fern pagoda's gentle
sway, or their ruined column
of anise, or a bent minaret of wild sage's solemn
bow—that's a copy, in grass and pollen,

of Babylon! Terzaromeville's verdant recent
version! The realm where, turning left, one's risking
ending up on the right side: everything's close, yet distant!
And a grasshopper in his pursuit of beauty—
of the cabbage butterfly in her pale tutu—
stalls, a knight at the crossroads, caught in dry blades' tutti.

II

Air, that's colorless in its core, seems, given
a landscape, blue—very often even
dark blue. The green perhaps gets enlivened
in a similar fashion. A passive grimace,
an eye's remoteness from the weed's the greenness
of the weed. In July, the seamless

flora's clear penchant to sunder
its ties with a botanist while darkening sanguine
leaves results in pale faces' suntan.

The sum of beautiful ones and ugly,
coming close or retreating, oddly
enough, can waste one's eye as badly

as these green/blue expanses. The color's humble
mask hides infinity's constant hunger
for details. Mass, after all, is hardly
the result of energy split by the square
of the speed of light (nay, sight!) somewhere
but the feeling of friction, of wear and tear

against one's own likes. Examine
space closely! Its selfsame garment
nearby and far away! Its ardent
obstinacy, with which green or bluish hollows—
their distance notwithstanding—always
sustain the pigment. Ah, this is almost

faith! A fanatic belief! The buzzing
of a fly stuck on flypaper doesn't
spell an agony but a dazzled
self-portrait in the Cyrillic *zh*. A semblance
of alphabet, warmth takes species across the sentence
of the horizon. A landscape shows just the settlers

left behind when their betters escaped to graceful
Asian palm trees. A July morning, faithful
to bedrooms, to shutters, flutters fistfuls
of jasmine banknotes, skipping
the acacia change of its seed pods splitting;
and the air's more diaphanous than a sleeping

beauty's lingerie. Sultry July! The surplus
of the green and the blue—of that threadbare surface
of existence. And a kind of solstice
of the luminary, stopped and splatter-

ing, like Attila before the battered
shield, fills one's orbs. The aforementioned outer

blue flaxlike stuff after all can't spin it
indefinitely. Light simply learns its limit
by means of a body because, within it,
light gets refracted, as at the finish
of too long a road whose beginning few wish
to consider. The finish, though, tends to furnish

III
butterflies, mallow, hay-scented fever,
a Seim or Oredezh type of river,
its banks strewn with luxuriating figures
of city-folk families; rosy naiads,
their risqué outfits which ignite us;
splutters, splashes; shrill jeremiads

of blue jays thrill pussy willows' bashful
branches obscuring the white parts of bathers
mooning as they wring swimsuits in bushes
upstream; ocher precipices, the pine-needle-
thick aroma, the heat, the nimble
sudden clouds tinting waves with a nickel,

fishlike sheen. Ah summer reservoirs! Most often
glimmering through foliage, molten
ponds or lakes—those orphan
parts of water surrounded by land; the rustle
of sedge and bulrush, moss-shammied muscles
of snarled snags, tender duckweed, and nascent

yellow nymphaeas, passionless water lilies,
algae or Paradise with no limits
for lines; and a water bug darts the liquid
blue, rather Christlike. And at times a perch is

splashing in order to catch a nervous
glimpse of the world, the way one peers out

a window and reels back afraid of falling.
Summer! The time for the shirt gone flapping,
for the old, animated polemic fumbling
about nightshades, toadstools, or garish,
wart-dotted, poisonous fly agarics;
for the quiet of forest clearings carried

by the peacefulness of their noontime slumber,
when your eyelids get lowered down by languor,
when a bumblebee, if it stung you,
did so because it was too myopic
and simply mistook you for blooming poppies
or a desirable cow dropping

and soared upward, distressed, in an awkward spiral.
The woods look like combs with their teeth in peril.
And a boy's revelation that he is "taller
than the bush though shorter than trees" will scramble
his brain for the rest of it! And a humble
nay! invisible skylark appears to tumble

his trills from on high. Summer! The season of exam cramming,
of formulae, of tossed coins, of a manic
pimpled look in boys, delays caused by panic
in girls; and the colonnade of a college
or bricks of some other seat of knowledge
haunt your dreams. Only fishing rods can abolish

with a swish those worries, the fears and burdens.
And we notice a singlet or else a bodice,
sandals, a bicycle in the grass; we notice
specifically its stainless pedals,

resembling a sergeant's bars or medals.
Indeed, their rubber pads, their metal

spell the future, the century, the whole deal,
Europe, a railroad whose branch, for real,
as though wind-shattered, produces rural
platforms—waterspouts, painted fences,
chickens, hedges, broad peasant faces
of women. In the meantime, each maggot forces

itself out of your tin can, soggy, sluggy,
homesick for its cowshed wall, for its muggy
shade. And then, later, a creaking buggy
lumped with burlap bushels, the clanging harness,
and the track that winds through the fields past harvest
time, and, at a distance, some church's harmless

bottle silhouette, haystacks, barns, stables—mainly
huts with their tarred sloping roofs and lonely
windows for whose sakes only
sunsets exist. And the spokes' shadow upon the shoulder
stretching all the way to the Polish border
runs along like some Fido, or a still bolder

Rover, catching foul mutterings of the driver;
and you stare at your toes or chomp on clover,
your thoughts drifting over to some freckled oval
in the town. And high up, in the very corner
of your eye, it's a crane, and not some infernal
thunderbird. Three cheers for normal

temperature: ten notches below the body's
standard. Three cheers for all things you notice.
For both the closest and the remotest
things. For everything that still matters,
for your shirt's drying tatters, for sunflowers' bent lanterns,
for the faint, distant waltz tune—"Manchurian Mountains."

IV

Summer twilight's fluttering window laces!
Cold cellars packed with milk jugs and lettuce,
a Stalin or a Khrushchev on the latest
news, jammed by cicadas' incessant rattle;
homemade bilberry jelly jars bat the rafters;
lime socks round apple orchards' ankles

look the whiter the darker it gets, like joggers
running beyond what the distance offers;
and farther still loom the real ogres
of full-size elms in the evening's bluing.
Kitchens, vast bottoms and head rugs brewing
something; the hellish fires phewing

in cookstoves' mica peepholes. Suppers on the verandas!
Potato in all its genres and genders,
onions and radishes in their grandest
fashion; tomatoes, dill, cucumbers—
all straight from the garden patch in great numbers;
and, finally, tired of their hide-and-seek, decanters

coated with dust! A soot-rich lantern,
a ballet of shadows dwarfing the wallpaper pattern,
geniuses of this high art, their ardent
admirers; samovar's armor; sugar
that you tell from salt by a fly, and shoo her
off. A nightjar's lonely pitch or super-

cilious frogs voicing every grievance
from their ditch. A silver pitcher glimmers
with your pink oval's distorted grimace,
rustling tabloids, burp-triggered tremors;
from the parlor wafts "Chopsticks," or else some tenor's
record. And Simonides' view on tendons

spares for a moment a keenly placid
stare at the wallpaper or hawthorn's flaccid

ramifications and twists: a glance at
a knee is never enough. The flesh is
dear indeed, since the fabric (bless its
patterns), by hiding the body, lessens

the resistance of skin—free of any pattern—
to one's upward gliding. Meantime, a patina
fogs half-empty tea glasses; prattling
dies; the flame in the lamp, too, suffers
shivers. And later, beneath the covers,
your brand-new pocket compass's needle quivers,

gleaming dully yet pointing north not any
less categorically than many
a prosecutor. Dogs barking, a dropping penny,
creaking joints of old chairs, or is that some invader?—
a sudden cackle in the hen coop, a whistling freight or
cattle train. Yet even these sounds later

cease. And naggingly, softly—even
softer perhaps than your ears are given
to discern—leaves, as countless as souls of all those who lived on
the earth before ourselves, blab something
in their burgeoning dialect; it's sounding
like dark tongues, though their tattered samplings—

smudges, cuneiforms, moon-spun vowels—
are unclear both to you and your wall for hours
as you toss and turn twixt the mounds and hollows
of the mattress, trying in vain to fathom
a sprouting hieroglyph, a phantom
comma, while outdoors the invisible rustling quantum

airs its China-like, powerful yellow anthem.

1981

Venetian Stanzas I

TO SUSAN SONTAG

I

The wet hitching post of the quay: a sulky hackney
fights off sleep in the twilight, twitching the iron bay
of her mane; napeless gondolas, fiddling numbly
the out-of-sync silence, sway.
As the Moor grows more trusting, words turn the paper darker,
and a hand, short of snapping a neck, though keen on the gothic lace
of a stone kerchief crushed in the palm of Iago,
presses it to its face.

II

The piazza's deserted, the quays abandoned.
The café walls are more crowded than the café inside:
a lute's being strummed by a frescoed, bejeweled maiden
to her similarly decked Said.
Oh, nineteenth century! oh, lure of the East! and oh, clifftop poses
of exiles! and, like leucocytes in the blood,
full moons in the works of bards burning with tuberculosis,
claiming it is with love.

III

At night, there's nothing to do here. No sweet Duses, no arias.
A solo heel's tapping out a basalt street.
Under lamps, your shadowy shuddered alias
like carbonari postpones its hit
and exhales a cloud. At night here we hold soliloquies
to an audience of echoes, whose breath won't warm up, alas,
this resonant marbled fish tank, nor fill it with
anything save steamed glass.

IV

Golden scales of tall windows bring to the rippled surface
wedges of grand piano, bric-a-brac, oils in frames.

That's what's hidden inside, blinds drawn, by perches
or, gills flapping, by breams.
The retina's sudden encounter with a white ceiling's goddess
shedding it all but her cobweb bra
makes one dizzy. A doorway's inflamed raw throat is
gaping to utter "Ahhhh."

V

How they flitted their tails here! How they flapped here, breamlike!
How spurning and spawning they streamed to score
the mirror! And how that cleaving, cream-white
bodice's plunge could stir—
like a sirocco that roils the waters. How, in the middle
of the promenade, squalls were turning their pantaloons and skirts
   into cabbage soup! Where are they all now—masks, stockings, middies,
harlequins, clowns, flirts?

VI

That's how chandeliers dim at the opera; that's how cupolas
shrink, like medusas, in volume, the tighter night hugs the place;
that's how streets coil and dwindle, like eels; that's how just-as-populous
squares mimic plaice.
That's how, treating his daughters, Nereus nears us,
pinching the combs from ladies' wind-ravaged curls,
leaving untouched the quays' yellow, nervous,
cheap electrical pearls.

VII

That's how orchestras fade. The city, while words are at it,
is akin to attempts to salvage notes from the silent beat,
and the palazzi, like music stands, stand scattered,
hoarded and poorly lit.
Only up where Perm's citizen sleeps his lasting sleep, a falsetto
star is vibrating through telegraph wires, reaches a minor key.
But the water applauds, and the quay is a hoarfrost settled
down on a do-re-mi.

VIII

And the loaded pupil of Claude, his limbs like half past eleven,
jettisoning his lines to the page's edge
in the struggle to keep all his gray mass level
despite the brandy's siege,
longs to undress, to cast off his woolen armor,
flop to the bed, press himself to the living, soft
bone's hot mirror from whose amalgam
no finger will scratch him off.

1982

Venetian Stanzas II

TO GENNADY SMAKOV

I

A sleep-crumpled cloud unfurls mealy mizzens.
Slapped by the baker, matte cheeks acquire
a glow. And in pawnbrokers' windows
jewelry catches fire.
Flat garbage barges sail. Like lengthy, supple
sticks run by hot-footed schoolboys along iron grates,
the morning rays strum colonnades, red-brick chimneys, sample
curled seaweed, invade arcades.

II

Dawn takes its time. Cold, naked, pallid marble
thighs of the new Susanna wade waves, being watched with glee
by new elders whose lenses squint, whirr, and gargle
at this bathing. Two-three
doves, launched from some pilaster, are turning
into gulls at the palaces opposite; that's the tax
here for flights over water—or else that's bed linen spurning
the ceiling for what it lacks.

III

Dampness creeps into the bedroom where a sleeping beauty,
dodging the world, draws her shoulder blades in.
That's how quail shrink sometimes at twig-snapping bootsteps,
how angels react to sin.
The window's sentient gauze gets fluttered by both exhaling
and inhaling. A pale, silky foam lashes stiff armchairs and
the mirror—an exit for objects, ailing
locally from their brown dead end.

IV

Light pries your eye—like a shell. Your helix,
in its turn like a shell, gets completely drowned

by the clamor of bells: that's the thirsty cupolas herding,
waterhole- and reflection-bound.
Parting shutters assault your nostrils with coffee, rags and
cinnamon, semen; with something transparent, pink.
And the golden St. George tips his lance at the writhing dragon's
maw, as though drawing ink.

V

Leaving all of the world, all its blue, in the rearguard,
the azure—squared to a weightless mass—
breasts the windowpane's gunport, falling headlong forward,
surrendering to the glass.
A curly-maned cloud pack rushes to catch and strangle
the radiant thief with his blazing hair—
a nor'easter is coming. The town is a crystal jumble
replete with smashed chinaware.

VI

Motorboats, rowboats, gondolas, dinghies, barges—
like odd scattered shoes, unmatched, God-size—
zealously trample pilasters, sharp spires, bridges'
arcs, the look in one's eyes.
Everything's doubled, save destiny, save the very
H_2O. Yet the idle turquoise on high
renders—like any "pro" vote—this world a merry
minority in one's eye.

VII

That's how some rise from the waters, their smooth skin stunning
the knobbly shore—while a flower may sway
in the hand—leaving the slipped dress scanning
the dry land from far away.
That's how they wash you in spray, for the immortals' ardent
perfume of kelp is what marks them from us and scares
pigeons off playing their crazy gambits
on the chessboards of squares.

307

VIII

I am writing these lines sitting outdoors, in winter,
on a white iron chair, in my shirtsleeves, a little drunk;
the lips move slowly enough to hinder
the vowels of the mother tongue,
and the coffee grows cold. And the blinding lagoon is lapping
at the shore as the dim human pupil's bright penalty
for its wish to arrest a landscape quite happy
here without me.

1982

Seaward

Darling, you think it's love, it's just a midnight journey.
Best are the dales and rivers removed by force,
as from the next compartment throttles "Oh, stop it, Bernie,"
yet the rhythm of those paroxysms is exactly yours.
Hook to the meat! Brush to the red-brick dentures,
alias cigars, smokeless like a driven nail!
Here the works are fewer than monkey wrenches,
and the phones are whining, dwarfed by to-no-avail.
Bark, then, with joy at Clancy, Fitzgibbon, Miller.
Dogs and block letters care how misfortune spells.
Still, you can tell yourself in the john by the spat-at mirror,
slamming the flush and emerging with clean lapels.
Only the liquid furniture cradles the dwindling figure.
Man shouldn't grow in size once he's been portrayed.
Look: what's been left behind is about as meager
as what remains ahead. Hence the horizon's blade.

1983

Galatea Encore

As though the mercury's under its tongue, it won't
talk. As though with the mercury in its sphincter,
immobile, by a leaf-coated pond
a statue stands white like a blight of winter.
After such snow, there is nothing indeed: the ins
and outs of centuries, pestered heather.
That's what coming full circle means—
when your countenance starts to resemble weather,
when Pygmalion's vanished. And you are free
to cloud your folds, to bare the navel.
Future at last! That is, bleached debris
of a glacier amid the five-lettered "never."
Hence the routine of a goddess, née
alabaster, that lets roving pupils gorge on
the heart of the color and temperature of the knee.
That's what it looks like inside a virgin.

1983

Variation in V

"Birds flying high above the retreating army!
Why do you suddenly turn and head toward our enemy,
contrary to the clouds? We are not yet defeated, are we?
True, we are scattered, but we still have some energy."

"Because your numbers diminish. You are less fit to listen
to our songs. You are no more an audience.
Vultures swoop in to replace us, and Valkyries. And the eastern
wind slams the fir horizons like jagged accordions."

"Cuneiform of the beaks! Explosions that sprout a palm tree!
Your tunes will be blown out of the sky, too, by the screaming westerly.
We commit them to memory, which is a larger country.
Nobody knows the future, but there is always yesterday."

"Ye-ah! but our life span's shorter. There is no tomb or pyre
for our kind, but chamomile, clover, chicory,
thyme. Your valedictory runs 'Fire! fire! fire!'
We are less comprehensible. That's why we need a victory."

1983

Letter to an Archaeologist

Citizen, enemy, mama's boy, sucker, utter
garbage, panhandler, swine, *refujew, verrucht*;
a scalp so often scalded with boiling water
that the puny brain feels completely cooked.
Yes, we have dwelt here: in this concrete, brick, wooden
rubble which you now arrive to sift.
All our wires were crossed, barbed, tangled, or interwoven.
Also: we didn't love our women, but they conceived.
Sharp is the sound of the pickax that hurts dead iron;
still, it's gentler than what we've been told or have said ourselves.
Stranger! move carefully through our carrion:
what seems carrion to you is freedom to our cells.
Leave our names alone. Don't reconstruct those vowels,
consonants, and so forth: they won't resemble larks
but a demented bloodhound whose maw devours
its own traces, feces, and barks, and barks.

1983

Kellomäki

I

Dumped in the dunes snatched from the witless Finns,
a small veneered burg whose walls let one's sneezing fits
be echoed at once by a "Bless you" cabled from Sweden, yet
sporting no ax to split enough wood to heat
up a dwelling. What's more, certain houses aimed
at warming winter itself, using their black walls, and
bred lush flowers at eventide on blue
glass veranda rhomboids or squares; and you,
as though plotting a trip to the polar zone,
were falling asleep there with your thick socks on.

II

Flat, lapping swells of the sea starting with B, in curves,
resembling bleak thoughts about oneself, ran course
onto the empty beach and froze
into wrinkles there. The twitching gauze
of the hawthorn twigs at times would compel one's stark-
naked eye to develop a rippling bark.
Or else a few gulls would issue from the snowy haze
like the curls of the soiled-by-nobody's-fingers page
of a pallid, quietly rustling day,
and no lamp would light up till they flapped away.

III

In small towns one recognizes folk
not by face but by their queuing backs that flock
to the store. And on Saturdays the populace strung out, bound
caravanlike for the sandlike ground
flour, or string bags of smelts rending one's balance sheets.
In a little town usually one eats
the same thing as others. And to distinguish one-
self from the rest, one could only try doodling on

a ruble with its sharp-*cum*-dull hardware
or seeing your things scattered everywhere.

IV

Notwithstanding all that, they were sturdy, those
abandoned matchboxes, stacked in white bundled rows
with two or three rattling, damp heads inside,
which, when feeding a sparrow, huddled to watch the sight,
family-strong, by the window whose trees as well
strove to merge into some baobab whose spill
of branches would overtake the sky's pink hem—
which indeed would happen round 6 p.m.,
when a book was slammed shut; and where once you sat
just two lips were remaining, like that vanished cat.

V

This outermost generosity, this—to denote true worth—
gift to exude, while freezing inside, the warmth
outside was binding tenants and habitats,
and winter considered the drying sheets its own linen. That's
what would stall conversations. A normal laugh
creaked like snow underfoot, leaving prints above
where it powdered the edges of sighs or shy
pronouns with hoarfrost, or turned some "I"
into a crystal, shot with hard turquoise,
that would melt like your tear to reduce the choice.

VI

Did it really happen, all that? And if yes, then why
now disturb the peace of these has-beens by
recalling details, testing shadowy pines by grip
—aping the afterlife (often accurately) when asleep?
Only those who believe (in angels, in roots) will rise
again. And what honestly could Kellomäki prize
as such, save its rail and its schedule of tin-plate links,
whistling from nonexistence, by which these things

would be gobbled up five minutes later, along with blurred
thoughts of love, plus those who have jumped aboard?

VII

Nothing. Winter expanses' slaked lime that would duly grab
from empty suburban platforms its daily grub
was leaving by conifer awnings, with their white load,
the present in its black overcoat, whose broad-
cloth, more sturdy than cheviot and *drap d'or*,
shielded one much better against the future or
the past than the station buffet's dim shack.
There is nothing more permanent than black.
That's what unleashes letters, or Carmen's breast;
that's why opponents of change hit their mattresses fully dressed.

VIII

Never again is that door to endure that key
with its curly goatee, nor is the switch to be
shoved up by one's heaving shoulder, to blind the stale loaf of bread.
This birdhouse has outlived its bird
and its cirrus or cumulous flocks. From time's point of view,
there is no "then," only "there." And "there," through
empty rooms, memory roams like a thief at dusk,
frisking the wardrobe, rummaging through the desk,
knocking over a novel by an unknown
—picking the pocket which is its own.

IX

In mid life's thick forest, in that dark wood,
man, like a runaway or, better still, a hood,
tends to glance backward: now branches creaking, now water's sound.
But the past is neither that panther nor some greyhound
that leaps onto one's stooped shoulders and, having thrown
the prey to the ground, strangles it in its brown
furry embrace—for its shanks ain't so sweet anymore, alas;
and the liquid, Narcissus-resistant glass

of the river gets icy (the fish, having pondered its
tin-can, flickering silver bits,

X

swims away beforehand). Probably you could state
that you simply were trying to dodge the great
metamorphosis, much as those smelts did. That
every point in space is indeed B-flat,
and a true express, skipping points A, B, and
C, slows down as a rule at the farthest end
of the alphabet, letting the steam out from
its comma-like nostrils. That water, too, runs home
from the basin much faster than it pours in
through a couple of pipes, making the bottom win.

XI

One may nod and admit that the Lobachevsky sleds'
lesson was lost on this terrain. Or let's
say that Finland's asleep, nurturing deep disdains
for ski poles, aluminum-made these days—
that is, better for hands, as they say, for turns;
still, they won't teach a youngster how bamboo burns,
won't evoke palm trees, tsetse flies, fox-trot,
monologues of a parrot—i.e., the sort
of parallels where, since the world there ends,
a naked scientist makes naked friends.

XII

In little towns' basements, storing all sorts of scraps,
like snapshots of strangers or playing cards, no maps
are ever kept, as though to block the thresh-
old for fate's bold attempts upon defenseless flesh.
The wallpaper suffices; a populated site
is relieved by its pattern from outer ties
so completely the smoke would in kind decide
to coil back in the chimney, whitewashing its pale façade,

316

so that the blending of two into one would yield
but a cloudy spot on the laundered field.

                         XIII
It's irrelevant now to remember your name, or mine.
For your blouse or my waistband will do just fine
to confirm in a trifoliate mirror's splits
that anonymity truly becomes us, fits,
as it does in the end all that's alive, that dwells
on this earth, till the aimless salvo of all one's cells.
Things have their limits—that is, their length
or immobility. And our claim on that piece of land-
scape extended no farther than, should I say,
the woodshed's sharp shadow, which, on a sunny day,

                         XIV
wedged a snowpile. Scanning an alien scene,
let's agree that that wedge can be simply seen
as our common elbow, thrust into the outside;
the elbow that neither of us can bite
or, moreover, kiss. In that sense, I bet,
we really blended—though our standard bed
barely squeaked. For it chose, in its turn, to swell
and become the wide world. In which, on the left as well
there is a door. Which, for all its domestic clout,
may only be good for one's getting out.

                                              [1982]

                         317

Ex Voto

TO JONATHAN AARON

Something like a field in Hungary, but without
its innocence. Something like a long river, short
of its bridges. Above, an unutterable umlaut
of eyes staining the view with hurt.
A posthumous vista where words belong
to their echo much more than to what one says.
An angel resembles in the clouds a blond
gone in an Auschwitz of sidewalk sales.
And a stone marks the ground where a sparrow sat.
In shop windows, the palms of the quay foretell
to a mosquito challenging the facade
of a villa—or, better yet, hotel—
his flat future. The farther one goes, the less
one is interested in the terrain.
An aimless iceberg resents bad press:
it suffers a meltdown, and forms a brain.

1983

Elegy

About a year has passed. I've returned to the place of battle,
to its birds that have learned their unfolding of wings from a subtle
lift of a surprised eyebrow, or perhaps from a razor blade
—wings, now the shade of early twilight, now of stale bad blood.

Now the place is abuzz with trading in your ankles' remnants, bronzes
of sunburnt breastplates, dying laughter, bruises,
rumors of fresh reserves, memories of high treason,
laundered banners with imprints of the many who since have risen.

All's overgrown with people. A ruin's a rather stubborn
architectural style. And the heart's distinction from a pitch-black cavern
isn't that great; not great enough to fear
that we may collide again like blind eggs somewhere.

At sunrise, when nobody stares at one's face, I often
set out on foot to a monument cast in molten
lengthy bad dreams. And it says on the plinth "Commander
in chief." But it reads "in grief," or "in brief," or "in going under."

1985

The Fly

TO IRENE AND ALFRED BRENDEL

I

While you were singing, fall arrived.
A splinter set the stove alight.
While you were singing, while you flew,
the cold wind blew.

And now you crawl the flat expanse of
my greasy stove top, never glancing
back to whence you arrived last April,
slow, barely able

to put one foot before the other.
So crushing you would be no bother.
Yet death's more boring to a scholar's eye
than torment, fly.

II

While you were singing, while you flew, the leafage
fell off. And water found it easier
to run down to the ground and stare,
disinterested, back into air.

But your eyesight has gone a bit asunder.
The thought of your brain dimming under
your latticed retina—downtrodden,
matte, tattered, rotten—

unsettles one. Yet you seem quite aware of
and like, in fact, this mildewed air of
well-lived-in quarters, green shades drawn.
Life does drag on.

320

III

Ah, buggie, you've lost all your perkiness;
you look like some old shot-down Junkers,
like one of those scratched flicks that score
the days of yore.

Weren't you the one who in those times so fatal
droned loud above my midnight cradle,
pursued by crossing searchlights into
my black-framed window?

Yet these days, as my yellowed finger-
nail mindlessly attempts to fiddle
with your soft belly, you won't buzz with fear
or hatred, dear.

IV

While you sang on, the gray outside grew grayer.
Damp door-frame joints swell past repair;
drafts numb the soles. This place of mine
is in decline.

You can't be tempted, though, by the sink's outrageous
slumped pyramids, unwashed for ages,
nor by sweet, shiftless honeymoons
in sugar dunes.

You're in no mood for that. You're in no mood to
take all that sterling-silver crap. Too good to
let yourself in for all that mess.
Me too, I guess.

V

Those feet and wings of yours! they're so old-fashioned,
so quaint. One look at them, and one imagines
a cross between Great-grandma's veil
et la Tour Eiffel

—the nineteenth century, in short. However,
by likening you to this and that, my clever
pen ekes out of your sorry end
a profit and

prods you to turn into some fleshless substance,
thought-like, unpalpable—into an absence
ahead of schedule. Your pursuer
admits: it's cruel.

VI

What is it that you muse of there?
Of your worn-out though uncomputed derring-
do orbits? Of six-legged letters,
your printed betters,

your splayed Cyrillic echoes, often
spotted by you in days gone by on open
book pages, and—misprints abhorring—
fast you'd be soaring

off. Now, though, since your eyesight lessens,
you spurn those black-on-white curls, tresses,
releasing them to real brunettes, their ruffles,
chignons, thick afros.

VII

While you were singing, while you flew, the birds went
away. Brooks, too, meander free, unburdened
of stickleback. Groves flaunt see-throughs—no takers.
The cabbage acres

crackle with cold, though tightly wrapped for winter,
and an alarm clock, like a time bomb, whimpers
tick-tock somewhere; its dial's dim and hollow:
the blast won't follow.

Apart from that, there are no other sounds.
Rooftop by rooftop, light rebounds
back into cloud. The stubble shrivels.
It gives one shivers.

VIII

And here's just two of us, contagion's carriers.
Microbes and sentences respect no barriers,
afflicting all that can inhale or hear.
Just us two here—

your tiny countenance pent up with fear
of dying, my sixteen, or near,
stones playing at some country squire—
plus autumn's mire.

Completely gone, it seems, your precious buzzer.
To time, though, this appears small bother—
to waste itself on us. Be grateful
that it's not hateful,

IX

that it's not squeamish. Or that it won't care
what sort of shoddy deal, what kind of fare
it's getting stuck with in the guise of
some large nose-divers

or petty ones. Your flying days are over.
To time, though, ages, sizes never
appear distinguishable. And it poses
alike for causes

as for effects, by definition. Even—
nay! notably—if those are given
in miniature: like to cold fingers,
small change's figures.

X

So while you were off there, busy flirting
around the half-lit lightbulb's flicker,
or, dodging me, amidst the rafters,
it—time—stayed rather

the same as now, when you acquire the stature
—due to your impotence and to your posture
toward myself—of pallid dust. Don't ponder,
decrepit, somber,

that time is my ally, my partner.
Look, we are victims of a common pattern.
I am your cellmate, not your warden.
There is no pardon.

XI

Outside, it's fall. A rotten time for bare
carnelian twigs. Like in the Mongol era,
the gray, short-legged species messes
with yellow masses,

or just makes passes. And yet no one cares
for either one of us. It seems what pairs us
is some paralysis—that is, your virus.
You'd be desirous

to learn how fast one catches this, though lucid,
indifference and sleep-inducing
desire to pay for stuff so global
with its own obol.

XII

Don't die! Resist! Crawl! though you don't feel youthful.
Existence is a bore when useful,
for oneself specially—when it spells a bonus.
A lot more honest

is to bound calendars' dates with a presence
devoid of any sense or reasons,
making a casual observer gather:
life's just another

word for nonbeing and for breaking rules. Were
you younger, my eyes'd scan the sphere
where all that is abundant. You are,
though, old and near.

XIII

So here's two of us. Outside, rain's flimsy
beak tests the windowpanes, and in a whimsy
crosshatches the landscape: its model.
You are immobile.

Still, there's us two. At least, when you expire,
I mentally will note the dire
event, thus mimicking the loops so boldly
spun by your body

in olden times, when they appeared so witless.
Death too, you know, once it detects a witness,
less firmly puts full-stops, I bet,
than tête-à-tête.

XIV

I hope you're not in pain, just lonely.
Pain takes up space; it therefore could only
creep toward you from outside, sneak near
you from the rear

and cup you fully—which implies, I reckon,
my palm that's rather busy making
these sentences. Don't die as long as
the worst, the lowest

still can be felt, still makes you twitch. Ah, sister!
to hell with the small brain's disaster!
A thing that quits obeying, dammit,
like that stayed moment,

XV

is beautiful in its own right. In other
words, it's entitled to applause (well, rather,
to the reversed burst), to extend its labor.
Fear's but a table

of those dependencies that dryly beckon
one's atrophy to last an extra second.
And I for one, my buzzy buddy,
I am quite ready

to sacrifice one of my own. However,
now such a gesture is an empty favor:
quite shot, my Shiva, is your motor;
your torpor's mortal.

XVI

In memory's deep faults, great vaults, among her
vast treasures—spent, dissolved, disowned or
forgotten (on the whole, no miser
could size them, either

in ancient days or, moreover, later)—
amidst existence's loose change and glitter,
your near-namesake, called the Muse, now makes a
soft bed, dear *Musca*

domestica, for your protracted
rest. Hence these syllables, hence all this prattling,
this alphabet's cortege: ink trailers,
upsurges, failures.

XVII

Outside, it's overcast. Designed for friction
against the furniture, my means of vision
gets firmly trained on the wallpaper.
You're in no shape to

take to the highest its well-traveled pattern,
to stun up there, where prayers pummel
clouds, feeble seraphs with the notion
of repetition

and rhythm—seen senseless in their upper
realms, being rooted in the utter
despair for which these cloudborne insects
possess no instincts.

XVIII

What will it end like? In some housefly heaven?
an apiary or, say, hidden
barn, where above spread cherry jam a heavy
and sleepy bevy

of your ex-sisters slowly twirls, producing
a swish the pavement makes when autumn's using
provincial towns? Yet push the doors:
a pale swarm bursts

right past us back into the world—out! out!—
enveloping it in their white shroud
whose winter-like shreds, snatches, forms
—whose swarm confirms

XIX

(thanks to this flicker, bustling, frantic)
that souls indeed possess a fabric
and matter, and a role in landscape,
where even blackest

things in the end, for all their throttle,
too, change their hue. That the sum total
of souls surpasses any tribe.
That color's time

or else the urge to chase it—quoting
the great Halicarnassian—coating
rooftops *en face*, hills in profile
with its white pile.

XX

Retreating from their pallid whirlwind,
shall I discern you in their winged
(a priori, not just Elysian)
a-swirling legion,

and you swoop down in your familiar fashion
onto my nape, as though you missed your ration
of mush that thinks itself so clever?
Fat chance. However,

having kicked off the very last—by eons—
you'll be the last among those swarming millions.
Yet if you're let in on a scene so private,
then, local climate

XXI

considered—so capricious, flippant—
next spring perhaps I'll spot you flitting
through skies into this region, rushing
back home. I, sloshing

through mud, might sigh, "A star is shooting,"
and vaguely wave to it, assuming
some zodiac mishap—whereas
there, quitting spheres,

that will be your winged soul, a-flurry
to join some dormant larva buried
here in manure, to show its nation
a transformation.

[1985]

Belfast Tune

Here's a girl from a dangerous town.
    She crops her dark hair short
so that less of her has to frown
    when someone gets hurt.

She folds her memories like a parachute.
    Dropped, she collects the peat
and cooks her veggies at home: they shoot
    here where they eat.

Ah, there's more sky in these parts than, say,
    ground. Hence her voice's pitch,
and her stare stains your retina like a gray
    bulb when you switch

hemispheres, and her knee-length quilt
    skirt's cut to catch the squall.
I dream of her either loved or killed
    because the town's too small.

1986

Afterword

I

The years are passing. On the palace's pumice façade appears
a crack. The eyeless seamstress's thread finally spears the midget
eye of the needle. And the Holy Family, the features drawn, severe,
comes half a millimeter more close to Egypt.

The bulk of the visible world consists of living types.
The streets are lit with a bright, extraneous
light. And at night an astronomer reckons, straining his
eyes, the total of sparkling tips.

II

I am no longer able to recall where or when events
occurred. This one, or any other.
Yesterday? A few years ago? On a garden bench?
In the air? In the water? Was I the matter?

And the event itself—an explosion or, say, a flood,
the lights of the Kuzbass derricks or some betrayal—
can't recall anything either, burying thus the trail
of myself or of those who either were saved or fled.

III

This, presumably, means that we are now in league
with life. That I, too, have become a segment
of that rustling matter whose fabric's bleach
infects one's skin with its neutral pigment.

In profile I, too, now can hardly be set
apart from some wrinkle, domino, patchwork, fig leaf,
fractions or wholes, causes or their effects—
from all that can be ignored, coveted, stood in fear of.

Touch me—and you'll touch dry burdock stems,
the dampness intrinsic to evenings in late Marchember,
the stone quarry of cities, the width of steppes,
those who are not alive but whom I remember.

Touch me—and you'll disturb a little that which does
exist regardless of me, obviously in the process
not trusting me, my overcoat, my face—
that in whose book we are always losses.

I am speaking to you, and it's not my fault
if you don't hear. The sum of days, by slugging
on, blisters eyeballs; the same goes for vocal cords.
My voice may be muffled but, I should hope, not nagging.

All the better to hear the crowing of a cockerel, the tick-tocks
in the heart of a record, its needle's patter;
all the better for you not to notice when my talk stops,
as Red Riding Hood didn't mutter to her gray partner.

1986

At Carel Willink's Exhibition

TO ADA STROEVE

I

Nearly a landscape. The full figure count,
appearing in it, gradually flees
the influx of bare statues. Like a coal
turned inside out, the marble's blondish, bleached,
and the locale seems northern. A plateau;
the cabbage tousled by a polar blast.
It's all so very horizontal that
no one will clasp you to an anxious breast.

II

Perhaps—this is the future. Backdrop of
repentance. An old colleague's vengeance. One
distinct yet muffled expletive, "Get out!"
A martial artist's unexpected veer.
And this—the future's town. Your lidless eyes
stay glued to rampant garden growth, alert,
like lizards scanning tropical hotel
façades. And skyscrapers even more.

III

It's possibly the past. Despair's last swoon,
its limit. Common summit. Verbs that wait
in line to view the preterit entombed.
A storm of crumpled velvet settled, passed.
And here's the past's dominion. Paths grown dense
while straying in reality. Lagoons
preserving lapsed reflections. Eggshells glimpsed
externally by yolk's unscrambled pools.

IV

Clearly—perspective. Calendar of sorts.
Or rather, from inflamed and swollen throats,

a tunnel sunk to psychological
beyonds, unfettered by our features. For
the voice, acquainted better with the thick
and thin of failure's landscape than is sight,
the greater evil's handier to pick—
it reckons on the echo's kind response.

V

Perhaps it's—still life. Far away it seems
that everything within the stretchers is
part dead and certainly immobile. Clouds.
A river, over which in circles flies
a bird. A plain, unable quite to stage
a transmutation, dons another shape,
becomes the prey of canvas, postcard, page,
the vindication Ptolemy awaits.

VI

Perhaps it's—tidal zebras or a half
a tiger hide. A hybrid barricade
and rumpled dress that licks the supple calves
of balusters immune to sunburn; and
the time approaches evening. Stifling heat;
a lone mosquito's stubborn solo, whose
pitch hoists the sweaty hammer from its soft and sweet
forge, dies amidst the bedroom's loud applause.

VII

Perhaps—the decoration for a set.
A staging of the classic "Cause's Rude
Indifference to Parting from Effect."
In greeting creature comforts singers prove
less gentle than myopic; "fa" resounds
a short-lived "far." And, trembling, brilliant, slight,
above the wire of notes like faucet drops,
the moonspun trill of the soprano glides.

VIII

Clearly—a portrait, but without a lick
of varnish. Dark, a subtly surfaced pall
whose earthy tints quite naturally arrest
the eye—of one who's up against the wall.
A ways away, a compromise with white,
Olympians amass in storm clouds, sense
the stare aimed at their backs, the inside-out-
ward gaze, the painter's—i.e., the suicide's.

IX

Which is the essence of self-portraiture.
A step aside from one's own flesh and frame,
the profile of a footstool kicked toward
you, a long view on life when dues are paid.
This, then, is "mastery": ability
to not take fright at the procedure of
nonbeing—as another form of one's
own absence, having drawn it straight from life.

[1985]

"Slave, Come to My Service!"

A VERSION FROM THE SUMERIAN

I

"Slave, come to my service!" "Yes, my master. Yes?"
"Quick, fetch my chariot, hitch up the horses: I'll drive to the palace!"
"Drive to the palace, my master. Drive to the palace.
The King will be pleased to see you, he will be benevolent to you."
"No, slave. I won't go to the palace!"
"Don't, my master. Don't go to the palace.
The King will send you on a faraway expedition,
down the unknown road, through hostile mountains;
day and night he will make you experience pain and hardship."

II

"Slave, come to my service!" "Yes, my master. Yes?"
"Fetch water, pour it over my hands: I am to eat my supper."
"Eat your supper, my master. Eat your supper.
Frequent meals gladden one's heart. Man's supper
is the supper of his god, and clean hands catch the eye of Shamash."
"No, slave. I won't eat my supper!"
"Don't eat your supper, master. Don't eat your supper.
Drink and thirst, food and hunger
never leave man alone, let alone each other."

III

"Slave, come to my service!" "Yes, my master. Yes?"
"Quick, fetch my chariot, hitch up the horses: I'll go for a ride in the
                                                                country."
"Do that, my master. Do that. A carefee wanderer
always fills his belly, a stray dog always
finds a bone, a migrating swallow is especially skilled in nesting,
a wild donkey finds the grass in the driest desert."
"No, slave. I won't go for a ride in the country."
"Don't go, my master. Don't bother.
The lot of a wanderer is always dicey.

A stray dog loses its teeth. The nest
of a migrating swallow gets buried in plaster.
Naked earth is a wild donkey's bedding."

IV

"Slave, come to my service!" "Yes, my master. Yes?"
"I feel like starting a family, like begetting children."
"Good thinking, my master. Start a family, start a family.
Who has children secures his name, repeated in posthumous prayers."
"No, slave. I won't start a family, I won't have children!"
"Don't start it, my master. Don't have them.
A family is like a broken door, its hinge is creaking.
Only a third of one's children are healthy; two-thirds always sickly."
"So, should I start a family?" "Don't start a family.
Who starts a family wastes his ancestral house."

V

"Slave, come to my service!" "Yes, my master. Yes?"
"I shall yield to my enemy;
in the court, I'll stay silent before my detractors."
"Right, my master, right. Yield to your enemy;
keep silence, my master, before your detractors."
"No, slave! I won't be silent, and I won't yield!"
"Don't yield, my master, and don't be silent.
Even if you don't open your mouth at all
your enemies will be merciless and cruel to you, as well as numerous."

VI

"Slave, come to my service!" "Yes, my master. Yes?"
"I feel like doing some evil, eh?"
"Do that, my master. By all means, do some evil.
For how otherwise can you stuff your belly?
How, without doing evil, can you dress yourself warmly?"
"No, slave. I shall do no evil!"
"Evildoers are either killed, or flayed alive and blinded,
or blinded and flayed alive and thrown into a dungeon."

337

VII

"Slave, come to my service!" "Yes, my master. Yes?"
"I'll fall in love with a woman." "Fall in love, my master. Fall in love!
Who falls in love with a woman forgets his griefs and sorrows."
"No, slave. I won't fall in love with a woman!"
"Don't love, my master. Don't love.
Woman is a snare, a trap, a dark pit.
Woman is a sharp steel blade slitting man's throat in darkness."

VIII

"Slave, come to my service!" "Yes, my master. Yes?"
"Quick, fetch water to wash my hands: I am to make an offering to my god."
"Make an offering, make an offering.
Who makes offerings to his god fills his heart with riches;
he feels generous, and his purse is open."
"No, slave. I won't make an offering!"
"Rightly so, my master. Rightly so!
Can you really train your god to follow you like a doggy?
All the time he demands obedience, rituals, sacrifices!"

IX

"Slave, come to my service!" "Yes, my master. Yes?"
"I'll invest with the interest, I will loan for the interest."
"Yes, invest with the interest, make loans for the interest.
Who does so preserves his own; his profit, though, is enormous."
"No, slave, I won't lend and I won't invest!"
"Don't invest, my master. Don't lend.
To lend is like loving a woman; to receive, like siring bad children:
people always curse those whose grain they eat.
They'll resent you or try to reduce your profit."

X

"Slave, come to my service!" "Yes, my master. Yes?"
"I shall do a good deed for my nation!"
"Very good, my master, very good. You do that!
Who does good deeds for his nation has his name in Marduk's gold signet."
"No, slave. I won't do a good deed for my nation."

"Don't do that, my master. Don't bother.
Get up and stroll across ancient ruins,
scan the skulls of simple folk and nobles:
which one of them was a villain, which one a benefactor?"

XI

"Slave, come to my service!" "Yes, my master. Yes?"
"If all this is so, then what is good?"
"To have your neck broken and my neck broken,
to be thrown into a river—that's what is good!
Who is so tall as to reach the heavens?
Who so broad as to embrace plains and mountains?"
"If that's so, I should kill you, slave: I'd rather you go before me."
"And does my master believe that he can survive for three days without me?"

1987

In Italy

TO ROBERTO AND FLEUR CALASSO

I, too, once lived in a city whose cornices used to court
clouds with statues, and where a local *penseur*, with his shrill "Pervért!
Pervért!" and the trembling goatee, was mopping
avenues; and an infinite quay was rendering life myopic.

These days evening sun still blinds the tenements' domino.
But those who have loved me more than themselves are no
longer alive. The bloodhounds, having lost their quarry,
with vengeance devour the leftovers—herein their very

strong resemblance to memory, to the fate of all things. The sun
sets. Faraway voices, exclamations like "Scum!
Leave me alone!"—in a foreign tongue, but it stands to reason.
And the world's best lagoon with its golden pigeon

coop gleams sharply enough to make the pupil run.
At the point where one can't be loved any longer, one,
resentful of swimming against the current and too perceptive
of its strength, hides himself in perspective.

1985

In Memoriam

The thought of you is receding like a chambermaid given notice.
No! like a railway platform, with block-lettered DVINSK or TATRAS.
But odd faces loom in, shivering and enormous,
also terrains, only yesterday entered into the atlas,
thus filling up the vacuum. None of us was well suited
for the status of statues. Probably our blood vessels
lacked in hardening lime. "Our family," you'd have put it,
"gave the world no generals, or—count our blessings—
great philosophers." Just as well, though: the Neva's surface
can't afford yet another reflection, brimming with mediogres.
What can remain of a mother with all her saucepans
in the perspective daily extended by her son's progress?
That's why the snow, this poor man's marble, devoid of muscle power,
melts, blaming empty brain cells for their not so clever
locks, for their failure to keep the fashion in which you, by putting powder
on your cheek, had meant to look forever.
What is left is to shield the skull, with raised arms, against idle glances,
and the throat, with the lips' nonstop "She has died, she has died," while
endless

cities rip the retinal sacs with lances
clanging loud like returning empties.

1985

341

SO

FORTH

.

TO MY WIFE

AND

TO MY DAUGHTER

Infinitive

TO ULF LINDE

Dear savages, though I've never mastered your tongue, free of pronouns and
                                      gerunds,
I've learned to bake mackerel wrapped in palm leaves and favor raw turtle
                                       legs,
with their flavor of slowness. Gastronomically, I must admit, these years
since I was washed ashore here have been a non-stop journey,
and in the end I don't know where I am. After all, one keeps carving
                                    notches only
so long as nobody apes one. While you started aping me even before I
                                    spotted
you. Look what you've done to the trees! Though it's flattering to be
                                    regarded
even by you as a god, I, in turn, aped you somewhat, especially with your
                                    maidens
—in part to obscure the past, with its ill-fated ship, but also to cloud the
                                    future,
devoid of a pregnant sail. Islands are cruel enemies
of tenses, except for the present one. And shipwrecks are but flights from
                                    grammar
into pure causality. Look what life without mirrors does
to pronouns, not to mention one's features! Perhaps your ancestors also
ended up on this wonderful beach in a fashion similar
to mine. Hence, your attitude toward me. In your eyes I am
at the very least an island within an island. And anyhow, watching my every
                                    step,
you know that I am not longing for the past participle or the past
                                    continuous
—well, not any more than for that future perfect of yours deep in some
                                    humid cave,
decked out in dry kelp and feathers. I write this with my index finger
on the wet, glassy sand at sunset, being inspired perhaps
by the view of the palm-tree tops splayed against the platinum sky like some

Chinese characters. Though I've never studied the language. Besides, the

breeze

tousles them all too fast for one to make out the message.

1994

A Song

I wish you were here, dear,
I wish you were here.
I wish you sat on the sofa
and I sat near.
The handkerchief could be yours,
the tear could be mine, chin-bound.
Though it could be, of course,
the other way around.

I wish you were here, dear,
I wish you were here.
I wish we were in my car,
and you'd shift the gear.
We'd find ourselves elsewhere,
on an unknown shore.
Or else we'd repair
to where we've been before.

I wish you were here, dear,
I wish you were here.
I wish I knew no astronomy
when stars appear,
when the moon skims the water
that sighs and shifts in its slumber.
I wish it were still a quarter
to dial your number.

I wish you were here, dear,
in this hemisphere,
as I sit on the porch
sipping a beer.
It's evening, the sun is setting;

boys shout and gulls are crying.
What's the point of forgetting
if it's followed by dying?

1989

A Footnote to Weather Forecasts

A garden alley with statues of hardened mud,
akin to gnarled, stunted tree trunks.
Some of them I knew personally; the rest
I see for the first time ever. Presumably they are gods
of local woods and streams, guardians of silence.
As for the feminine shapes—nymphs and so forth—they look
thought-like, i.e., unfinished;
each one strives to keep, even here,
in the future that came, her vagrant's status.

A chipmunk won't pop up and cross the path.
No birdsong is audible, nor, moreover, a motor.
The future is a panacea
against anything prone to repetition.
And in the sky there are scattered, like a bachelor's
clothes, clouds, turned inside out
or pressed. It smells of conifer—
this prickly substance of not so familiar places.
Sculptures loom in the twilight, darkening
thanks to their proximity to each other, thanks
to the indifference of the surrounding landscape.

Should any one of them speak, you would
sigh rather than gasp or shudder
upon hearing well-known voices, hearing
something like "The child wasn't yours" or "True,
I testified against him, but out of fear,
not jealousy"—petty, twenty-
odd-year-old secrets of purblind hearts
obsessed with a silly quest for power
over their likes. The best ones among them were
at once the executioners and the victims.

It's good that someone else's memories
interfere with your own. It's good that some
of these figures, to you, appear
alien. Their presence hints
at different events, at a different sort of fate—
perhaps not a better one, yet clearly
the one that you missed. This unshackles
memory more than imagination—
not forever, of course, but for a while. To learn
that you've been deceived, that you've been completely
forgotten, or, the other way around,
that you are still being hated
is extremely unpleasant, but to regard yourself
as the hub of even a negligible universe,
unbearable and indecent.

                        A rare,
perhaps the only, visitor to these parts,
I have, I suppose, a right
to describe the observed. Here it is, our little
Valhalla, our long overgrown estate
in time, with a handful of mortgaged souls,
with its meadows where a sharpened sickle
won't roam, in all likelihood, with abandon,
and where snowflakes float in the air as a good example
of poise in a vacuum.

1986

Star of the Nativity

In the cold season, in a locality accustomed to heat more than
to cold, to horizontality more than to a mountain,
a child was born in a cave in order to save the world;
it blew as only in deserts in winter it blows, athwart.

To Him, all things seemed enormous: His mother's breast, the steam
out of the ox's nostrils, Caspar, Balthazar, Melchior—the team
of Magi, their presents heaped by the door, ajar.
He was but a dot, and a dot was the star.

Keenly, without blinking, through pallid, stray
clouds, upon the child in the manger, from far away—
from the depth of the universe, from its opposite end—the star
was looking into the cave. And that was the Father's stare.

December 1987

New Life

Imagine that war is over, that peace has resumed its reign.
That you can still make a mirror. That it's a cuckoo
or a magpie, and not a Junkers, that chirps in the twigs again.
That a window frames not a town's rubble but its rococo,
palms, magnolias, pine trees, tenacious ivy, grass,
laurel. That the cast-iron lace the moon used to shepherd
clouds in, in the end endured the onslaught of mimosa, plus
bursts of agave. That life must start from the very threshold.

People exit their rooms, where chairs like the letter *b* or else
h shield them from vertigo on occasion.
They are of use to nobody save themselves,
pavement flagstones, the rules of multiplication.
That's the impact of statues. Of their empty niches, more
accurately. Well, failing sanctity, one still can use its byword.
Imagine that this is all true. Imagine you speak of your-
self while speaking of them, of anything extra, sideward.

Life starts anew indeed like this—with a painted view
of a volcanic eruption, of a dinghy high waves beleaguer.
With the attendant feeling it's only you
who survey the disaster. With the feeling that you are eager
to shift your gaze any moment, catch sight of a couch, a blast
of peonies in a Chinese vase, sallow against the plaster.
Their garish colors, their wilting mouths must
be, in their turn, harbingers of a disaster.

Each thing is vulnerable. The very thought about
a thing gets quickly forgotten. Things are, in truth, the leeches
of thought. Hence their shapes—each one is a brain's cutout—
their attachment to place, their Penelope features;
that is their taste for the future. At sunrise, a rooster's heard.

Stepping out of the tub, wrapped in a bedsheet's linen
in a hotel in the new life, you face the herd
of four-legged furniture, mahogany and cast iron.

Imagine that epics shrink into idylls. That words are but
the converse of flame's long tongues, of that raging sermon
which used to devour your betters greedily like dry wood.
That flame found it difficult to determine
your worth, not to mention warmth. That's why you've survived intact.
That's why you can stomach apathy, that's why you feel fit to mingle
with the pomonae, vertumni, ceres this place is packed
with. That's why on your lips is this shepherd's jingle.

For how long can one justify oneself? However you hide the ace,
the table gets hit with jacks of some odd suit and tailor.
Imagine that the more sincere the voice, the less in it is the trace
of love for no matter what, of anger, of tears, of terror.
Imagine your wireless catching at times your old anthem's hum.
Imagine that here, too, each letter is trailed by a weaning
retinue of its likes, forming blindly now "betsy," now "ibrahim,"
dragging the pen past the limits of alphabet and meaning.

Twilight in the new life. Cicadas that don't relent.
A classicist perspective that lacks a tank or,
barring that, dank fog patches to obfuscate its end;
a bare parquet floor that never sustained a tango.
In the new life, no one begs the moment, "Stay!"
Brought to a standstill, it quickly succumbs to dotage.
And your features, on top of that, are glazed enough anyway
for scratching their matte side with "Hi" and attaching the postage.

The white stuccoed walls of a room are turning more white because
of a glance shot in their direction and boding censure,
steeped not so much in far meadows' morose repose
as in the spectrum's lack of their self-negating tincture.
A thing can be pardoned plenty. Especially where it cones,

where it reaches its end. Ultimately, one's unbound
curiosity about these empty zones,
about these objectless vistas, is what art seems to be all about.

In the new life, a cloud is better than the bright sun. The rain,
akin to self-knowledge, appears perpetual.
On the other hand, an unexpected train
you don't wait for alone on a platform arrives on schedule.
A sail is passing its judgment on the horizon's lie.
The eye tracks the sinking soap, though it's the foam that's famous.
And should anyone ask you "Who are you?" you reply, "Who—I?
I am Nobody," as Ulysses once muttered to Polyphemus.

1988

354

Angel

A white, pure-cotton angel
till this day hovering in my closet
on a metallic hanger. It's thanks to him
that nothing untoward in all these years
has ever happened to me, or to these very quarters.
A modest radius, one might say, though clearly
delineated. Having been made unlike
ourselves in the image and in the likeness
but incorporeal, angels possess just color
and velocity. The latter explains their being
everywhere. That's why you are still
with me. Wings and shoulder straps can indeed
manage without a proper torso,
shapely limbs, or love per se, and cherish
anonymity, letting the body burgeon
with happiness whose diameter lies somewhere in evergreen
California.

1992

An Admonition

I

Trekking in Asia, spending nights in odd dwellings, in
granaries, cabins, shacks—timber abodes whose thin
squinted windowpanes harness the world—sleep dressed,
wrapped in your sheepskin, and do your best
always to tuck your head into the corner, as
in the corner it's harder—and in darkness at that—to swing an ax
over your heavy, booze-laden gourd
and to chop it off nicely. Square the circle, in short.

II

Fear broad cheekbones (including the moon's), pockmarked
skin, and prefer blue eyes to brown eyes. Search hard
for the blue ones, especially when the road takes you into the wood,
into its heart. On the whole, as for eyes, one should
watch for their cut. For at your last instant it's
better to stare at that which, though cold, permits
seeing through: ice may crack, yet wallowing in an ice
hole is far better than in honey-like, viscous lies.

III

Always pick a house with baby clothes hanging out
in the yard. Deal only with the over-fifty crowd:
a hick at that age knows too much about fate to gain
anything by attempting to bust your brain;
same thing, a squaw. Hide the money in your fur coat's
collar or, if you are traveling light, in your brown culottes
under the knee—but not in your boots, since they'll find the dough
easily there. In Asia, boots are the first to go.

IV

In the mountains, move slowly. If you must creep, then creep.
Magnificent in the distance, meaningless closer up,

mountains are but a surface standing on end. The snail-
like and, it seems, horizontal meandering trail
is, in fact, vertical. Lying flat in the mountains, you
stand. Standing up, you lie flat. Which suggests your true
freedom's in falling down. That's the way, it appears,
to conquer, once in the mountains, vertigo, raptures, fears.

V

If somebody yells "Hey, stranger!" don't answer. Play deaf and dumb.
Even though you may know it, don't speak the tongue.
Try not to stand out—either in profile or
full face; simply don't wash your face at times. What's more,
when they rip a cur's throat with a saw, don't cringe.
Smoking, douse your butts with spittle. And besides, arrange
to wear gray—the hue of the earth—especially underclothes,
to reduce the temptation to blend your flesh with earth.

VI

When you halt in the desert, make an arrow from pebbles, so,
if suddenly woken up, you'll fathom which way to go
in the darkness. At night, demons in deserts try
travelers' hearts. He who heeds their cry
gets easily disoriented: one step sideways and—well, *c'est tout*.
Ghosts, specters, demons are at home in the desert. You
too will discover that's true when, sand creaking under your sole,
all that remains of you is your soul.

VII

Nobody ever knows anything for a fact.
Gazing ahead at your stooping guide's sturdy back,
think that you gaze at the future and keep your distance (if
that is possible) from him. Since, in principle, life
is itself but a distance between here and there, and
quickening the pace pays only when you discern the sound
behind of those running after you down the path
with lowered heads—be they murderers, thieves, the past.

In the sour whiff of rags, in the burnt dung's fume,
prize the indifference of things to being regarded from
afar, and in turn lose your own silhouette, turning, thus,
unattainable to binoculars, gendarmes, mass.
Coughing in a cloud of dust, wading through mud, muck, map—
what difference does it make how you would look close up?
It's even better if some character with a blade
figures out you are a stranger a bit too late.

IX

Rivers in Asia are longer than elsewhere, more rich
in alluvium—that is, murkier. As you reach
for a mouthful, your cupped fingers ladle silt,
and one who has drunk this water would prefer it spilt.
Never trust its reflection. Crossing it, cross it on
a raft built with no other hands but the pair you own.
Know that the gleam of a campfire, your nightly bliss,
will, by sliding downstream, betray you to enemies.

X

In your letters from these parts don't divulge whom and
what you've seen on your way. If anything should be penned,
use your varying feelings, musings, regrets, et al.:
a letter can be intercepted. And after all,
the movement of a pen across paper is,
in itself, the worsening of the break between you and those
with whom you won't any longer sit or lie down—with whom,
unlike the letter, you won't share—who cares why—a home.

XI

When you stand on an empty stony plateau alone
under the fathomless dome of Asia in whose blueness an airplane
or an angel sometimes whips up its starch or star—
when you shudder at how infinitesimally small you are,
remember: space that appears to need nothing does

crave, as a matter of fact, an outside gaze,
a criterion of emptiness—of its depth and scope.
And it's only you who can do the job.

1986

In Memory of My Father: Australia

You arose—I dreamt so last night—and left for
Australia. The voice, with a triple echo,
ebbed and flowed, complaining about climate,
grime, that the deal with the flat is stymied,
pity it's not downtown, though near the ocean,
no elevator but the bathtub's indeed an option,
ankles keep swelling. "Looks like I've lost my slippers"
came through rapt yet clear via satellite.
And at once the receiver burst into howling *"Adelaide! Adelaide!"*—
into rattling and crackling, as if a shutter,
ripped off its hinges, were pounding the wall with inhuman power.

Still, better this than the silky powder
canned by the crematorium, than the voucher—
better these snatches of voice, this patchwork
monologue of a recluse trying to play a genie

for the first time since you formed a cloud above a chimney.

1989

So Forth

Summer will end. September will come. Once more it's okay to shoot
duck, woodcock, partridge, quail. "You've grown long in the tooth,"
a belle may sigh, and you'll cock up your double-barrel,
but to inhale more oxygen rather than to imperil
grouse. And the keen lung will twitch at a sudden whiff
of apricots. On the whole, the world changes so fast, as if
indeed at a certain point it began to mainline
some muck obtained from a swarthy alien.

The point, of course, is not autumn. And not one's own features, which
alter like those of an animal approaching the one who'll catch
it. But this feeling of a puny paintbrush left idle
by the painting that lacks a frame, a beginning, an end, a middle.
Not to mention a gallery, not to mention a nail.
And a train in the distance runs whistling along the rail,
though you will spot no smoke inspecting its inventory.
But in a landscape's view, motion is mandatory.

That goes for autumn; that goes for time per se,
like when you quit smoking, or else when the trees you see
ape fanning-out tracks at last freed of their wheels' malfunction
and the edge of the forest echoes a rustling junction.
And it's not a lump but a hedgehog that fills your throat,
for you can't enjoy any longer the silhouette
of a steamship at sea, and an airplane's callous
profile looks odd on high, having lost its halos.

That's what speed's all about. The belle was right. What would
an ancient Roman, had he risen now, recognize? A wood-
pile, the blue yonder, a cloud's texture,
flat water, something in architecture,
but no one by face. That's how some folk still do
travel abroad at times, but, not entitled to

afterlife, scurry back home hiding their eyes in terror.
And not yet settled after the farewell tremor

a hanky still flits in the air. The others who had the luck
of loving something much more than life, knowing all along
that decrepitude is, after all, that after-
life, loom marble-white in the sun getting no tan and often,
partial in their way to history's pleasures, gaze
fixedly at some point in the distance. And the greater the latter's haze,
the more there are points like this defying one's aim and cartridge,
the more speckled turn the eggs of quail, woodcock, grouse, partridge.

[1987]

Constancy

Constancy is an evolution of one's living quarters into
a thought: a continuation of a parallelogram or a rectangle
by means—as Clausewitz would have put it—
of the voice and, ultimately, the gray matter.
Ah, shrunken to the size of a brain-cell parlor
with a lampshade, an armoire in the "Slavic
Glory" fashion, four studded chairs, a sofa,
a bed, a bedside table with
little medicine bottles left there standing like
a kremlin or, better yet, manhattan.
To die, to abandon a family, to go away for good,
to change hemispheres, to let new ovals
be painted into the square—the more
volubly will the gray cell insist
on its actual measurements, demanding
daily sacrifice from the new locale,
from the furniture, from the silhouette in a yellow
dress; in the end—from your very self.
A spider revels in shading especially the fifth corner.
Evolution is not a species'
adjustment to a new environment but one's memories'
triumph over reality, the ichthyosaurus pining
for the amoeba, the slack vertebrae of a train
thundering in the darkness, past
the mussel shells, tightly shut for the night, with their
spineless, soggy, pearl-shrouding contents.

1989

Brise Marine

Dear, I ventured out of the house late this evening, merely
for a breath of fresh air from the ocean not far away.
The sun was smoldering low like a Chinese fan in a gallery
and a cloud reared up its huge lid like a Steinway.

A quarter century back you craved curry and dates from Senegal,
tried your voice for the stage, scratched profiles in a sketch pad,
dallied with me—but later alloyed with a chemical
engineer and, judging by letters, grew fairly stupid.

These days you've been seen in churches in the capital and in provinces,
at rites for our friends or acquaintances, now continuous;
yet I am glad, after all, that the world still promises
distances more inconceivable than the one between us.

Understand me correctly, though: your body, your warble, your middle
                                                                name
now stir practically nothing. Not that they've ceased to burgeon;
but to forget one life, a man needs at minimum
one more life. And I've done that portion.

You got lucky as well: where else, save in a snapshot perhaps,
will you forever remain free of wrinkles, lithe, caustic, vivid?
Having bumped into memory, time learns its impotence.
Ebb tide; I smoke in the darkness and inhale rank seaweed.

1989

Centaurs I

They briskly bounce out of the future and having cried "Futile!"
immediately thud back up to its cloud-clad summit.
A branch bends, burdened with birds larger than space—new style,
stuffed not with dawn or feathers but only with "Damn it, damn it."
A horizontal *mare* stained with sunset. A winter evening,
tired of its eye-batting blueness, fondles
like a witless atom on the eve of being
split the remaining hours' golden
chain. A burnt matchstick's residue, a myopic
naked statue, a pergola looming wanly
are excessively real, excessively stereoscopic
since there's nothing they can turn themselves into. Only
horizontal properties, in their fusion, can spawn a monster
with a substantial fallout or follow-
up. For an explosion-sponsored
profile, there is no tomorrow.

Centaurs II

Part ravishing beauty, part sofa, in the vernacular—Sophie,
after hours filling the street whose windows are partly faces
with the clatter of her six heels (after all, a catastrophe
is something that always ogles the guises a lull refuses),
is rushing to a rendezvous. Love consists of tulle, horsehair,
blood, bolsters, cushions, springs, happiness, births galore.
Two-thirds a caring male, one-third a race car—Cary
for short—greets her joyfully with his idling roar
and whisks her off to a theater. Every thigh, from the age of swaddles,
shows the craving of muscles for furniture, for the antics
of mahogany armoires whose panels, in turn, show a subtle
yen for two-thirds, full-face, profiles anxious
for a slap. Whisks her off to a theater in whose murkiness—perspiring,
                                                        panting,
running each other over, kneading veneer with tire—
they enjoy off and on a drama about the life of puppets

which is what we were, frankly, in our era.

Centaurs III

A marble-white close-up of the past-*cum*-future hybrid,
cast as a cross between muscular torso and horse's ibid,
or else as a simple grammatical "was" and "will" in
the present continuous. Cast this thing as a million
boring details! in the fairy tale's hut on chicken
feet! Plus, ourselves in its chairs—to cheapen
the sight. Or merged with those whom we loved, or loved to
merge with on horizontal sheets. Or in the nubile auto-
mobile, i.e., as a perspective's captives. Or willy-nilly
in the brain's gray recesses. Cast it out loud, shrilly,
as a thought about death—frequent, tactile, aching.
Cast it as life right now mixed with afterlife where, like eggs in
a string bag, we all are alike and equally petrifying
to the mother hen who, sparing its yolk the frying
pan, flutters up by the means of our era
the six-winged mixture of faith and the stratosphere.

Centaurs IV

The instep-shaped landscape, the shade of a jackboot, with nothing moving.
The century's serial number matches a rooster's croak.
At dusk, dappled mutanks repair from far fields, a-mooing—
a bulky unicorn flock.
Only the seasons appear to know how to take a hint.
Chasing her slippery soap, a hausfrau sheds a tear
over her man's failure to hold the hilt
of his sword turning into a plowshare.
Still, a framed watercolor depicts a storm;
in a novel, the second letter is the previous one's dead ringer.
Near the cinema youngsters linger
like tightly corked bottles with frozen sperm.
The evening sky offers little to hope for, still less to cope
with. And only a veteran can still recall the foreign
name of a trench that a star has fallen
into, escaping the telescope.

1988

Epitaph for a Centaur

To say that he was unhappy is either to say too much
or too little: depending on who's the audience.
Still, the smell he'd give off was a bit too odious,
and his canter was also quite hard to match.
He said, They meant just a monument, but something went astray:
the womb? the assembly line? the economy?
Or else, the war never happened, they befriended the enemy,
and he was left as it is, presumably to portray
Intransigence, Incompatibility—that sort of thing which proves
not so much one's uniqueness or virtue, but probability.
For years, resembling a cloud, he wandered in olive groves,
marveling at one-leggedness, the mother of immobility.
Learned to lie to himself, and turned it into an art
for want of a better company, also to check his sanity.
And he died fairly young—because his animal part
turned out to be less durable than his humanity.

1988

Axiom

The world was wrought of a mixture of dirt, water, fire,
and air, with the scream "Don't touch me!" embedded in that mire,
rupturing first a plant, eventually a face,
so that you'd never presume the world was a naked place.
Then there rose vast rooms, furniture, ardent loves,
the past's appetite for the future, the tenor's for busted lungs.
Letters broke into motion, making the eyeball roll,
and emptiness grew fearful for its very soul.
Birds were the first to detect this, although a star,
too, signals the fate of a stone that's slung astray.
Any sound, be it music, a whisper, the howling wind,
is the fruit of anything's friction against its kind.
In shrieking beaks, in cumulus, in blazing pulsars none see,
the ear makes out a nagging "No vacancy,"
either an echo of the carpenter's boy or else
addressless stone-cold suns sputtering SOS.
And heeding the shrill "Amscray! Beat it! Vanish! Grab
your junk and get lost!" space itself, alias the backdrop
of life, rendered blind by a surfeit of plots,
heads toward pure time, where no one applauds.
Don't be afraid, though: I've been there. There in its bowels looms
a huge, wrinkle-spinning wheel, its roots
plugged into a raw material whose supply
we, the deposits, eagerly multiply.

1990

North of Delphi

Gedenke meiner,
flüstert der Staub.
—PETER HUCHEL

The plight of a pawn tells the king what it's all about.
A speck of land in the distance—that you are traveling on a boat.
Slight, sated notes in the voice of your sweetheart in the receiver—
that you've got a successor: a surgeon? an engineer?
a student? A junction's veneer—that you're getting nearer,
that the boiled egg won't sport its battered shell forever.

In each one of us sits a peasant, a real ace
at weather forecasting. For instance, leaves falling face-
down in autumn mean meager crops. The oracle is no better
when the law in a raincoat crosses your threshold: your
days are numbered—by a jury, or
they are pussycat lacrimae, scarce and bitter.

Say what you will but nature won't rob us of omens, hints.
A cherub might not distinguish his front from his
rear. Not so man. To man, every perspective empties
itself of his silhouette, echo, smell.
Whenever something rings a bell,
it sure rings for him, as they clink, drink, and round up the empties.

So your option is bravery. The palm's tangled lines,
thirteens and, moreover, sixty-nines,
plus the stucco effect in Balthazar's bedchamber
prove only that fate, alas,
has fewer options than victims to find itself at a loss:
you'll end up exactly the way a Gypsy foresaw your neighbor,
your sister, your brother, your colleague's wife
—but not you. The pen creaks in a silence that clearly vies
for its posthumous version, for a dance-hall reversal—
it's that deafening! A kind of anti-war.

371

All that means, however, that you've grown old, that a tired worm
in a beak quits coiling, becomes a morsel.

The dust settles down on objects in summer like winter snow.
This owes to surface, to flatness; essentially to its own
upward pull: toward snow, dust, et cetera; toward blissful
nonexistence. And, as a verse line does,
"Don't forget me," whispers the settled dust
to the hand with the cloth, and the wet cloth absorbs this whisper.

The strength of contempt tells you new times won't wait.
The glare of a star—that pity is rendered void,
as the concession of energy to low temperature
or as a sign that you'd better put
out your lamp, that the pen creaking across the pad
in the limitless silence is bravery in miniature.

Harken then to these words as to the worm's true song
and not to the music of spheres for centuries and so on.
Worse than a bird's tune, it might get a better billing
than the aria of a fish. What's coming no padlock can
check. Yet evil can't happen to an evil man.
It's the fear of tautology that guarantees well-being.

1989

Exeter Revisited

Playing chess on the oil tablecloth at Sparky's
Café, with half & half for whites,
against your specter at noon, two flights
down from that mattress, and seven years later. Scarcely
a gambit, by any standard. The fan's dust-plagued
shamrock still hums in your window—seven
years later and pints of semen
under the bridge—apparently not unplugged.
What does it take to pledge allegiance
to another biography, ocean, creed?
The expiration date on the Indian Deed?
A pair of turtledoves, two young pigeons?
The Atlantic, whose long-brewed invasion looks,
on the beaches of Salisbury, self-defeating?
Or the town hall cupola, still breast-feeding
its pale, cloud-swaddled Lux?

1988

Vertumnus

IN MEMORY OF GIOVANNI BUTTAFAVA

I

I met you the first time ever in latitudes you'd call foreign.
Your foot never trod that loam; your fame, though, had reached those
quarters
where they fashion the fruit habitually out of plaster.
Knee-deep in snow, you loomed there: white, moreover naked,
in the company of one-legged, equally naked trees,
in your part-time capacity as an expert
on low temperatures. "Roman Deity"
proclaimed a badly faded notice,
and to me you were a deity, since you knew
far more of the past than I (the future
for me in those days was of little import).
On the other hand, apple-cheeked and curly-
haired, you might well have been my agemate; and though you knew not a
word
of the local dialect, somehow we got to talking.
Initially, I did the chatting. Something about Pomona,
our stubbornly aimless rivers, obstinate foul weather,
the absence of greens and money, leapfrogging seasons
—about things, I thought, that should be up your alley
if not in their essence, then in their common pitch
of lament. Little by little (lament is the universal
ur-tongue; most likely, in the beginning
was either "ouch" or "ai") you began to respond: to squint,
to blink, to furrow your brow; then the lower part of your oval
sort of melted, and your lips were slowly set in motion.
"Vertumnus," you squeezed out finally. "I am called Vertumnus."

II

It was a wintry, pallid—more exactly, a hueless day.
The limbs, the shoulders, the torso—as we proceeded
from subject to subject—were gradually turning pinkish,

374

and were draped with fabric: a shirt, a jacket, trousers,
a moss-colored coat, shoes from Balenciaga.
The weather got warmer also, and you, at times falling still,
would listen intently into the park's soft rustle,
picking up and examining occasionally a gluey leaf
in your search for just the right word, the right expression.
At any rate, if I am not mistaken,
by the time I, now excessively animated,
was holding forth on history, wars, lousy crops,
brutal government, the lilac had already drooped past its bloom,
and you sat on the bench, from a distance looking
like an average citizen, impoverished by the system;
your temperature was ninety-eight point six.
"Let's go," you muttered, touching me on the elbow.
"Let's go. I'll show you the parts where I was born and grew up."

III

The road there led quite naturally through the clouds,
resembling gypsum in color and, later, marble
so much that it crossed my mind that you had in mind precisely
this: washed-out outlines, chaos, the world in ruins—
though this would have signaled the future, while you already
existed. Shortly afterwards, in an empty
café in a drowsy small town fired white-hot by noon,
where someone who dreamt up an arch just couldn't stop more from
coming,
I realized I was wrong when I heard you chatting
with some local crone. The language turned out to be
a mix of the evergreen rustle and the ever-blue bubbling of
waves, and so rapid that in the course of the conversation,
you several times, in front of my eyes, turned into
her. "Who is she?" I asked when we ventured out.
"She?" You just shrugged your shoulders. "No one. To you, a goddess."

IV

It got a bit cooler. We started to chance more often
upon passersby. Some of them would be nodding,

others looked sideways, becoming thus mere profiles.
All of them, however, were noticeably dark-haired.
Each one behind his back had an impeccable perspective,
not excluding the children. As for old men, in their
cases, it coiled like a shell of some snail or other.
Indeed, the past in these parts was much more abundant
than the present! The centuries outnumbered
cars, parked or passing. People and sculpted figures,
as they drew near and as they receded,
neither grew large nor petered out, thus proving
they were, as it were, invariable magnitudes.
It was strange to observe you in your natural circumstances!
Stranger still was the fact that nearly everybody
understood me. This had to do, perhaps,
with the ideal acoustics, caused by the architecture,
or with your intervention—with the basic penchant of an
absolute ear for garbled sounds.
"Don't be surprised. My field is metamorphosis.
Whomsoever I glance at acquires at once my features.
To you, this may come in handy. You are, after all, abroad."

                                    V

A quarter century later I hear your voice, Vertumnus,
uttering these words, and I sense with my skin the steady
stare of your pearl-gray eyes,
odd in a southerner. In the backdrop there are palm trees,
like Chinese characters tousled by the *tramontana*,
and cypresses like Egyptian obelisks.
Noon; a decrepit balustrade somewhere
in Lombardy; and its sun-splattered mortal visage
of a deity! A provisional one for a
deity, but for me the only
one. With widow's peak, with mustachio
(à la Maupassant more than Nietzsche),
with a much thickened—for the sake of disguise, no doubt—
torso. On the other hand, it is not
for me to flash my diameter, to mimic Saturn,

to flirt with a telescope. Everything leaves a spoor,
time especially. Our rings are
those of fat trees with their prospective stump,
not the ones of a rustic round dance in the dooryard,
let alone of a hug. To touch you is to touch a truly
astronomical sum of cells,
which fate always finds affordable, but to which
only tenderness is proportionate.

VI

And I have ensconced myself in the world where your word and gesture
were imperative. Mimicry, imitation
were regarded as loyalty. I've mastered the art of merging
with the landscape the way one fades into the furniture or the curtains
(which, in the end, influenced my wardrobe).
Now and then in the course of a conversation
the first-person-plural pronoun would start to dribble
off my lips, and my fingers acquired the agility of hedged hawthorn.
Also, I quit glancing back over my padded shoulder. Hearing
footsteps behind me, nowadays I don't tremble:
as previously a chill in my shoulder blades,
nowadays I sense that behind my back also stretches
a street overgrown with colonnades, that at its far end
also shimmer the turquoise crescents
of the Adriatic. Their total is, clearly,
your present, Vertumnus—small change, if you will; some loose
silver with which, occasionally, rich infinity
showers the temporary. Partly out of superstition,
partly, perhaps, because it alone—
the temporary—is capable of sensation,
of happiness. "In this sense, for the likes of me,"
you would squint, "your brethren are useful."

VII

With the passage of years I came almost to the conviction
that the joy of life had become, for you, second nature.
I even started to wonder whether joy is indeed that safe

for a deity. Whether it's not eternity
that a deity pays with in the end for the joy of life.
You'd just brush all this off. But nobody, my Vertumnus,
nobody ever rejoiced so much in the transparent
spurt, in the brick of a basilica, in pine needles,
in wiry handwriting. Much more than we! I even
started to think that you'd gotten infected with
our omnivorousness. Indeed, a view
of a square from a balcony, a clangor of *campanili*,
a streamlined fish, the tattered coloratura
of a bird seen only in profile, laurels'
applause turning into an ovation
—they can be appreciated only by those who do
remember that, come tomorrow, or the day after tomorrow,
all this will end. It's precisely from them, perhaps,
that the immortals learn joy, the knack of smiling
(since the immortals are free from all manner of apprehension).
To the likes of you, in this sense our brethren are useful.

VIII

Nobody ever knew how you were spending nights.
But then that's not strange, taking into consideration
your origins. Once, well past midnight, at the hub of the universe,
I bumped into you, chased by a drove of dimming
stars, and you gave me a wink. Secretiveness? But the cosmos
isn't that secretive. In the cosmos one can see all
things with the naked eye, and they sleep there without blankets.
The intensity of a standard star is such
that its cooling alone can produce an alphabet,
vegetation, sincerity; in the end, ourselves,
with our past, present, future, et cetera—but with the
future especially. We are only
thermometers, brothers and sisters of
ice, not of Betelgeuse. You were made of warmth,
hence your omnipresence. It is difficult to imagine
you in any particular, no matter how shining, dot.
Hence your invisibility. Gods leave no blotches

on a bedsheet, not to mention offspring,
being content with a handmade likeness
in a stony niche, at the end of a garden alley,
happy as a minority; and they are.

IX

An iceberg sails into the tropics. Exhaling smoke, a camel
promotes a pyramid made of concrete, somewhere in the North.
You too, alas, learned to shirk
your immediate duties. To say the least, the four seasons
are more and more one another, eventually getting jumbled
like lire, pounds, dollars, marks, kroner
in a seasoned traveler's wallet.
The papers mutter "greenhouse effect" and "common market,"
but the bones ache at home and overseas alike.
Just look: even that loafer Christo's stone-faced precursor,
which for years used to snake through minefields, is crumbling down.
As a result, birds don't fly away on time
to Africa; characters like myself
less and less often return to the parts they came from;
the rent rises sharply. Apart from having
to exist, one has to pay for that existence monthly.
"The more banal the climate," you once remarked,
"the faster the future becomes the present."

X

On a scorched July dawn, the temperature of a body
plummets, aiming at zero. A horizontal bulk
in the morgue looks like raw material
for garden statuary. Due to a ruptured heart
and immobility. This time around, words
won't do the trick: to you my tongue
is no longer foreign enough to pay
heed to. Besides, one can't
step twice into the same cloud. Even
if you are a god. Especially, if you are not.

In winter the globe sort of shrinks, mentally flattens out.
The latitudes crawl, in twilight especially, upon one another.
The Alps for them are no obstacle. It smells of an ice age,
it smells, I would add, of neolith and of paleolith;
to use the vernacular, of the future. Since
an ice age is a category of the future, which is
that time when finally one loves no one,
even oneself. When you put on clothes
without planning to drop them off all of a sudden
in somebody's parlor. And when you can't walk out into
the street in your blue shirt alone, not to mention naked.
(I've learned quite a bit from you, but not this.) In a certain sense,
the future's got nobody. In a certain sense,
there is nobody in the future that we'd hold dear.
Of course, there are all those moraines and stalagmites everywhere
looming like louvres and skyscrapers with their meltdown contours.
Of course, something moves there: mammoths, mutant
beetles of pure aluminum, some on skis.
But you were a god of subtropics, with the power of supervision
over mixed forests and the black-earth zone—
that birthplace of the past. In the future it has no place,
and you've got nothing to do there. So that's why it crawls in winter
on the foothills of the Alps, on the sweet Apennines, snatching
now a small meadow with its clear brook, now something
plain evergreen: a magnolia, a bunch of laurels;
and not only in winter. The future always
arrives when somebody dies. Especially
if it's a man. Moreover, if it's a god.

XII

A dog painted in bright hues of sunrise
barks at the back of a passerby of midnight color.

XIII

In the past those whom you love don't ever
die. In the past they betray you or peter out into a perspective.

380

In the past the lapels are narrower, the only pair of loafers
steams by a heater like the ruins of boogie-woogie.
In the past a frozen garden bench
with its surplus of slats resembles
an insane equal sign. In the past the wind
to this day animates the mixture
of Cyrillic and Latin in naked branches:
Ж, Ч, Ш, Щ, plus X, Y, Z,
and your laughter is ringing: "As your head honcho said,
there is nothing that matches abracadabra."

XIV

A quarter century later, a streetcar's broken
vertebrae strike a spark in the evening yonder
as a civic salute to a forever darkened
window. One Caravaggio equals two Bernini,
turning either into a cashmere scarf
or a night at the opera. Now these cited
metamorphoses, left apparently unattended,
continue by pure inertia. Other objects, however, harden
in the condition you left them in,
thanks to which, from now on, they can be afforded by
no one. Display of loyalty? Plain predilection for
monumentality? Or is it simply the brazen future
barging in through the doors, and a sellout-resistant soul
acquires before our eyes the status
of a classic, of solid mahogany, of a Fabergé
egg? Most likely, the latter, which is also a metamorphosis,
and to your credit as well.
                         I've got nothing to plait a wreath with
so as to adorn your cold brow in proper fashion
at the closure of this extraordinarily dry year.
In a tastelessly furnished but large apartment,
like a cur that's suddenly lost its shepherd,
I lower myself onto all fours and scratch
the parquet with my claws, as though underneath were hidden—
because it's from down there that wafts the warmth—

your current existence. At the corridor's distant end dishes are rattling. Under the tightly shut door the frigid air thickens, rubbed by incessantly rustling dresses. "Vertumnus," I whisper, pressing my wet cheek hard against yellow floorboards. "Return, Vertumnus."

[December] 1990
[Milan]

Nativity

No matter what went on around them; no matter
what message the snowstorm was straining to utter;
or how crowded they thought that wooden affair;
or that there was nothing for them anywhere;

first, they were together. And—most of all—second,
they now were a threesome. Whatever was reckoned—
the stuff they were brewing, accruing, receiving—
was bound to be split into three, like this evening.

Above their encampment, the sky, cold and idle,
and leaning as big things will do over little,
was burning a star, which from this very instant
had no place to go, save the gaze of the infant.

The campfire flared on its very last ember.
They all were asleep now. The star would resemble
no other, because of its knack, at its nadir,
for taking an alien for its neighbor.

December 1990

Postcard from Lisbon

Monuments to events that never took place: to bloody
but never waged wars; to ardent phrases
swallowed once one's arrested; to a naked body
fused with a conifer, and whose face is
like St. Sebastian's; to aviators
who soared on winged pianos to a cloudy duel;
to the inventor of engines that foiled invaders
using discarded memories for fuel;
to the wives of seafarers bent over one-egged omelettes;
to voluptuous Justice awaiting suitors
and to carnal Respublica; to the comets
that missed this place in their hot pursuit of
infinity—whose features are echoed very
frequently by local vistas (alas, more photo-
genic than habitable); to the discovery
of Infarctica—an unknown quarter
of the afterworld; to the red-tiled seaside
village which dodged the cubist talent
for almost a century; to the suicide
—for unrequited love—of the Tyrant;
to the earthquake greeted by far too many
—say the annals—with cries of "A bargain!";
to the hand which never fondled money,
not to mention a reproductive organ;
to the green leaf choirs' bias against their callous
soloists getting the last ovation;
to happiness; and to dreams which imposed their chaos
on matter, by dint of the population.

1988

August Rain

In broad daylight it starts to get dark with breathless
speed, and a cumulous cloak grows into an uneasy
fur coat off some astral back. An acacia, under the pressure
of rain, becomes too noisy.
Neither thread nor needle, but something to do with sewing,
almost Singer-made, mixed with a rusty cistern's
spurt, is heard in this chirr, and a geranium bares the sinewed
vertebrae of a seamstress.

How familial is the rustling of rain! how well it darns and stitches
rents in a worn-out landscape, be that a pasture,
alleyway, puddles, tree-intervals—to foil one's eyesight, which is
capable of departure
from its range. Rain! vehicle of nearsightedness,
a scribe without his cell, greedy for Lenten fare,
mottling the loamy parchment with his cuneiform brand of silence,
with his smallpox care.

To turn away from the window! to behold a greatcoat with epaulets
on the brown varnished rack, a red fox on the chair, neglected,
the fringe of a yellow cloth which, having mastered the shibboleths
of gravity, has resurrected
itself and covered the table where late at night, a threesome,
we sit for supper, and you say in your drowsy, quiet
—almost my own but muted by years' vast distance—
baritone: What a climate.

1988

Venice: Lido

A rusty Romanian tanker, wallowing out in the azure
like a down-at-heel shoe discarded with sighing pleasure.

The crew, stripped to their pants—womanizers and wankers—
now that they're in the south, sun themselves by the anchors,

without a coin in their pockets to do the city,
which closely resembles a distant pretty

postcard pinned to the sunset; across the water, flocking
clouds, the smell of sweaty armpits, guitars idly plucking.

Ah, the Mediterranean! After your voids, a humble
limb craves a labyrinth, a topographic tangle!

A camel-like superstructure, on its decaying basis,
through binoculars scans the promenade's oasis.

Only by biting the sand, though, all tattoos faded,
can the eye of the needle truly be negotiated

to land at some white table, with a swarthy darling
of local stock, under a floral garland,

and listen as wide-splayed palms, above the bathhouse pennant,
rustle their soiled banknotes, anticipating payment.

1989

Fin de Siècle

The century will soon be over, but sooner it will be me.
That's not the message, though, of a trembling knee.
Rather, the influence of not-to-be

on to-be. Of the hunter upon—so to speak—his fowl,
be that one's heart valve or a red brick wall.
We hear the whiplash's foul

whistle recalling vainly the surnames of those who have loved us back,
writhing in the slippery palms of the local quack.
The world has just lost the knack

of being the place where a sofa, a fox-trot, a lampshade's cream
trimmings, a bodice, a risqué utterance reigned supreme.
Who could foresee time's grim

eraser wiping them off like some chicken scrawl
from a notepad? Nobody, not a soul.
Yet time's shuffling sole

has accomplished just that. Censure it, go ahead.
Now everywhere there are antennae, punks, stumps instead
of trees. No chance of your spotting at

a little café your confreres ruined by kismet, or
at the bar the silk-clad angel who failed to soar
above herself and her whiskey sour

on ice. And all over the place people obscure the view,
now forming a solid mass, now a lengthy queue.
A tyrant's no longer a bugaboo

but a plain mediocrity. Likewise, a car at last
isn't a luxury but the means of extracting dust
out of a street where the cast-

iron leg of a veteran fell silent for good, off course.
And the child is convinced that the wolf is worse
than infantry or the air force.

And somehow your hanky, bypassing your nose more and more often, leaps
to your organ of sight, trained on rustling leaves,
taking personally the least

new gap in their emptiness-shielding fence,
the letters *ed* heralding the past tense,
an aria of suspense

sung by a cuckoo's voice. Now it sounds more crude
than, say, Cavaradossi's. Approximately like "Hey, dude,"
or at best like "You should

quit drinking," and your limp palm glides off the decanter's skin,
though it's neither the priest nor the rabbi that's barging in
but the era called "fin

de siècle." Black things are in vogue: camisole, bloomers, hose.
When in the end you relieve your playmate of those
items, your humble house

suddenly gets lit up by something like a twenty-watt.
But instead of an exuberant *"Vivat!"*
the lips drop a flat

"Sorry." New times! Lamentable, sorry times!
Goods in shop windows, sporting nicknames, entice
us into telling the types

of things which are managed easily from the kinds
which we, technologically behind,
now equate to mankind's

ancient quest not so much for something that lets you save
energy as for an inanimate sort of slave;
on the whole, for a safe

anonymity. That's the logical, though unwelcome end
of multiplying, of the demographic trend
whose source is neither the Orient

nor zippers but electricity. The century's winding down. The rush
of time, demanding a ruin, a victim, rejects as trash
Baalbek. And a man won't wash

either. No, give it sentiments! give it ideas, plus
memories. Such is time's, alas,
sweet tooth. Well, I make no fuss

and give. I am not yellow; I am ready to play a thing
of the past, if that's so interesting
to time, eyeing

absentmindedly over its shoulder its measly catch—
which still shows some movement, though not much
else, and is still warm to touch.

I am ready to sink for good in those shifting sands. And I
am prepared that a traveler shambling by
won't focus the beady eye

of his camera on me, and that he won't succumb
to some powerful feeling on my account.
It so happens I can't

stand time that moves on. Time that stands still I still
can stand. Like a solid façade whose style
echoes now a stockpile,

now a chessboard. The century was indeed
not so bad. Well, perhaps the dead
ran a surplus. Yet the living did

that as well. So substantially, in fact,
that presently they could be pickled, packed,
and sealed to attract

stellar customers known for their grand deep-freeze
machinery. Unless, of course, they insist on cheese.
Which could be, with equal ease,

arranged; the holes in the collective memory are the proof.
To the accompaniment of air crashes in not-far-off
spots, the century ends. A prof

mumbles, poking his finger upward, about the atmosphere's
layers, explaining the heat and attendant fears,
but not how one steers

from here to where the cumulous bulky front
is suffused with our "forgive" and "don't
forsake me," which daunt

the ray into changing its gold into some silver roe.
Yet the century, rummaging through its bureau,
treats as retro

even that. Well, small wonder: the more it ticks
and tocks, the busier are young dicks,
the more numerous the antiques

and relics, including the planet, stuck
in its orbit and courting, a sitting duck,
the runaway cul-de-sac

of a comet; including the dog-eared files
of the fallen giants, since every bullet flies
from the future, which plies

its urgent trade with the present and thus needs room
now. Therefore no heirloom
lasts in the dooryard bloom

for long. At the North Pole a husky barks and a flag still twists.
In the West they stare eastward through their clenched fist
making out at least

the barracks, gone suddenly lively. Spooked by the forest of hands,
birds too
flutter and then take wing rapidly, heading due
south, to its wadis, to

its minarets, turbans, palm trees—and farther down tom-toms roll.
But the longer you scan strange features, the more they gall
you. You conclude that all

over the place the kinship between plain old dirt
and, say, a great painting of the classical sort
lies in that you won't hoard

either's original, ever. That nature, like minstrels of yesteryear
longing for carbons, like a thalamus holding dear
black letters, like a honeybee near

its hive, truly cherishes the mass scale, profuse
outputs, dreading uniqueness for its abuse
of energy, whose

best guardian is licentiousness. Space is fully settled. Time
is welcome to rub against its new surface, I'm
sure, infinitely. All the same,

your eyelid is drooping. Only the seas alone
remain unruffled and blue, telling the dawn "Go on,"
which sounds, from afar, like "gone."

And upon hearing that, one wants to quit one's travail,
shoveling, digging, and board a steamship and sail
and sail, in order to hail

in the end not an island nor an organism Linnaeus never found,
nor the charms of new latitudes, but the other way around:
something of no account.

1989

Porta San Pancrazio

The bees haven't buzzed away, nor has a horseman galloped
off. In the bar Gianicolo, old-timers enjoy their salad
days, and the ice cube melts, cooling the ailing motor
grateful for sipping twice the proverbial water.

Eight years have scurried by. Wars have flared up and smoldered,
families crumbled, scum bared its teeth grown older;
airplanes fell from the sky and the radio mumbled "Jesus."
The linen can still be washed, but the dermal creases

won't yield to the gentlest palm. The sun high above a winter
Rome is jostling the purple smoke with bare rays. The cinder
reeks of burnt leaves, and the fountain is glittering like a wobbly
medal pinned to a cannon at noon for its aimless volley.

Stone is employed worldwide to keep memory captive.
Yet cropping up is much harder than vanishing in a perspective
running out of the city straight through the years and further
in its pursuit of pure time, devoid of love and future.

Life without us is, darling, thinkable. It exists as
honeybees, horsemen, bars, habitués, columns, vistas,
and clouds over this battlefield whose every standing statue
triumphs, with its physique, over a chance to touch you.

[January 18] 1989

Transatlantic

The last twenty years were good for practically everybody
save the dead. But maybe for them as well.
Maybe the Almighty Himself has turned a bit bourgeois
and uses a credit card. For otherwise time's passage
makes no sense. Hence memories, recollections,
values, deportment. One hopes one hasn't
spent one's mother or father or both, or a handful of friends entirely
as they cease to hound one's dreams. One's dreams,
unlike the city, become less populous
the older one gets. That's why the eternal rest
cancels analysis. The last twenty years were good
for practically everybody and constituted
the afterlife for the dead. Its quality could be questioned
but not its duration. The dead, one assumes, would not
mind attaining a homeless status, and sleep in archways
or watch pregnant submarines returning
to their native pen after a worldwide journey
without destroying life on earth, without
even a proper flag to hoist.

1992

View from the Hill

Here is your frozen city cut into marble cubes.
Geometry is bewailing its ravaged quarry.
First, you hear a trio, then a Negro's piano flurry.
The river, as yet unfrozen, still coils and loops,
failing to make the ocean. The meandering urge
is stronger perhaps in a city planned personally by Pollyanna.
Then at the corner flares up an electric birch.
The fat river shines like a black piano.

Once you exit your lair, footsteps ring out behind.
That's the perspective's extra: no murderer keen to follow.
Two years of this place, and yesterday's tomorrow.
And the square, like a record, lets grooves unwind,
an obelisk for spindle. Something took place, that's why.
Say, a century back. Of the triumphant order.
Hence, this oomph of the triumph. Basically, you are small fry.
You are, at best, simply echo fodder.

Snow is falling pell-mell; "cyclone," all sets repeat.
Don't leave the bar, don't leave the bar, stay cozy.
High beams of some automouse make colonnades stampede
madly like Hannibal's elephants, scared and woozy.
There is a stench of desert recalling a widow's laughs.
"Baby, what's wrong?" Sinatra wonders.
Also an echo, though taped. Like the Senate's contours,
blizzard, boredom, low temperature, you, your loves.

Here is your hard-boiled egg, here its nest; here is
its yolk that glows through a shell cracked by the dead of winter.
On the highway, your taxi still overtakes a hearse
loaded with wreaths, apparently rolling in the
same direction as yours, thanks to a comfy rut.
That's the perimeter's spin-off, the call of suburbs,

those stubby districts absorbing, while they sleep, the hubbub
of freight trains, northeasters, fate's gargling throat.

And then—the ocean. An unresponsive tract.
A level expanse, no built-up isthmus.
Where if you are a historian, you've got no business,
nor if you are a doctor, an actor, an architect,
or, moreover, an echo. Since this expanse
lacks a past. All that it hears is the total
of its own waves—that unprecedented tattle
whose volume could be suppressed but once

by Gabriel's trumpet. Here is your splendid set
of horizontal lines. Indeed, the leaf spring
of the cosmos. In which one makes out a lisping
solo by Parker. True; not the pitch you get
from an archangel, judging by the spit it yields.
And beyond that, northbound and getting smaller
in the darkness, now vanishes, now pops up a trawler,
like a church, lost somewhere amid the fields.

[February 2] 1992

Homage to Girolamo Marcello

Once in winter I, too, sailed in
here from Egypt, believing that I'd be greeted
on the crowded quay by my wife in resplendent furs
and a tiny veiled hat. Yet I was greeted
not by her but by two small, decrepit
Pekinese with gold teeth. Their German owner
told me later that, should he be
robbed, the Pekinese might help him
to make ends meet; well, at least initially.
I was nodding and laughing.

The quay was infinite and completely
vacant. The otherworldly
winter light was turning palazzi into porcelain crockery
and the populace into those who won't
dare to touch it.
Neither veil nor, for that matter, furs
were at issue. The sole transparent
thing was the air and its pinkish laced
curtain in the hotel "Meleager and Atalanta,"
where, as far back as then, eleven years ago,
I could have surmised, I gather,
that the future already
had arrived. When a man's alone,
he's in the future—since it can manage
without the supersonic stuff,
streamlined bodies, an executed tyrant,
crumbling statues; when a man's unhappy,
that's the future.
                    Nowadays I don't get
on all fours any longer in the hotel
room, imitating its furniture and safeguarding
myself against my own maxims. Now to die of grief

would mean, I'm afraid, to die
belatedly, while latecomers
are unwelcome, particularly in the future.

The quay swarms with youngsters chattering in Arabic.
The veil has sprouted into a web of rumors,
dimmed later into a net of wrinkles.
And the Pekinese long ago got consumed by their canine Auschwitz.
No sign of the owner, either. What seems to have survived
is but water and me, since water also
has no past.

1988

Elegy

Sweetheart, losing your looks, go to live in a village.
Mirrors there crave mildew, no maiden's visage.
A river, too, comes with ripples; and fields, in furrows,
clearly forgot for good about stocky fellows.

Nothing but kids around. And as to whose this litter
is, that's known but to those who jail the suckers later,
or to nobody; or to a cobwebbed icon.
And only the law comes to plow in springtime.

Move to a village, sweetheart. A grove or a glebe are where
it's simpler to ponder humus, or what to wear.
There for a hundred miles yours is the only lipstick,
though its slug will do better with no ballistics.

You know, it's better to age where a milepost is nodding,
where beauty means absolutely nothing,
or it means not youthfulness, bosom, semen
—since time, on the whole, is indeed all seasons.

That should cure ennui, though one would be loath to patent
this. And the woods there clamor that everything has happened
already; and not just once. And the total number
of what happened already is the root of their constant clamor.

It's better to age in a village. There, even though a recluse,
you'd easily spot a tiny crucifix in a reckless
stark-naked birch, in a shepherd's purse, in manly
burdocks, in moths aflutter for twenty-four hours only.

And I'll come to join you there. Still, in this ardent cry of
joining you read not your but those beings' triumph,

since, like a bedsheet, earth better follows
not the parlance of love but that of ruts, gulches, hollows.

And even if I won't come! Any sinkhole or crater,
or some dark well's razor-blade-tasting water,
road-shoulder brambles, a hobbling scarecrow
is, frankly, me: that is, what you don't care for.

Go to a village, sweetheart. You know, a ruined
face only proves there exist more fluent
ways of tying the knot—ah, many other methods!
Yet we seldom see what is staring at us.

You know, a landscape is what you never
know. Think of that when you think it's over.
Squinting one day at some colorless brushstrokes, dear,
you'll make out yourself, and a colorless brushstroke near.

1992

Anti-Shenandoah: Two Skits and a Chorus

I. Departure
"Why don't we board a train and go off to Persia?
Persia doesn't exist, obviously, but inertia
does. It's a better vehicle than any old engine, Johnny,
and we may have a comfortable, an eventful journey."

"Why do you call me Johnny when you know I am Billy, Mary?
Perhaps because of inertia? It's Johnny you want to marry,
not me. But he is not in Persia, he went off to Warsaw,
although after 1945 it's a different city also."

"Of course, you are Billy, Billy; and I'm not Mary, either.
Actually, I am Suzy: you are welcome to check my Visa.
But let's be Mary and Johnny, like in the Ark of Noah,
or nameless, the way we were when we were spermatozoa."

"Because there are but two sexes, there is a lot of nuance,
and history's where our exes join kings and ruins.
When someone's whereabouts become a mystery,
you should take the train of thought that goes to history."

"Ah, there is so much action! In history, willy-nilly,
Mary becomes just Suzy, and Johnny Billy,
B.C. becomes A.D., and Persia Warsaw.
For history breeds inertia, and vice versa."

"Ah, mixing inertia with history bespeaks individuality!
Mary, let's take a chance, this father of causality:
let's take the express to where folks live in utter penury
and where the reality quickly becomes a memory."

"Oh, he is my dear boy, my slowly peeled banana!"
"And she is my sweetheart filled with Tampax Americana!"

"The future arrives on time whistling *Domini Gloria*,
and we must take it eastward, where it's always earlier."

II. Arrival
"What is this place? It looks kind of raw.
The trees stand as if they are about to draw,
their rustle is so menacing. They, no doubt,
have seen too many movies—but were they dubbed?"

"I don't mind the place, but who are these guys?
Is this their true appearance, or disguise?
They all sell shoelaces but wear no shoes.
Can we explain to them that we are not Jews?"

"I never knew that history is so much
inhabited and curious, and prone to touch.
Oh, do they have a leader? A shah? A khan?
Frankly, I regret I don't have my gun."

"But I've read many people can't wish the same
wish. Unless, of course, they are insane.
I think we are quite safe; they don't want to kill,
though frankly I regret I am off the pill."

"Ah, this is the past, and it's rather vast,
and in the land of the cause its effects go bust
or else get outnumbered in more ways than one:
we've brought them all the future, and we are left with none."

"One shouldn't speak for others when things get tight.
You might not have the future, but I just might.
The future is derivative; they may crack skulls,
but because they've been so primitive, we've had Pascals."

"So it's goodbye, dear Mary. Hope all goes well.
We'll meet not in the future but, say, in hell."

"Oh, that would be nice, dear Johnny, that would be great.
But the afterlife in history occurs quite late."

III. Chorus
Here they are, for all to see,
the fruits of complacency.
Beware of love, of A.D., B.C.,
and the travel agency.

A train may move fast, but time is slow.
History's closer
to the Big Bang than to Roman law,
and you are the loser.

So, our advice to you is, Stay put
if you can help it.
Always be ready to say Kaput,
but wear a helmet.

1992

Daedalus in Sicily

All his life he was building something, inventing something.
Now, for a Cretan queen, an artificial heifer,
so as to cuckold the king. Then a labyrinth, this time for
the king himself, to hide from bewildered glances
an unbearable offspring. Or a flying contraption, when
the king figured out in the end who it was at his court
who was keeping himself so busy with new commissions.
The son on that journey perished falling into the sea,
like Phaeton, who, they say, also spurned his father's
orders. Here, in Sicily, stiff on its scorching sand,
sits a very old man, capable of transporting
himself through the air, if robbed of other means of passage.
All his life he was building something, inventing something.
All his life from those clever constructions, from those inventions,
he had to flee. As though inventions
and constructions are anxious to rid themselves of their blueprints
like children ashamed of their parents. Presumably, that's the fear
of replication. Waves are running onto the sand;
behind, shine the tusks of the local mountains.
Yet he had already invented, when he was young, the seesaw,
using the strong resemblance between motion and stasis.
The old man bends down, ties to his brittle ankle
(so as not to get lost) a lengthy thread,
straightens up with a grunt, and heads out for Hades.

[Winter] 1993
[Amsterdam]

Clouds

Ah, summer clouds
of the Baltic! I swear
you are nowhere
to be outclassed.

Isn't your free state
the afterworld's border—
stallions, a warrior,
sometimes a saint?

The Almighty alone
glimpses by lightning
your crumbling lining,
fraying cretonne.

Hence, I, an old
hand at premonitions,
take your omniscience
for non-being's mold,

afterlife's mask.
Steadily running
over the granite,
over the most

humble of seas,
you are the limpid
sculptures of limit-
less genesis.

Cupolas, peaks,
profile of Tolstoy,

muscular torso,
bachelor digs,

candlesticks' vain
meltdown, or Hapsburg
Vienna, an iceberg-
alias-brain,

Eden's debris.
Ah, save the northeaster,
you wouldn't master
geometry!

Your cirric ploys
or cumulous domus
make both the nomads
and the settled rejoice.

Thanks to your reams,
patches, and tatters,
words that one utters
equal one's dreams.

It's you who let
me with your nimbus
trust not in numbers
but in the complete

spurning of weights
and measures in favor
—once and forever—
of phantoms and grace.

It was you, too,
who made the salient
planet an island
paltry for two.

Ah, your rent-free
castles! Those lofty
soft hotbeds of the
heart's tyranny!

Frothy cascades
of seraphs and ball gowns;
crashing of bogus
starched barricades;

conjugal bouts
of butterflies and
the Himalayan
glaciers—ah, clouds,

high in pristine
skies of the Baltic!
Whose stern and vatic
calls have you been

heeding? To whose
might do you yield? Or
who is your builder?
Your Sisyphus?

Who, having found
shapes to your grandeur,
made it surrender
sound? For sound-

less is your great
miracle! Heavy
or scattered, your bevy,
cohort, parade

silently hedge
toward some finish

line, where you'll vanish
—toward the edge

etched by your shoal
that charged it more boldly,
and was lighter than body,
better than soul.

1989

Cappadocia

A hundred and forty thousand warriors of Mithridates Ponticus—
cavalry, archers, armor, swords, lances, helmets, shields—
cross into a foreign territory which is called Cappadocia.
The army has stretched for miles. Horsemen cast gloomy, ominous
glances around. The space, ashamed of its bareness, feels
that, with their every step, the far-off turns cautiously
into the nearby. Especially in the mountains, whose
summits, equally tired of purple
at dawn, of lilac at twilight, of clouds' burnous,
gain, because of the strangers' keensightedness, in their marble
sharpness, if not in distinctness. The army looks
from afar like a river snaking among the rocks,
whose source does its best not to fall too far behind its mouth,
which, in turn, glances back now and then at its lagging source.
And the farther the troops move eastward, the more this sparse
terrain, as though facing a mirror, from a muddy, forsaken chaos

turns, temporarily, into an impassive, sublime backdrop
of history. Shuffling of many feet,
cursing, clinking of harnesses, of stirrups against the sheath,
hubbub, a thicket of spears. Suddenly, with an abrupt
cry, the outrider freezes; is it a phantom, or . . . ?
In the distance, replacing the landscape, across the whole plateau
stand the legions of Sulla. Sulla, forgetting Marius,
brought here legions to clarify to whom,
despite the brand of the winter moon,
Cappadocia belongs. Having come to a halt, the army is
settling now for a battle. The stony, wide
plateau for the last time looks like a place where no one died.
Sparks of bonfire, bursts of laughter, of singing "The fox was crafty."
Stretched on the naked stone, King Mithridates' hefty
bulk is beholding a dream's perennial milky breast,
hamstrings, wet ringlets, smooth thighs, the torso.

The same is beheld by the rest of his troops, and also
by the legions of Sulla. Which proves, at least,
not the absence of choice but the fullness of moon. In Asia
space tends to hide from itself, and the frequent charge
of monotony, in its conqueror; by and large
in his head, his armor, his beard, which, to make things easier,
it shrouds with the moonlight. Under this silver shroud,
the troops are no longer a river proud
of its length but a sizable lake, whose depth, apparently,
is exactly what space, living here in seclusion, needs,
since that depth is proportionate to those many covered leagues.
That's why often the Pontians, sometimes the Romans (currently
both of them), wander into Cappadocia. Armies are
essentially water, without which neither plateaus nor a
mountain would know how they look in profile, much less

en face. Two sleeping lakes, with the same floating piece of flesh
inside, glow at night like the triumph of flora over
fauna, aiming to coalesce at dawn,
in a ravine, into one common mirror quite fit to own
Cappadocia's all: boulders, lizards, skies—save the oval
of one's face. Only, perhaps, a big
eagle up there in the dark, used to its wing and beak,
knows what lies in the future. Glancing below with utter
apathy, common in birds, since, unlike a king,
a bird is repeatable, an eagle soaring
in the present soars naturally in the future
and of course in the past: in history; in its late-
running show, in its friction—the way it's sounding—
of something temporary against something
permanent, the way matches grate

sandpaper, a dream the reality, troops a terrain. In Asia
daybreaks are rapid. Something chirps. As soon
as you rise, a shiver runs down your spine
infecting with chilliness the stubborn, earth-hugging, drowsy,
long-legged shadows. The milky haze

of dawn, with its coughing, neighing, half-yawn, half-phrase,
rattling of armor, commands to rise.
And, witnessed by half a million eyes,
the sun sets in motion limbs, spears, all manner of sharpened metal,
horsemen, foot soldiers, archers, chariots. Helmets shine,
and the troops march toward each other like line after line
of a book slamming shut in the very middle;
like, more aptly, two mirrors, two shields; like two
faces, two parts of addition, instead of *summa*
resulting in difference and subtracting Sulla
from Cappadocia. Whose grass—which, too,

never knew what it looks like—gains more than anyone
from the screams, the clangor, the noise, the gore
of this smashing and crashing, as its green eyes pore
over the smithereens of a shattered legion
and the fallen Pontians. Waving widely his sharp sword, King
Mithridates, not thinking of anything,
rides ahead amid chaos, crossed weapons, babel.
The battle looks from afar like—"aaagh" carved in stone;
or else like a mirror's silver gone
berserk facing its shiny double.
And with each body falling next, from the ranks, onto this stony glade,
the terrain, akin to a dulling blade,
loses its sharpness, gets blurred in the south and mossier
in the east; the silhouette seems to resume its fair
reign. That's how the fallen take into the next world their
trophy: the features of nobody's Cappadocia.

1992

411

Ab Ovo

Ultimately, there should be a language
in which the word "egg" is reduced to O
entirely. The Italian comes the closest,
naturally, with its *uova*. That's why Alighieri thought
it the healthiest food, sharing the predilection
with sopranos and tenors whose pear-like torsos
in the final analysis embody "opera."
The same pertains to the truly Romantic, that is,
German poets, with practically every line
starting the way they'd begin a breakfast,
or to the equally cocky mathematicians
brooding over their regularly laid infinity,
whose immaculate zeros won't ever hatch.

1996

Via Funari

Ugly gargoyles peek out of your well-lit window,
the Caetani palace exhales turpentine and varnish,
and Gino's, where the coffee was good and I used to pick up the keys,
has vanished. In Gino's stead
came a boutique; it sells socks and neckties,
more indispensable than either him or us
—from any standpoint, actually. And you are far off in Tunisia
or in Libya, contemplating the lining of
the waves whose lace keeps adorning the Italian coastline:
an homage to Septimus Severus? I doubt whether all this should
be blamed on money, or the passage of time, or me.
In any case, it's no less probable
that the famous inanimateness
of the cosmos, tired of its pretty vicious
infinitude, seeks for itself an earthly
abode; and we come in handy. And, frankly, one should be grateful
when it confines itself to an apartment,
some facial expression, a few brain cells,
and doesn't drive us directly under,
the way it did parents, your kid brother and sister, G.
The doorbell button is but a crater
in miniature, modestly gaping in the
wake of some cosmic touch, the crumb of a meteorite;
all doorways are peppered with this otherworldly smallpox.
Well, we've failed to connect. I think the next opportunity
won't arise very soon. Probably not at all.
Don't regret this, however. I don't believe I could
reveal to you more than Sirius to Canopus,
though it's precisely here, on your doorstep, where
they bump into one another, in broad daylight,
and not in the vigilant, telescope-hugging nighttime.

1995
[Hotel Quirinale, Rome]

Portrait of Tragedy

Let's look at the face of tragedy. Let's see its creases,
its aquiline profile, its masculine jawbone. Let's hear its rhesus
contralto with its diabolic rises:
the aria of effect beats cause's wheezes.
How are you, tragedy? We haven't seen you lately.
Hello, the medal's flip side gone lazy.
Let's examine your aspects, lady.

Let's look into her eyes. Into her wide-with-senseless-
pain hazel pupils aimed like lenses
at us in the stalls, or touring in someone else's
predicament, on false pretenses.
Welcome, tragedy, with gods and heroes,
with the curtain exposing your feet, dirty with other eras,
with proper names sunk in the maddening chorus.

Let's put our fingers into her mouth that gnashes
scurvy-eaten keyboards inflamed by wolfram flashes
showing her spit-rich palate with blizzards of kinfolk's ashes.
Let's yank her hem, see if she blushes.
Well, tragedy, if you want, surprise us.
Show us a body betrayed or its demise, devices
for lost innocence, inner crisis.

Ah, but to press ourselves against her cheek, her Gorgon
coiling hairdo! Against the golden
icon's coarse wooden backside that hoards the burden
of proof the better the more her horizons broaden.
Greetings, tragedy, dressed slightly out of fashion,
with lengthy sentences making time look ashen.
Though you feel fine alfresco, it's the morgue you've got a crush on.

Let's tumble into her arms with a lecher's ardor!
Let's drown in her flabby rubble; yes, let's go under.
Let's burrow through her and make mattress fodder.
Who knows, she may carry. A race always needs a founder.
What's new on the schedule, tragedy, in your cartridge?
And re stuffing wombs, what takes more courage
to star in: a scene of carnage or a pile of garbage?

Ah, to inhale her stench of armpits and feces
mixed with the incense clouding subtracted faces;
to exclaim hysterically, You save this
for the sissies! And throw up into her laces.
Thanks, tragedy, for your attempts to cheer up
(since there is no abortion without a cherub),
for jackboots kicking the groin as though it's a stirrup.

Her face is abominable! It's never hidden
by the domino, makeup, duckweed, by heathen
ignorance, or by a fishnet mitten
involved in a stormy ovation, completely smitten.
Thanks, tragedy, for playing decent.
For being direct like a bullet, albeit distant.
For not wasting time, for happening in an instant.

Who are we, after all, neither oils nor statues,
not to allow the mangling of our lives as much as
one wishes? Which, too, could be seen as a boon. The catch is,
a thing must become unpalpable to look matchless.
Don't spurn that, tragedy, the genre of martyrs!
How about the loss of all that's sacred to us for starters?
Small wonder that togas become you as much as tatters.

Look at her, she is scowling! She says, "Good evening,
let me begin. In this business, folks, the beginning
matters more than the end. Give me a human being
and I'll begin with misfortune, so set the wristwatch for grieving."

Go ahead, tragedy! Among our vowels,
pick out the *yi*, born in the Mongol bowels,
and turn it, ripping our gushing ovals,

into a noun, a verb, an adjective! *yi*, our common gargle!
yi, we barf out as our gains and our losses ogle
us, or as we storm the exit. But there, an ogre,
you're looming large with your oblong cudgel and bulging goggle!
Tragedy, hit us like a relative. Make clowns of us.
Knead us into a pulp on our bunks and sofas.
Spit into our souls till you find a surface,

and afterwards also! Make it a swamp, and stir it,
so that neither the Father and Son nor the Holy Spirit
will clear it up. Curdle it into the serried
rubble. Plant there aspens, shoot up acid, and leave needles buried.
Let soul be like nature, tragedy; that won't wear badly.
Let's graft a seraph to the night-work buggy.
As the fruit told the botanist, Fine, make me ugly.

Once you were, dear, a beauty, a power, a non-stop torrent.
You'd come after midnight and flash a warrant.
You were quoting Racine; obscene you weren't.
Now you are the perspective stewed in the dead end. A worried
herd, though, finds its address, and a lamb an oven
by spotting your footprint that's fresh and cloven.
Come on! Fly the gates of your pigsty open.

1991

Törnfallet

There is a meadow in Sweden
where I lie smitten,
eyes stained with clouds'
white ins and outs.

And about that meadow
roams my widow
plaiting a clover
wreath for her lover.

I took her in marriage
in a granite parish.
The snow lent her whiteness,
a pine was a witness.

She'd swim in the oval
lake whose opal
mirror, framed by bracken,
felt happy broken.

And at night the stubborn
sun of her auburn
hair shone from my pillow
at post and pillar.

Now in the distance
I hear her descant.
She sings "Blue Swallow,"
but I can't follow.

The evening shadow
robs the meadow

of width and color.
It's getting colder.

As I lie dying
here, I'm eyeing
stars. Here's Venus;
no one between us.

1990/1993

Persian Arrow

TO VÉRONIQUE SCHILTZ

Your wooden shaft has vanished; so has the body
which you clearly missed way back in zero
B.C. Nonetheless, oxidized and badly
chipped, you have reached me, dear devotee of Zeno.

Clockworks tick on. Yet, to put it archly,
they are, like a corked liquid, settled
and immobile. While you are starkly
mobile, heedless of any second.

Could you really guess what lay ahead when bidding
farewell to your string? What grand hiatus
you embarked on, snapping the bow and hitting
the blue yonder the other side of the Euphrates?

Even now, resting in my warm fingers
on a cold afternoon, in an alien chamber,
resembling, thanks to your greenish pigment,
a bay leaf that has outlived its chowder,

you are rushing away, target-free, defiant.
There is no way to catch up with you in a desert; also
in the jungle-like present. For every warmth is finite.
That of the human hand is more so.

[February] 1993

Song of Welcome

Here's your mom, here's your dad.
Welcome to being their flesh and blood.
Why do you look so sad?

Here's your food, here's your drink.
Also some thoughts, if you care to think.
Welcome to everything.

Here's your practically clean slate.
Welcome to it, though it's kind of late.
Welcome at any rate.

––––––––

Here's your paycheck, here's your rent.
Money is nature's fifth element.
Welcome to every cent.

Here's your swarm and your huge beehive.
Welcome to the place with its roughly five
billion like you alive.

Welcome to the phone book that stars your name.
Digits are democracy's secret aim.
Welcome to your claim to fame.

––––––––

Here's your marriage, and here's divorce.
Now that's the order you can't reverse.
Welcome to it; up yours.

Here's your blade, here's your wrist.
Welcome to playing your own terrorist;
call it your Middle East.

Here's your mirror, your dental gleam.
Here's an octopus in your dream.
Why do you try to scream?

———————

Here's your corncob, your TV set.
Your candidate suffering an upset.
Welcome to what he said.

Here's your porch, see the cars pass by.
Here's your shitting dog's guilty eye.
Welcome to its alibi.

Here are your cicadas, then a chickadee,
the bulb's dry tear in your lemon tea.
Welcome to infinity.

———————

Here are your pills on the plastic tray,
your disappointing, crisp X-ray.
You are welcome to pray.

Here's your cemetery, a well-kept glen.
Welcome to a voice that says "Amen."
The end of the rope, old man.

Here's your will, and here's a few
takers. Here's an empty pew.
Here's life after you.

———————

And here are your stars which appear still keen
on shining as though you had never been.
They might have a point, old bean.

Here's your afterlife, with no trace
of you, especially of your face.
Welcome, and call it space.

Welcome to where one cannot breathe.
This way, space resembles what's underneath,
and Saturn holds the wreath.

1992

Elegy

Whether you fished me bravely out of the Pacific
or I pried your shell wide open by the Atlantic
now matters little. A different kind of ocean
erodes nowadays what seemed fairly rocky
and presumably insinuates itself
into your hairdo as well—obliterating
as much as conquering. And, as the poet said,
thou art far in humanity, what with your offspring now
breaking new hearts and balls across this continent,
which is what, I hope, we still have in common.
Still, they are only half you. In a court of law
the inheritance of your mesmerizing beauty
that I thought immortal will be awarded
to nobody, including yourself. For although the gods or genes
are generous lending their properties—say, for a trial run
in these precincts—ultimately they are selfish;
at any rate, they are more vain than you,
having eternity. Which is a far cry from
yet another rented abode in a snowbound village
somewhere up north, where perhaps at this
very moment you stare at your flimsy mirror
returning you surely less than my equally one-dimensional
memory, though to you this makes indeed no difference.

1995

423

Kolo

In march the soldiers
with rifles on their shoulders.
Out run through brambles
the locals with their bundles.

Off fly the envoys
contemplating new ways
of creating symmetry
in a future cemetery.

Up go the pundits
explicating bandits.
Clearly outworded,
down go the murdered.

The expensive warriors,
sailing by on carriers
flying Old Glory,
signal hunky-dory.

Far is the neighbor,
loveless or unable,
neutral or bullied.
Near is a bullet.

Deep dig new hermits
sporting blue helmets.
Reasonable offers
manufacture orphans.

Blood as a liquid
shows no spilling limit;

one might build finally
here a refinery.

Home stay the virtuous
with their right to watch this
live, while they are dining:
it's a mealtime dying.

Soiled turns the fabric
of the great republic.
Ethics by a ballot
is what it's all about.

Mourn the slaughtered.
Pray for those squatted
in some concrete lair
facing betrayal.

1995

425

Lullaby

Birth I gave you in a desert
not by chance,
for no king would ever hazard
its expanse.

Seeking you in it, I figure,
won't be wise
since its winter cold is bigger
than its size.

As you suck my breast, this vastness,
all this width,
feeds your gaze the human absence
it's filled with.

Grow accustomed to the desert
as to fate,
lest you find it omnipresent
much too late.

Some get toys, in piles and layers,
wrapped or bound.
You, my baby, have to play with
all the sand.

See that star, at terrifying
height, aglow?
Say, this void just helps it, eyeing
you below.

Grow accustomed to the desert.
Uniform
underfoot, for all it isn't,
it's most firm.

In it, fate rejects a phantom
faint or gross:
one can tell for miles a mountain
by a cross.

Paths one sees here are not really
human paths
but the centuries', which freely
through it pass.

Grow accustomed to the desert:
flesh is not—
as the speck would sigh, wind-pestered—
all you've got.

Keep this secret, child, for later.
That, I guess,
may just help you in a greater
emptiness.

Which is like this one, just ever-
lasting; and
in it love for you shows where
it might end.

Grow accustomed to the desert
and the star
pouring down its incandescent
rays, which are

just a lamp to guide the treasured
child who's late,
lit by someone whom that desert
taught to wait.

December 1992

Homage to Chekhov

Sunset clings to the samovar, abandoning the veranda,
but the tea has gone cold, or is finished; a fly scales a saucer's *dolce*.
And her heavy chignon makes Varvara Andreevna look grander
than ever. Her starched cotton blouse is staunchly
buttoned up to her chin. Vialtsev, deep in his chair, is nodding
over the rustling weekly with Dubrovo's latest swing
at the Cabinet. Varvara Andreevna under her skirts wears not a
thing.

The drawing room's dark piano responds to a dry ovation
of hawthorns. The student Maximov's few random chords
stir the garden's cicadas. In the platinum sky, athwart,
squadrons of ducks, foreshadowing aviation,
drift toward Germany. Hiding in the unlit
library, Dunia devours Nikki's letter, so full of cavils.
No looker; but, boy, what anatomy! And so unlike
hardcovers.

That is why Erlich winces, called in by Kartashov
to join Prigozhin, the doctor, and him at cards. "With pleasure."
Ah, but swatting a fly is simpler than staving off
a reverie of your niece, naked upon the leather
couch and fighting mosquitoes, fighting heat—but to no avail.
Prigozhin deals as he eats: with his belly virtually
crushing the flimsy table. Can the doctor be asked about this little boil?
Perhaps eventually.

Oppressive midsummer twilight; a truly myopic part
of day, when each shape and form loses resolve, gets eerily
vague. "In your linen suit, Piotr Lvovich, it's not so hard
to take you for one of the statues down in the alley." "Really?"
Erlich feigns embarrassment, rubbing his pince-nez's rim.
It's true, though: the far-off in twilight looks near, the near, alien;

and Erlich tries to recall how often he had Natalia
Fiodorovna in his dream.

But does Varvara Andreevna love the doctor? Gnarled poplars crowd
the dacha's wide-open windows with peasant-like abandon.
They are the ones to be asked: their branches, their crow-filled crowns.
Particularly, the elm climbing into Varvara's bedroom:
it alone sees the hostess with just her stockings on.
Outside, Dunia calls for a swim in the night lake: "Come, lazies!"
To leap! overturning the tables! Hard, though, if you are the one
with aces.

And the cicada chorus, with the strength of the stars' display,
burgeons over the garden, sounding like their utterance.
Which is, perhaps, the case. Where am I, anyway?
wonders Erlich, undoing his braces at the outhouse entrance.
It's twenty versts to the railroad. A rooster attempts its *lied*.
The student Maximov's pet word, interestingly, is "fallacy."
In the provinces, too, nobody's getting laid,
as throughout the galaxy.

1993

Ischia in October

TO FAUSTO MALCOVATI

Once a volcano here belched with zest.
Later, a pelican plucked its breast.
Virgil dwelt not too far away,
and Wystan Auden held drinks at bay.

These days, the palaces' stucco peels,
frightful prices make longer bills.
Yet I somehow still make, amid
all these changes, my line ends meet.

A fisherman sails into the azure,
away from the drying bed linen's lure.
And autumn splashes the mountain ridge
with a wave unknown to the empty beach.

On the balustrade, my wife and child
peer at a distant piano lid
of sail, or at the small balloon
of Angelus fleeing the afternoon.

Unreachable, as it were, by foot,
an island as a kind of fate
suits solely the sirocco; but
we also are fluent at

banging the shutters. A sudden draft
scattering papers right and left
is proof that in this limestone
place we are not alone.

The rectangular, mortar-held eggshell,
enduring the wind's solid brow, as well

as the breakers' wet hammer works,
reveals at dusk three yolks.

The bougainvillea's tightly wound
scrawl helps the isolated ground
to shade its limited shame a bit,
avenging thus space with writ.

Almost no people; so that pronouns
sharpen one's features all at once,
as though speech makes them definite like a lens
at the vista's expense.

And should someone sigh longingly "Home," your hand
more willingly than to the continent
might point to the cumulous peaks where great
worlds rise and disintegrate.

We are a threesome here and I bet
what we together are looking at
is three times more addressless and more blue
than what Aeneas saw sailing through.

1993

Anthem

Praised be the climate
for putting a limit,
after a fashion,
to time in motion.

Of all prisons
the Four Seasons
has the best diet
and welcomes riot.

Asked for its origin
a climate cites oxygen,
but gives no reasons
for its omnipresence.

Detached like Confucius,
hardly conscious,
it may not love us,
but murmurs, "Always."

Being finite,
we certainly find it
promising and heartwarming,
though it's a warning.

A climate's permanence
is caused by the prevalence
of nothingness in its texture
and atmospheric pressure.

Hence, the barometer,
with its Byronic air,

should be, I reckon,
our only icon.

Since the accuracy of mercury
beats that of memory
(which is also mortal),
climate is moral.

When it exhibits
its bad habits,
it blames not parents
but ocean currents.

Or charged with the tedium
and meaninglessness of its idiom,
it won't seek legal
aid and goes local.

Keen on history,
it's also well versed in the mystery
of the hereafter
and looks like their author.

What I have in common
with the ancient Roman
is not a Caesar,
but the weather.

Likewise, the main features
I share with the future's
mutants are those curious
shapes of cumulus.

Praised be the entity
incapable of enmity
and likewise finicky
when it comes to affinity.

Yet if one aspect
of this highly abstract
thing is its gratitude
for finding latitude,

then a rational anthem
sung by one atom
to the rest of matter
should please the latter.

1995

In Front of Casa Marcello

The sun's setting, and the corner bar bangs its shutters.
Lampposts flare up, as though an actress

paints her eyelids dark violet, looking both rum and scary.
And the headache is parachuting squarely

behind enemy wrinkles. While five enormous
pigeons on the Palazzo Minelli's cornice

are copulating in the last rays of sunset,
paying no heed, as our Stone Age ancest-

ors did, no doubt, to their scruffy neighbors,
already asleep or a little nervous.

The booming bells of the slant bell tower
rooted in the ultramarine sky over

this town are like fruits keen on falling rather
than hitting the ground. If there is another

life, someone picks them up there. Well, pretty
soon we'll find out. Here, where plenty

of saliva, rapturous tears, and even
seed has been shed, in a nook of the earthly Eden,

I stand in the evening, absorbing slowly
with the dirty sponge of my lungs the lovely,

transparent, autumn-*cum*-winter, lucent
local oxygen, pink with loosened

tiles and a windowsill's carnation,
and giving the scent of cells' liberation

from time. The money-like, crumpled water
of the canal, buying off the palazzo's outer

riches, ends up with a somewhat shady,
peeling-off deal that includes a shaky

caryatid shouldering still the organ
of speech, with its cigarette, and ogling

the scenes, breathtaking for their oblivion
of propriety, happening in the avian

bedroom, exposed to a passing party,
and resembling now a windswept palm tree,

now a jumble of numerals insane with their quest for timing,
now a line scrawled in haste and rhyming.

1995

After Us

After us, it is certainly not the flood,
and not drought either. In all likelihood, the climate
in the Kingdom of Justice, with its four seasons, will
be temperate, so that a choleric, a melancholic,
a sanguinic, and a phlegmatic could rule by turns
three months each. From the standpoint of an encyclopedia,
that's plenty. Although, no doubt, caprices
of atmospheric pressure or those of temperature
might confuse a reformer. Still, the god of commerce
only revels in a rising demand for tweeds,
English umbrellas, worsted topcoats. His most dreaded enemies
are darned stockings and patched-up trousers.
It would seem that the rain outside the window
advocates precisely this distinctly frugal
approach to the landscape—more generally to all creation.
But the Constitution doesn't mention rain.
There's not a single reference in the Constitution
to barometers or, for that matter, to anyone
who, perched on a stool, holding a ball of yarn,
like some muscular Alcibiades, passes the
night poring over a fashion magazine's dog-eared pages
in the anteroom of the Golden Age.

1994

437

A Tale

I

In walks the Emperor, dressed as Mars;
   his medals clink and sway.
The General Staff sports so many stars,
   it looks like the Milky Way.

The Emperor says, "I guess you guess
   what you are here for."
The generals rise and bark, "Oh yes,
   Sire! To start a war."

"Right," says the Emperor. "Our enemy
   is powerful, mean, and brash.
But we'll administer him such an enema
   his toilet won't need a flush.

"Move your artillery! Move your warships!
   Where is my gorgeous horse?
Forward! May God, whom our nation worships,
   join our brave air force!"

"Yes!" cry the warriors. "Our job is carnage,
   ruin, destruction, void.
We promise, Sire: we'll find a Carthage
   and we'll leave it destroyed."

"Great!" cries the Emperor. "What one conquers
   is up to the scholars' quills.
And let the Treasury boys go bonkers
   trying to pay the bills."

The generals thunder: "Well said, Sire.
   Our coin is of tolling bells.

May the sun that won't set over your empire
    rise for nobody else!"

And off roars the turbine, off clangs the metal,
    off they march, hand on hilt,
as many a rose curls its tender petal
    ready to wait and wilt.

II

It's no Armageddon, it's not some smarmy
    earthquake or H-bomb test.
No, it's just the Imperial Army
    trying to do its best.

The sky is falling, the earth is gaping,
    the ocean simply boils.
"Life," says the Emperor, "is just aping
    popular abstract oils.

"War," he continues, "is like a museum."
    And the Top Brass agree:
"Sire, we'll paint like that ad nauseam,
    since Art equals History!

"History never says it's sorry,
    nor does it say, What if.
To enter History, a territory
    first has to come to grief."

"History never says it's sorry,"
    join the enlisted men.
"Who needs memento when we've got mori?
    History must know when."

"Ah, tell them to turn the good old horizon
    vertical, save its sail,"

adds the Emperor, with his eyes on
   the most minute detail.

"Yes," cry the generals. "Yes, for heaven's
   sake. That's what's been amiss.
Let's push the button and see what happens.
   This must be a masterpiece."

And lo, the world turns topsy-turvy,
   in other words, goes bust.
"Gosh," says the Emperor. "That was nervy,
   but, in the context, just."

III

Now there's nothing around to argue
   over: no pros or cons.
"Hey, enemy!" the Emperor shouts. "Are you
   there?" —There's no response.

Now it's pure space, devoid of mountains,
   plains, and their bric-a-brac.
"Let's," says the Emperor, "sing our anthem's
   lyrics and raise the flag."

Up flies the pennant, attended only
   by two or three evening bats.
"A victory often makes one lonely,"
   the Emperor says, then adds:

"Let's have a monument, since my stallion,
   white as a hyacinth,
is old and looks, as it were, quite alien;
   and write on the granite plinth:

" 'Tight was the enemy's precious anus.
   We, though, stood strong and firm.'

The critics might say that we went bananas.
  But we've got it all on film.

"Lest her sweet mutants still cry, the mother
  may sing them the ancient lay.
The future as such has no purpose, other
  than pushing down Replay."

At sunset, everything looks quite pretty.
  Down goes the temperature.
The world lies motionless, like a treaty
  without a signature.

The stars start to twinkle, remote and jolly.
  The eye travels rather far.
One feels a little bit melancholy.
  But there is one's cigar.

1995

Ode to Concrete

You'll outlast me, good old concrete,
as I've outlasted, it seems, some men
who had taken me, too, for a kind of street,
citing color of eyes, or mien.

So I praise your inanimate, porous looks
not out of envy but as the next
of kin—less durable, plagued with loose
joints, though still grateful to the architects.

I applaud your humble—to be exact,
meaningless—origins, roar and screech,
fully matched, however, by the abstract
destination, beyond my reach.

It's not that nothing begets its kind
but that the future prefers to court
a date that's resolutely blind
and wrapped in a petrified long skirt.

1995

At the City Dump in Nantucket

The perishable devours the perishable in broad daylight,
moribund in its turn in late November:
the seagulls, trashing the dump, are trying to outnumber
the snow, or have it at least delayed.

The reckless primordial alphabet, savaging every which
way the oxygen wall, constitutes a preface
to the anarchy of the refuse:
in the beginning, there was a screech.

In their stammering Ws one reads not hunger but
the prurience of comma-sharp talons toward
what outlasts them, or else a torn-out
page's flight from the volume's fat,

while some mad anemometer giddily spins its cups
like a haywire tea ceremony, and the Atlantic
is breasting grimly with its athletic
swells the darkening overcast.

1995–96

A Photograph

We lived in a city tinted the color of frozen vodka.
Electricity arrived from afar, from swamps,
and the apartment, at evening, seemed
smudged with peat and mosquito-bitten.
Clothes were cumbersome, betraying
the proximity of the Arctic. At the corridor's farthest end
the telephone rattled, reluctantly coming back
to its senses after the recently finished war.
The three-ruble note sported coal miners and aviators.
I didn't know that someday all this would be no more.
In the kitchen, enameled pots
were instilling confidence in tomorrow
by turning stubbornly, in a dream, into headgear or
a Martian army. Motorcars also were
rolling toward the future and were mostly black,
gray, and sometimes—the taxis—
even light brown. It's strange and not very pleasant
to think that even metal knows not its fate
and that life has been spent for the sake of an apotheosis
of the Kodak company, with its faith in prints
and jettisoning of the negatives.
Birds of Paradise sing, despite no bouncing branches.

1994

444

A Postcard

The country is so populous that polygamists and serial
killers get off scot-free and airplane crashes
are reported (usually on the evening news) only when they occur
in a wooded area—the difficulty of access
is most grievous if it's tinged with feelings for the environment.
Theaters are packed, both stalls and stage.
An aria is never sung by a single tenor:
normally they use six at once, or one that's as fat as six.
And the same goes for the government, whose offices stay lit up
through the night, working in shifts, like factories,
hostage to the census. Everything is pandemic.
What is loved by one is loved by many,
be it an athlete, a perfume, or bouillabaisse.
Therefore, no matter what you say or do *is* loyal.
Nature too seems to have taken note of the common denominator,
and whenever it rains, which is seldom, clouds linger longest over
not the army and navy stadium but the cemetery.

1994

Reveille

Birds acquaint themselves with leaves.
Hired hands roll up their sleeves.
In a brick malodorous dorm
boys awake awash in sperm.

Clouds of patently absurd
but endearing shapes assert
the resemblance of their lot
to a cumulative thought.

As the sun displays its badge
to the guilty world at large,
scruffy masses have to rise,
unless ordered otherwise.

Now let's see what one can't see
elsewhere in the galaxy:
life on earth, of which its press
makes a lot and comets less.

As a picture doomed to sneak
previews only, it's unique
even though some action must
leave its audience aghast.

Still, the surplus of the blue
up on high supplies a clue
as to why our moral laws
won't receive their due applause.

What we used to blame on gods
now gets chalked up to the odds

of small particles whose sum
makes you miss the older sham.

Yet regardless of the cause,
or effects that make one pause,
one is glad that one has been
caught this morning in between.

Painted by a gentle dawn
one is proud that like one's own
planet now one will not wince
at what one is facing, since

putting up with nothing whose
company we cannot lose
hardens rocks and—rather fast—
hearts as well. But rocks will last.

1996

Blues

Eighteen years I've spent in Manhattan.
The landlord was good, but he turned bad.
A scumbag, actually. Man, I hate him.
Money is green, but it flows like blood.

I guess I've got to move across the river.
New Jersey beckons with its sulphur glow.
Say, numbered years are a lesser evil.
Money is green, but it doesn't grow.

I'll take away my furniture, my old sofa.
But what should I do with my windows' view?
I feel like I've been married to it, or something.
Money is green, but it makes you blue.

A body on the whole knows where it's going.
I guess it's one's soul that makes one pray,
even though above it's just a Boeing.
Money is green, and I am gray.

1992

At a Lecture

Since mistakes are inevitable, I can easily be taken
for a man standing before you in this room filled
with yourselves. Yet in about one hour
this will be corrected, at your and at my expense,
and the place will be reclaimed by elemental particles
free from the rigidity of a particular human shape
or type of assembly. Some particles are still free. It's not all dust.

So my unwillingness to admit it's I
facing you now, or the other way around,
has less to do with my modesty or solipsism
than with my respect for the premises' instant future,
for those aforementioned free-floating particles
settling upon the shining surface
of my brain. Inaccessible to a wet cloth eager to wipe them off.

The most interesting thing about emptiness
is that it is preceded by fullness.
The first to understand this were, I believe, the Greek
gods, whose forte indeed was absence.
Regard, then, yourselves as rehearsing perhaps for the divine encore,
with me playing obviously to the gallery.
We all act out of vanity. But I am in a hurry.

Once you know the future, you can make it come
earlier. The way it's done by statues or by one's furniture.
Self-effacement is not a virtue
but a necessity, recognized most often
toward evening. Though numerically it is easier
not to be me than not to be you. As the swan confessed
to the lake: I don't like myself. But you are welcome to my reflection.

1994

In Memory of Clifford Brown

It's not the color blue, it's the color cold.
It's the Atlantic's color you've got no eyes for
in the middle of February. And though you sport a coat,
you're flat on your naked back upon the ice floe.

It's not a regular ice floe, meltdown-prone.
It's an argument that all warmth is foreign.
It's alone in the ocean, and you're on it alone,
and the trumpet's song is like mercury falling.

It's not a guileless tune that chafes in the darkness, though;
it's the gloveless, frozen to C-sharp fingers.
And a glistening drop soars to the zenith, so
as to glance at the space with no retina's interference.

It's not a simple space, it's a nothing, with
alts attaining in height what they lose in color,
while a spotlight is drifting into the wings,
aping the ice floe and waxing polar.

[February] 1993

450

Love Song

If you were drowning, I'd come to the rescue,
    wrap you in my blanket and pour hot tea.
If I were a sheriff, I'd arrest you
    and keep you in a cell under lock and key.

If you were a bird, I'd cut a record
    and listen all night long to your high-pitched trill.
If I were a sergeant, you'd be my recruit,
    and boy, I can assure you, you'd love the drill.

If you were Chinese, I'd learn the language,
    burn a lot of incense, wear funny clothes.
If you were a mirror, I'd storm the Ladies',
    give you my red lipstick, and puff your nose.

If you loved volcanoes, I'd be lava,
    relentlessly erupting from my hidden source.
And if you were my wife, I'd be your lover,
    because the Church is firmly against divorce.

1995

To My Daughter

Give me another life, and I'll be singing
in Caffè Rafaella. Or simply sitting
there. Or standing there, as furniture in the corner,
in case that life is a bit less generous than the former.

Yet partly because no century from now on will ever manage
without caffeine or jazz, I'll sustain this damage,
and through my cracks and pores, varnish and dust all over,
observe you, in twenty years, in your full flower.

On the whole, bear in mind that I'll be around. Or rather,
that an inanimate object might be your father,
especially if the objects are older than you, or larger.
So keep an eye on them always, for they no doubt will judge you.

Love those things anyway, encounter or no encounter.
Besides, you may still remember a silhouette, a contour,
while I'll lose even that, along with the other luggage.
Hence, these somewhat wooden lines in our common language.

1994

Flourish

O if the birds sang while the clouds felt bored by singing,
and the eye gaining blue as it traced their trill
could make out the keys in the door and, beyond, a ceiling,
and those whose address at present begins with nil.

And other than that, it's just shifting of chairs and sofas,
and flowers on walls and in vases obstruct their view.
And if there was ever a bee sans beehive or solace
with extra spores on its paws, it's you.

O if the transparent things in their blue garret
could hold their eye-dodging matter in second gear
to curdle themselves one day into a tear or star at
this end of the universe. Afterwards, everywhere.

Yet oxygen seems to be just the raw material
for lace strung out on spokes in the tsars' back yard,
and the statues freeze as though they smell a serial
Decembrist, beheaded later and breathing hard.

[Spring] 1994

MCMXCIV

Lousy times: nothing to steal and no one to steal from.
The legions return empty-handed from their faraway expeditions.
A sibyl confuses the past with the future as if she were a tree.
And actors whom nobody now applauds
forget the great lines. Forgetting, however, is the mother
of classics. Eventually these years
too will be seen as a slab of marble
with a network of capillaries (the aqueduct, the system
of taxation, the catacombs, the gossip),
with a tuft of grass bursting up from within its crack.
Whereas this was a time of poverty and of boredom,
when there was nothing to steal, still less to buy,
not to mention to offer somebody as a present.
The fault was not Caesar's, more suffering than the rest
because of the absence of luxury. Nor should one blame the stars,
since the low overcast relieves the planets of responsibility
toward the settled terrain: an absence
cannot influence a presence. And here's precisely where
a marble slab starts, because one-sidedness
is the enemy of perspective. Perhaps it's simply
that things, more quickly than men, have lost
their desire to multiply. In this white captivity.

1994

MCMXCV

The clowns are demolishing the circus. The elephants have run off to India;
tigers sell, on the sidewalk, their stripes and hoops;
under the leaky cupola, there is hanging, off the trapeze,
as in a wardrobe, the limp tuxedo
of a disillusioned magician;
and little horses, casting off their embroidered blankets, pose
for a portrait of the new engine. In the arena,
knee-deep in sawdust, clowns, wildly wielding
sledgehammers, demolish the circus.
The public is either absent or doesn't clap.
Only a miniature shaggy poodle
still yelps incessantly, feeling she's getting closer
to her sugar lump: feeling that any second
she'll be hitting nineteen ninety-five.

1995

View with a Flood

A somewhat familiar landscape, currently flooded. Currently
it's only cupolas, spires, treetops, a rainy gauze.
The throat wells up with a gurgling, passionate commentary,
but out of the bunch of words all that remains is was.

That's how, toward the end, a mirror reflects a veteran's
baldness, but not his face, let alone his butt.
Below, sheer washed-out scribblings and swallowed utterance.
Above, the snatch of a cloud. And you stand in water. Cut.

It seems the scene is somewhere in the Netherlands; very probably
prior to their having dikes, and names like Van Dam, De Vries.
Or else it's Southeast Asia, with the monsoon soberly
softening up the paddies. But you are no rice.

Clearly it rose drop by drop, for years, attempting a neverscape
whose potable swells now crave new distances: salty, vast.
And it's high time to shoulder the child like a periscope
to spot the faraway enemy battleships steaming fast.

1993

Taps

I've been reproached for everything save the weather
and in turn my own neck was seeking a scimitar.
But soon, I'm told, I'll lose my epaulets altogether
and dwindle into a little star.

I'll twinkle among the wires, a sky's lieutenant,
and hide in clouds when thunder roars,
blind to the troops as they fold their pennant
and run, pursued by the pen, in droves.

With nothing around to care for, it's of no import
if you are blitzed, encircled, reduced to nil.
Thus wetting his dream with the tumbled ink pot,
a schoolboy can multiply as no tables will.

And although the speed of light can't in nature covet
thanks, non-being's blue armor plate,
prizing attempts at making a sifter of it,
might use my pinhole, at any rate.

1994

UNCOLLECTED POEMS

POEMS

·

TRANSLATIONS

Rio Samba

Come to Rio, oh come to Rio.
Grow a mustache and change your bio.
Here the rich get richer, the poor get poorer,
here each old man is a *Sturmbahnführer*.

Come to Rio, oh come to Rio.
There is no other city with such brio.
There are phones by Siemens, and even Jews
drive around like crazy in VWs.

Come to Rio, oh come to Rio.
Here Urania rules and no trace of Clio.
Buildings ape Corbusier's beehive-*cum*-waffle,
though this time you can't blame this on the Luftwaffe.

Come to Rio, oh come to Rio.
Here every bird sings "O sole mio."
So do fish when caught, so do proud snow geese
in midwinter here, in Portuguese.

Come to Rio, oh come to Rio.
It's the Third World all right, so they still read Leo
Trotsky, Guevara, and other sirens;
still, the backwardness spares them the missile silos.

Come to Rio, oh come to Rio.
If you come in duo, you may leave in trio.
If you come alone, you'll leave with a zero
in your thoughts as valuable as one cruzeiro.

[1978]

461

A Season

The time of the hawk counting chickens, of haystacks in
fog, of small change in the pocket that burns the skin;
of the northern rivers whose ripples, freezing in a far-off mouth,
recall their sources, their godforsaken south,
and warm up for a second. The time of the daylight's ups
and downs; of the raincoat hanging, swollen boots, mishaps
in the stomach due to the soft-boiled, fallow
turnip; of winds tearing apart gonfalons
of sod-fearing warriors. The season of card-built kremlins;
days resemble each other like "when" and "where,"
and the bark is stripped by fire's shameless, trembling
fingers that grope for more than damp underwear.

[1980?]

Shorts

Epitaph for a Tyrant

He could have killed more than he could have fed
but he chose to do neither. By falling dead
he leaves a vacuum and the black Rolls-Royce
to one of the boys who will make the choice.

To a Fellow Poet

Sir, you are tough, and I am tough.
But who will write whose epitaph?

Abroad

Tickets are expensive. So are the hotels.
Names range from Rita to Juanita.
In walks a policeman, and what he tells
is "You are *persona non grata* in *terra incognita.*"

Future

High stratosphere winds with their juvenile whistle.
A thought-like white cloud, in search of mankind.
"O where are you flying" said missile to missile.
"There is nothing ahead and nothing behind."

Epitaph to a Tyrant

He was in charge of something large.
Some call it Hell; some Paradise.
Now that he's gone, let's drop the grudge:
We are still alive. Surprise! Surprise!

———

I sit at my desk
My life's grotesque.

A Postcard from France

Now that I am in Paris
I wish I were where my car is.

———

Hail the vagina
that peopled China!

———

I went to a museum,
saw art ad nauseam.

Oysters

Oysters, like girls, like pearls.
Pearls like darkness and moisture.
With pearls round her neck or amidst her curls,
my girl makes my world my oyster.

A Valentine

You are too young, and I am scared to touch you
'cause that means trouble.
Let's discover an island and build a statue
of puberty in the harbor.

An island won't know how to spell the word "daughter,"
itself an orphan.
And you will be, if you don't mind, the water
and I, your dolphin.

And all day long we will keep our eyes on each other
instead of the police-blue horizon
marred by your father.

I've seen the Atlantic.
Pretty but frantic.

I've seen the Pacific.
Nothing specific.

The Indian Ocean
stirred no emotion.

But dry land, I confess,
I like still less,

For there I find
my kind.

New York Lullaby

Buenas noches.
Don't mind the roaches.

Weather

Weather wears many dresses.
Weather's wardrobe is best.
Her parties are great successes.
But what is she like undressed?

History of the Twentieth Century
(A Roadshow)

The Sun's in its orbit,
yet I feel morbid.

Act I

PROLOGUE

Ladies and gentlemen and the gay!
All ye made of sweet human clay!
Let me tell you: you are okay.

Our show is to start without much delay,
So let me inform you right away:
this is not a play but the end of the play

that has been on for some eighty years.
It received its boos and received its cheers.
It won't last for long, one fears.

Men and machines lie to rest or rust.
Nothing arrives as quick as the Past.
What we'll show you presently is the cast

of characters who have ceased to act.
Each of these lives has become a fact
from which you presumably can subtract

but to which you blissfully cannot add.
The consequences of that could be bad
for your looks or your blood

for they are the cause, you are the effect.
Because they lie flat, you are still erect.
Citizens! Don't neglect

history! History holds the clue
to your taxes and to your flu,
to what comes out of the blue.

We'll show you battlefields, bedrooms, labs,
sinking ships and escaping subs,
cradles, weddings, divorces, slabs.

Folks! The curtain's about to rise!
What you'll see won't look like a Paradise.
Still, the Past may moisten a pair of eyes,

for its prices were lower than our sales,
for it was ruining cities: not blood cells;
for on the horizon it's not taut sails

but the wind that fails.

1900. A quiet year, you bet.
True: none of you is alive as yet.
The "00" stands for the lack of you.
Still, things are happening, quite a few.
In China, the Boxers are smashing whites.
In Russia, A. P. Chekhov writes.
In Italy, Floria Tosca screams.
Freud, in Vienna, interprets dreams.
The Impressionists paint, Rodin still sculpts.
In Africa, Boers grab the British scalps
or vice versa (who cares, my dear?).
And McKinley is re-elected here.
There are four great empires, three good democracies.
The rest of the world sports loincloths and moccasins,
speaking both figuratively and literally.
Upstaging "Umberto's" in Little Italy,
in the big one Umberto the First's shot dead.
(Not all that's written on walls is read.)
And marking the century's real turn,

Friedrich Nietzsche dies, Louis Armstrong's born
to refute the great Kraut's unholy
"God is dead" with "Hello, Dolly."
The man of the year, though, is an engineer.
John Browning is his name.
He's patented something. So let us hear
about John's claim to fame.

(John Moses Browning)

"I looked at the calendar, and I saw
that there are a hundred years to go.
That made me a little nervous
for I thought of my neighbors.
I've multiplied them one hundred times:
it came to them being all over!
So I went to my study that looks out on limes
and invented this cute revolver!"

1901. A swell, modest time.
A T-bone steak is about a dime.
Queen Victoria dies; but then Australia
repeats her silhouette and, *inter alia*,
joins the Commonwealth. In the humid woods
of Tahiti, Gauguin paints his swarthy nudes.
In China, the Boxers take the rap.
Max Planck in his lab (not on his lap
yet) is studying radiation.
Verdi dies, too. But our proud nation,
represented by Mrs. Disney, awards the world
with a kid by the name of Walt,
who'll animate the screen. Off screen,
the British launch their first submarine.
But it's a cakewalk or a Strindberg play
or Freud's *Psychopathology of Everyday
Life* that really are not to be missed!
And McKinley's shot dead by an anarchist.

The man of the year is Signore Marconi.
He is an Italian, a Roman.
His name prophetically rhymes with "Sony":
they have a few things in common.

(Guglielmo Marconi)
"In a Catholic country where the sky is blue
and clouds look like cherubs' vestiges,
one daily receives through the air a few
wordless but clear messages.
Regular speech has its boring spoils:
it leads to more speech, to violence,
it looks like spaghetti, it also coils.
That's why I've built the wireless!"

1902. Just another bland
peaceful year. They dissect a gland
and discover hormones. And a hormone
once discovered is never gone.
The Boer War (ten thousand dead) is over.
Elsewhere, kind Europeans offer
railroad chains to a noble savage.
A stork leaves a bundle in a Persian cabbage
patch, and the tag reads "Khomeini." Greeks, Serbs, Croats,
and Bulgars are at each other's throats.
Claude Monet paints bridges nevertheless.
The population of the U.S.
is approximately 76
million: all of them having sex
to affect our present rent.
Plus Teddy Roosevelt's the President.

The man of the year is Arthur Conan Doyle,
a writer. The subjects of his great toil
are a private dick and a paunchy doc;
occasionally, a dog.

(Sir Arthur Conan Doyle)
"Imagine the worst: your subconscious is
as dull as your conscience. And you, a noble
soul, grab a Luger and make Swiss cheese
out of your skull. Better take my novel
about the Hound of the Baskervilles!
It'll save a handful of your brain cells
and beef up your dreams. For it simply kills
time and somebody else!"

1903. You may start to spy
on the future. Old Europe's sky
is a little dim. To increase its dimness,
the Krupp Works in Essen erect their chimneys.
(Thus the sense of Geld breeds the sense of guilt.)
Still, more smoke comes from London, from a smoke-filled
room where with guile and passion
Bolsheviks curse Mensheviks in Russian.
Speaking of Slavs: the Serbian King and Queen
are done by local well-wishers in.
Painters Whistler, Gauguin, Pissarro are gone.
Panama rents us its Canal Zone.
While bidding their maidens bye-bye and cheerio,
the Tommies sail off to grab Nigeria
and turn it into a British colony:
to date, a nation's greatest felony
is if it's neither friend nor foe.
My father is born. So is Evelyn Waugh.

Man of the year, I am proud to say
is two men. They are brothers. Together, they
sport two heads, four legs, and four hands—which brings
us to their bird's four wings.

(The Wright Brothers)
"We are Orville and Wilbur Wright.
Our name simply rhymes with 'flight'!

471

This may partially explain
why we decided to build a plane.
Oh, there are no men in the skies, just wind!
Cities look like newspaper print.
Mountains glitter and rivers bend.
But the ultimate plane'd rather bomb than land!"

1904. Things which were in store
hit the counter. There is a war:
Japan, ever so smiling, gnashes
teeth and bites off what, in fact, is Russia's.
Other than that, in Milan police
crack local skulls. But more common is
the touch of the new safety razor blade.
The nuances of the White Slave Trade,
Mont Ste.-Victoire by Monsieur Cézanne
and other trifles under the sun,
including popular French disgust
with the Vatican, are discussed
in every Parisian cafeteria.
Radioactivity—still a theory—
is stated by Rutherford (when a particle
brings you a lordship, we call it practical).
And as the first Rolls-Royce engines churn,
Chekhov dies but Graham Greene is born,
so is George Balanchine, to upgrade the stage,
so too—though it's sin to disclose her age—
is Miss Dietrich, to daunt the screen.
And New York hears its subway's first horrid scream!

The man of the year is a Hottentot.
Southwest Africa's where he dwells.
In a German colony. And is being taught
German. So he rebels.

(A Hottentot)

"Germans to me are extremely white.
They are white in broad daylight and, what's more, at night.
Plus if you try to win minds and hearts
of locals, you don't call a black guy 'schwarz'—
'Schwarz' sounds shoddy and worse than 'black.'
Change your language and then come back!
Fly, my arrow, and hit a Hans
to cure a Hans of his arrogance!"

1905. In the news: Japan.
Which means that the century is upon
us. Diminishing the lifespan
of Russian dreadnoughts to nought, Japan
tells *urbi et orbi* it's loath to lurk
in the wings of geography. In Petersburg
those whose empty stomachs churn
take to the streets. Yet they won't return
home, for the Cossacks adore long streets.
A salesman of the Singer sewing devices greets
in Latvia the arrival of yet another
daughter, who is to become my mother.
In Spain, unaware of this clever ploy,
Pablo Picasso depicts his *Boy
with Pipe* in blue. While the shades of blond,
Swedes and Norwegians, dissolve their bond
And Norway goes independent; yet
that's not enough to turn brunette.
Speaking of things that sound rather queer,
E is equated to MC^2
by Albert Einstein, and the Fauvists
(*les fauves* is the French for unruly beasts)
unleash Henri Matisse in Paris.
The Merry Widow by Franz Lehár is
the toast of the town. Plus Transvaal gets its
constitution called by the natives "the pits."

And Greta Garbo, *la belle dame sans*
merci, is born. So are neon signs.

The man of the year, our record tells,
is neither Strindberg nor H. G. Wells,
he is not Albert Schweitzer, not Oscar Wilde:
his name is obscured by his own brainchild.

(Camouflage)
"I am what gentlemen wear in the field
when they are afraid that they may be killed.
I am called camouflage. Sporting me, each creature
feels both safer and close to Nature.
The green makes your sniper's pupil sore.
That's what forests and swamps are for.
The planet itself wears me: the design
is as French as it is divine."

1906. Time stands at ease.
Having one letter in common with
his subject, Freud adds to our bookshelf
preparing the century for itself.
On the whole, Europeans become much nicer
to each other: in Africa. Still, the Kaiser,
when asked of the growth of his navy, lies.
The Japs, for some reason, nationalize
their railroads, of whose existence none,
save several spies, had known.
Along the same, so to speak, cast-iron
lines, aping the rod of Aaron,
the Simplon Tunnel opens to hit your sight
with a smoking non-stop Vis-à-vis. Aside
from that, the civilized world condemns
night shifts (in factories, though) for dames.
Prime ministers are leapfrogging in
Russia, as though they've seen

in a crystal ball that the future keeps
no room for these kinds of leaps.
The French government warily says "Pardon"
to Captain Dreyfus, a Jew who's done
ten years in the slammer on the charge of treason.
Still, this distinction between a prison
and a Jew has no prophetic air.
The U.S. troops have a brief affair
with the Island of Cuba: their first *tête-à-tête*.
Samuel Beckett is born. Paul Cézanne is dead.

The man of the year is, Herr von Pirquet.
He stings like a honeybee.
The sting screams like Prince Hamlet's sick parakeet:
TB or not TB.

(Dr. Clemens von Pirquet)
"What I call allergy, you call rash.
I'll give you an analogy; each time you blush,
it shows you're too susceptible to something lurid,
obscene, and antiseptical to hope to cure it.
This, roughly, is the principle that guides my needle.
To prove you are invincible it hurts a little;
it plucks from your pale cheeks the blooming roses
and checks their petals for tuberculosis!"

As for 1907, it's neither here
nor there. But Auden is born this year!
This birth is the greatest of all prologues!
Still, Pavlov gets interested in dogs.
Next door Mendeleev, his bearded neighbor
who gave the universe the table
of its elements, slips into a coma.
The Cubists' first show, while Oklahoma
becomes the Union's 46th
state. Elsewhere New Zealand seeks

to fly the Union Jack. Lumière
develops the colored pictures ere
anyone else (we all owe it to him!).
The Roman Pope takes a rather dim
view of modernism: jealous Iago!
Having squashed (4–0) Detroit, Chicago
forever thirsting for *Gloria Mundi*
wins the World Series. In Swinemünde
Nicholas the Second meets the German Kaiser
for a cup of tea. That, again, is neither
here nor there, like Kalamazoo.
And Karl Hagenbeck opens his cageless zoo
where walruses swim, lions pace, birds fly
proving: animals also can live a lie.

The man of the year, you won't believe,
is Joseph Stalin, then just a thief.
He is young; he is twenty-eight;
but History's there, and he cannot wait.

    (Joseph Dzhugashvili, alias Stalin)
"My childhood was rotten, I lived in mud.
I hold up banks 'cause I miss my dad.
So to help the Party, for all my troubles
one day I took four hundred grand in rubles.
Thus far, it was the greatest heist
in the Russian history after Christ.
Some call me eager, some call me zealous;
I just like big figures with their crowd of zeroes."

1908 is a real bore
though it provides a new high in gore
by means of an earthquake in the southern part
of Calabria, Italy. Still, the world of art
tries to replace those one hundred fifty
thousand victims with things as nifty

as Monet's depiction of the Ducal Palace
in Venice, or with Isadora's galas,
or with the birth of Ian Fleming: later
his books'll sell in the millions: to fill the crater.
In the World Series, Chicago's again a winner.
In the Balkans, Bosnia and Herzegovina
are taken by Austria (for what it took
it will pay somewhat later with its Archduke).
And the fountain pen is in vogue worldwide.
The gas of helium's liquified
in Holland, which means the rising of
that flat country a bit above
sea level, which means thoughts vertical.
The King and the Crown Prince are killed in Portugal,
for horizontality's sake no doubt.
Also, the first Model T is out
in Dearborn to roam our blissful quarters
trailed by the news that General Motors
is incorporated. The English Edward
and Russia's Nicholas make an effort
to know each other aboard a yacht.
The Germans watch it but don't react—
or do, but that cannot be photographed.
And the Republic calls on William Taft.

The man of the year is a German scientist,
Paul Ehrlich. He digs bacterias
and sires immunology. All the *sapiens*
owe a lot to his theories.

(Paul Ehrlich)

"The world is essentially a community
and to syphilis, nobody has immunity.
So what I've invented beefs up your arsenal
for living a life that's a bit more personal.
I've made Salvarsan. Oh my Salvarsan!

It may cure your wife, it may cure your son,
it may cure yourself and your mistress fast.
Think of Paul Ehrlich as you pull or thrust!"

1909 trots a fine straight line.
Three Lives are published by Gertrude Stein.
(On the strength of this book, if its author vies
for the man of the year, she sure qualifies.)
Other than that, there is something murky
about the political life in Turkey:
in those parts, every man has a younger brother,
and as sultans they love to depose each other.
The same goes apparently in Iran:
Ahmed Shah tells Mohammed Ali: "*I* run
the show," though he's twelve years old.
In Paris, Sergei Diaghilev strikes gold
with his Ballets Russes. While in Honduras,
screaming the usual "God, endure us!"
peasants slaughter each other: it's a civil war.
Sigmund Freud crosses the waters for
to tell our Wonderland's cats and Alices
a few things about psychoanalysis.
But David Griffith of Motion Pictures,
boggling one's dreams, casts Mary Pickford.
The Brits, aping the Royal Dutch
Shell Company, too, legalize their touch
on the Persian oil. The Rockefeller
Foundation is launched to stall a failure
and to boost a genius. Leaving all the blight,
glitter and stuff made of Bakelite
(that heralds the Plastic Age) far below, the weary
bearded and valiant Captain Robert Peary
reaches the North Pole, and thus subscribes
virginal white to the Stars and Stripes.
Ah those days when one's thoughts were glued
to this version of the Absolute!

The man of the year is the unknown
nameless hairdresser in London Town.
Stirred either by its cumulous firmament
or by the British anthem, he invents the permanent.

(A London hairdresser)
"The Sun never sets over this Empire.
Still, all empires one day expire.
They go to pieces, they get undone.
The wind of history is no fun.
Let England be England and rule the waves!
And let those waves be real raves.
Let them be dark, red, chestnut, blond
unruffled by great events beyond!"

1910 marks the end of the first decade.
As such, it can definitely be okayed.
For there is clearly a democratic
trend. Though at times things take an erratic
turn. Like when Egypt's Prime Minister, through no fault
of his, gets murdered. But the revolt
in Albania is the work of masses
(although how they tell their oppressed from their ruling class is
anyone's guess). Plus Portugal bravely rids
itself of its King and, as he's hugged by the Brits,
becomes a republic. As for the Brits themselves,
one more generation of them learns God saves
no king, and mourning the sad demise
of Edward the Seventh, they fix their eyes
on George the Fifth. Mark Twain and Tolstoy die, too.
But Karl May has just published his *Winnetou*
in German. In Paris, they've seen and heard
Stravinsky-*cum*-Diaghilev's *Firebird*.
That causes some riot, albeit a tiny one.
Whereas the twangs of the Argentinian
tango do to the world what the feared and hailed
Halley's comet, thank heavens, failed

to do. And our watchful Congress
finds it illegal if not incongruous
to take ladies across state lines
for purposes it declines
to spell out, while Japan moves nearer
to Korea: a face that invades a mirror.

The man of the year is an architect.
His name is Frank Lloyd Wright.
Things that he's built still stand erect,
nay! hug what they stand on tight.

(Frank Lloyd Wright)
"Nature and space have no walls or doors,
and roaming at will is what man adores.
So, a builder of houses, I decide
to bring the outside inside.
You don't build them tall: you build them flat.
That's what Nature is so good at.
You go easy on bricks and big on glass
so that space may sashay your parquet like grass."

1911 is wholly given
to looking balanced albeit uneven.
In Hamburg, stirring his nation's helm
the German Kaiser (for you, Wilhelm
the Second) demands what sounds weird for some:
"A Place for Germany in the Sun."
If you were French, you would say *C'est tout.*
Yet Hitler is barely twenty-two
and things in the sun aren't so hot besides.
The activity of the sun excites
the Chinese to abolish pigtails and then
proclaim a republic with Sun Yat-sen
their first President. (Although how three hundred
twenty-five million can be handled
by a parliament, frankly, beats

me. That is, how many seats
would they have had in that great pavilion?
And even if it's just one guy per million
what would a minority of, say, 10 percent
add up to? This is like counting sand!
For this democracy has no lexicon!)
Along the same latitude, the Mexican
civil war is over, and saintly, hesitant
Francisco Madero becomes the President.
Italy, finding the Turks too coarse
to deal with, resorts to the air force
for the first time in history, while da Vinci's
Mona Lisa gets stolen from the Louvre—which is
why the cops in Paris grab Monsieur Guillaume
Apollinaire, who, though born in Rome,
writes in French, and has other energies.
Rilke prints his Duinese Elegies
and in London, suffragettes poke their black
umbrellas at Whitehall and cry Alack!

Man of the year is a great Norwegian.
The crucial word in their tongue is *Skoal*.
They are born wearing turtlenecks in that region.
When they go South, they hit the Pole.

(Roald Amundsen)
"I am Roald Amundsen. I like ice.
The world is my oyster, for it's capped twice
with ice: first, Arctical, then Antarctical.
Human life in those parts is a missing article.
O! when the temperature falls sub-zero
the eyes grow blue, the heart sincere.
There are neither doubts nor a question mark:
it's the tails of your huskies which pull and bark."

1912. Captain Robert Scott
reaches the South Pole also. Except he got

there later than Amundsen. He stares at ice,
thinks of his family, prays, and dies.
Ice, however, is not through yet.
S.S. *Titanic* hits an iceberg at
full speed and goes down. The bell grimly tolls
at Lloyd's in London. Fifteen hundred souls
are lost, if not more. Therefore, let's turn
to Romania, where Eugène Ionesco's born
or to Turkey and her Balkan neighbors: each
one of them feels an itch to reach
for the gun; on reflection, though, they abandon
the idea. It's peace everywhere. In London
by now there are five hundred movie theaters
which makes an issue of baby-sitters.
At home, after having less done than said,
Woodrow Wilson becomes the Prez. Dead-set
to pocket the dizzy with flipping coin
New Mexico and Arizona join
the Union. For all its steel mills and farms
the Union keeps currently under arms
only one hundred thousand men. That's barmy
considering five million in the Russian Army,
or four million in Germany, or the French
who, too, have as many to fill a trench.
This sounds to some like a lack of caution.
But then there is the Atlantic Ocean
between the Continent and the U.S.,
and it's only 1912, God bless,
and the hemispheres luckily seem unable
to play the now popular Cain and Abel.

The man of the year is both short and tall.
He's nameless, and well he should
stay nameless: for spoiling for us free fall
by using a parachute.

(Captain Albert Berry)

"Leaving home with umbrella? Take a parachute!
When it rains from below, that is when they shoot
down a plane and its pilot objects to die,
when you want to grab Holland or drop a spy
behind enemy lines, you need parachutes.
O, they'll be more popular than a pair of shoes.
In their soft descent they suggest a dove.
Ay! it's not only love that comes from above!"

1913. Peace is wearing thin
in the Balkans. Great powers try their pristine
routine of talks, but only soil white gloves:
Turkey and the whole bunch of Slavs
slash one another as if there is no tomorrow.
The States think there is; and, being thorough,
introduce the federal income tax.
Still, what really spells the *Pax*
Americana is the assembly line
Ford installs in Michigan. Some decline
of capitalism! No libertine or Marxist
could foresee this development in the darkest
possible dream. Speaking of such a dream,
California hears the first natal scream
of Richard Nixon. However, the most
loaded sounds are those uttered by Robert Frost
whose *A Boy's Will* and *North of Boston*
are printed in England and nearly lost on
his compatriots eyeing in sentimental
rapture the newly built Grand Central
Station, where they later would
act as though hired by Hollywood.
In the meantime, M. Proust lets his stylus saunter
the Swann's Way, H. Geiger designs his counter;
probing nothing perilous or *perdu*,
Stravinsky produces *Le Sacre du*
printemps, a ballet, in Paris, France.

But the fox-trot is what people really dance.
And as Schweitzer cures lepers and subs dive deeper,
the hottest news is the modest zipper.
Think of the preliminaries it skips
timing your lips with your fingertips!

The man of the year is, I fear, Niels Bohr.
He comes from the same place as danishes.
He builds what one feels like when one can't score
or what one looks like when one vanishes.

(Niels Bohr)
"Atoms are small. Atoms are nice.
   Until you split one, of course.
Then they get large enough to play dice
   with your whole universe.
A model of an atom is what I've built!
   Something both small and big!
Inside, it resembles the sense of guilt.
   Outside, the lunar dig."

1914
Nineteen-fourteen! Oh, nineteen-fourteen!
Ah, some years shouldn't be let out of quarantine!
Well, this is one of them. Things get raw:
In Paris, the editor of *Figaro*
is shot dead by the wife of the French finance
minister, for printing this lady's—*sans
merci*, should we add?—steamy letters to
—ah, who cares! . . And apparently it's *c'est tout*
also for a socialist and pacifist
of all times, Jean Jaurès. He who shook his fist
at the parliament, urging hot heads to cool it,
dies, as he dines, by some bigot's bullet
in a café. Ah, those early, single
shots of nineteen-fourteen! ah, the index finger
of an assassin! ah, white puffs in the blue acrylic! . . .

There is something pastoral, nay! idyllic
about these murders. About that Irish enema
the Brits suffer in Dublin again. And about Panama
Canal's grand opening. Or about that doc
and his open heart surgery on his dog . . .
Well, to make these things disappear forever,
the Archduke is arriving at Sarajevo;
and there is in the crowd that unshaven, timid
youth, with his handgun . . . *(To be continued)*

[1986?]

Swiss Blue

The place is so landlocked that it's getting mountainous.
Glaciers and summits ski 'cross air.
The stage, where they give *Corsair*,
moonlights as an airfield, and Mr. Matthews,
for all his trilby, his UFO
glasses, his bad blood pressure,
never knows whether he comes here for business or
for pleasure.

A more accurate guess is of course the lake:
the picture of tranquility and harmony.
The weather and language come from Germany,
and at times Mr. Matthews is forced to rack
his brain to find out if it truly rains,
or if he simply misspelled the epithet
for the vista. It's common to hinge one's appetite
to windowpanes.

Farmland has always been scarce; so finally
the natives rose and rolled up their quilt.
Mr. Matthews thinks it was he who built
the local Laocoön-like refinery,
since topless bathers who crave pure gold
for their torsos still gain some honey
while Mr. Matthews in the vault
minds his money.

The nightclubs reek of cheese, spices, spies,
yet the more neutral you are, the less you are finicky.
In places like this, one craves infinity
with double intensity. Hence the spires,
perspectives. And no matter how much Mr. Matthews begs

his company stay, he cannot stop it
from petering out into small, shrill, spotted
quail eggs.

[June 1990?]

Lines for the Winter Recess

A hard-boiled egg cupped by the marble cold
cracks, showing its evening yolk. The infinite
avenue gobbles up cubes, rhomboids, parallelepipeds
with preglacial appetite, unseemly in geometry.
A snowbound airfield is lapping the neither milk nor honey
of the meandering local river,
sluggish, reluctant to make the ocean.
Gentlemen, these are the good old days.
Your taxicab on the highway still overtakes a hearse.
A wolf lies down eagerly with a lamb or a lame duck, citing
low temperature. Green hues survive
nevertheless in the streetlights. The more one bungles
things overseas, the richer one's cuisine.
And if stocks don't shoot up any longer like obelisks
they still bear a resemblance to Doric columns
holding a portico tight, while beggars
murder beggars. Lyrical and myopic,
stars blink in the winter sky like suburbia after hours,
full of prayers, sensitive to a lapse
in gravity, but unconscious of its limits;
in fact, quite expanding. And yet the future
surrounding your tender issue with bathroom tiles
from Onana Republic, or manufactured locally,
is nowhere in sight. These are the good old days
still, with their quaint attractions, with their unfinished business.
Since, frankly, even a single swan
equals 2 in profile, which foils reflection
if not applause. Since your window past midnight gleams
like a Chinaman scanning the yellow pages,
stalling dreams—with their routine flat tire,
with red meat courting knives, or a pasture its herbivores.

[1992]

Fossil Unwound

6 p.m. Curling his upper lip,
Spermatozaurus Rex invades her driveway.
Music, he says, dear Helga, is just the tip
of a Steinway.
Look, he cries, at these palm trees swaying like them Chinese
characters, bent to destroy the message.
Your kid is collecting stamps, Helga!, and underneath
the album there is the Rites of Passage!
Come closer, my little Oedipus, us sphinxes we dig no vibes.
Now he quotes Torricelli and waxes lyrical:
Helga, love is like water in unconnected pipes
seeking a faucet. Isn't that a miracle?
I fought through the whole Pleistocene just to hit this swamp!
The rank was Gruppensexführer, a medal for every cushion.
I am so charged, he cries, I can stick my thumb
into my ass and suffer electrocution.
Nobody ever caught geology in the act!
Once, he brags, I knew History; it had brittle tendons.
The Monument to its Victims should stand not in front of the jail but at
the maternity ward's main entrance.
Some still go for the jugular, Helga, but hit the bow tie.
Likewise every carpet bombing is followed by cries, "Excuse us!"
There is only one way to be born, but so many ways to die.
Stars look like beggars turned lucky choosers.

[1992]

489

Bosnia Tune

As you sip your brand of scotch,
crush a roach, or scratch your crotch,
as your hand adjusts your tie,
people die.

In the towns with funny names,
hit by bullets, caught in flames,
by and large not knowing why,
people die.

In small places you don't know
of, yet big for having no
chance to scream or say goodbye,
people die.

People die as you elect
brand-new dudes who preach neglect,
self-restraint, etc.—whereby
people die.

Too far off to practice love
for thy neighbor/brother Slav,
where your cherubs dread to fly,
people die.

While the statues disagree,
Cain's version, history
for its fuel tends to buy
those who die.

As you watch the athletes score,
check your latest statement, or

sing your child a lullaby,
people die.

Time, whose sharp bloodthirsty quill
parts the killed from those who kill,
will pronounce the latter band
as your brand.

[1992]

To the President-elect

You've climbed the mountain. At its top,
the mountain and the climbing stop.
A peak is where the climber finds
his biggest step is not mankind's.

Proud of your stamina and craft
you stand there being photographed
transfixed between nowhere-to-go
and us who give you vertigo.

Well, strike your tent and have your lunch
before you stir an avalanche
of brand-new taxes whose each cent
will mark the speed of your descent.

[1992]

Robinsonade

A brand-new heaven over outlandish earth.
Newborns squall, craving a stork's attention.
Old men hide their heads under a wing, like ostriches
burying their beaks, at that, not in feathers but graying armpits.
One can go blind with this surplus of azure
innocent of a sail. Agile outriggers
look like fish gnawed down past entrail to bone.
The rowers stick out of them, betraying
the mystery of motion. A victim of shipwreck,
in twenty years I've sufficiently domesticated
this island (though perhaps it's a continent),
and the lips move all on their own, as while reading, muttering:
"Tropical vegetation, tropical vegetation."
Most likely it's due to the breeze, particularly
in the second half of the day. That is, when the already glazed
eye no longer distinguishes the print of one's own flat sole
in the sand from Friday's. This is the real beginning
of *écriture*. Or its very end. Especially

from the point of view of the whispering evening ocean.

[1994]

493

Once More by the Potomac

Here is a Jolly Good Fellow,
he's painted the White House yellow.

Here are the Mighty Generals,
bemedaled for fighting memories.

Here are the Hallowed Offices,
groggy with foggy prophecies.

Here are the Strategic Centers,
filled with their caviar emptors.

Here is our Congress, scrupulous
in making their marbles the cupola's.

And here are We, the People;
each one a moral cripple

or athlete, well trained in frowning
on someone else's drowning.

[1995]

Cabbage and Carrot

One afternoon Cabbage visited Carrot
and found Carrot wearing something transparent.

"Oh, that looks quite fancy, that looks like fun.
But where are you off to in this cellophane?"

"You really think so?" blushed Carrot. "Well, I've . . .
Well, I've been invited tonight by the Knife.

"And I've been invited—please, don't get me wrong—
alone. I don't think I can bring you along."

"The Knife!" Cabbage shouted, disgusted. "Big deal!
Who cares for that cheap imitation of steel?

"I'm going out tonight, too, without you.
Two Spoons have invited myself for a stew."

[July 1995]

At the Helmet and Sword

One evening the Fork said to the Knife:
You are my husband and I am your wife.
Let's leave our teaspoons tonight to the Ladle.
It will sing them songs and put them in the cradle
While we hit the town and perhaps have a meal.
To me this idea has a certain appeal.

To me it has also, replied the breadwinner.
But what do you think you would have for a dinner?
You know, said the Fork, I can take what you take.
I think, said the Knife, we should order a steak.
And off they went both to the Helmet and Sword,
Where I ate alone and had no dessert.

[1995]

by Marina Tsvetaeva

I will win you away from every earth, from every sky,
For the woods are my place of birth, and the place to die,
For while standing on earth I touch it with but one foot,
For I'll sing your worth as nobody could or would.

I will win you from every time and from every night,
From all banners that throb and shine, from all swords held tight;
I'll drive dogs outside, hurl the keys into dark and fog,
For in the mortal night I'm a more faithful dog.

I will win you from all my rivals, and from the one;
You will never enjoy a bridal, nor I a man.
And in the final struggle I'll take you—don't make a sound!—
From him by whom Jacob stood on the darkened ground.

But until I cross your fingers upon your breast
You possess—what a curse!—yourself: you are self-possessed;
Both your wings, as they yearn for the ether, become unfurled,
For the world's your cradle, and your grave's the world.

1916

by Marina Tsvetaeva

TO OSIP MANDELSTAM

Seeing off the beloved ones, I
Give them songs, so that we get even
Through these tokens which may supply
Them again with what I was given.

By the overgrown lane at noon
I'd lead them to the crossroads where . . .
You, the wind, sing your tireless tune,
You, the road, treat their steps with care.

Dove-blue cloud, don't shed your tears—
Spare their Sunday best for good weathers!
Coiling dragon, don't gnash your teeth,
Drop, you bullyboys, your sly razors.

You, a loitering beauty, be
A gay bride for them, do a favor:
Strain your lips for a while for me—
You'll be paid by the Precious Saviour!

Rage, bonfires, light up, dark trees,
Drive each animal to its lair!
Virgin Mary in Heaven, please,
For my passersby say a prayer.

1916

Tristia

by Osip Mandelstam

I've mastered the great craft of separation
amidst the bare unbraided pleas of night,
those lingerings while oxen chew their ration,
the watchful town's last eyelid's shutting tight.
And I revere that midnight rooster's descant
when shouldering the wayfarer's sack of wrong
eyes stained with tears were peering at the distance
and women's wailings were the Muses' song.

Who is to tell when hearing "separation"
what kind of parting this may resonate,
foreshadowed by a rooster's exclamation
as candles twist the temple's colonnade;
why at the dawn of some new life, new era
when oxen chew their ration in the stall
that wakeful rooster, a new life's town crier,
flaps its torn wings atop the city wall.

And I adore the worsted yarn's behavior:
the shuttle bustles and the spindle hums;
look how young Delia, barefooted, braver
than down of swans, glides straight into your arms!
Oh, our life's lamentable coarse fabric,
how poor the language of our joy indeed.
What happened once, becomes a worn-out matrix.
Yet, recognition is intensely sweet!

So be it thus: a small translucent figure
spreads like a squirrel pelt across a clean
clay plate; a girl bends over it, her eager
gaze scrutinizes what the wax may mean.

To ponder Erebus, that's not for our acumen.
To women, wax is as to men steel's shine.
Our lot is drawn only in war; to women
it's given to meet death while they divine.

February 1916

Achilles. Penthesilea

by Zbigniew Herbert

When Achilles with his short sword pierced the breast of Penthesilea
and as usual twisted the blade thrice in the wound, he noticed
that the queen of the Amazons was lovely.
He laid her carefully on the sand, took off her heavy helmet, unclasped her
hair,
and gently arranged her hands on her bosom. He lacked, however, the
courage
to shut her eyes.
He gave her one more, last, farewell look and, as though suddenly
overpowered
by an outer force, cried—the way neither he nor other
heroes of that great war ever cried—in a quiet, mesmeric, dawdling,
aimless voice, ebbing with grief and with
rue, whose cadence was new to the offspring of Thetis. The cry's lengthy
vowels, like
leaves, were falling upon the neck, breasts, knees of Penthesilea,
wrapping the length of her grown-cold body.
She herself was preparing for Eternal Hunts in the fathomless forests.
Her still-open eyes stared from afar at the victor
with azure, steady hatred.

[late 1980s]

501

End and Beginning

by Wisława Szymborska

After each war
somebody has to clear up,
put things in order,
by itself it won't happen.

Somebody's got to push
rubble to the highway shoulder
making way
for the carts filled up with corpses.

Someone must trudge
through muck and ashes,
sofa springs,
splintered glass,
and blood-soaked rugs.

Somebody has to haul
beams for propping a wall,
another put glass in a window
and hang the door on hinges.

This is not photogenic
and takes years.
All the cameras have left already
for another war.

Bridges are needed,
also new railroad stations.
Tatters turn into sleeves
for rolling up.

Somebody, broom in hand,
still recalls how it was.
Someone whose head was not
torn away listens nodding.
But nearby already
begin to bustle those
who'll need persuasion.

Somebody still at times
digs up from under the bushes
some rusty quibble
to add it to burning refuse.

Those who knew
what this was all about
must yield to those
who know little
or less than little,
essentially nothing.

In the grass that has covered
effects in causes
somebody must recline,
a stalk of rye in the teeth,
ogling the clouds.

1993

Selected Bibliography

VERSE

Ostanovka v pustyne [A Halt in the Desert]. New York: Chekhov Publishing Company, 1970; revised edition, Ann Arbor, MI: Ardis, 1989; reissued, St. Petersburg: Pushkin Fund, and New York: Slovo/Word Publishing House, 2000.

Joseph Brodsky: Selected Poems, translated by George L. Kline. London: Penguin Books, 1973, and New York: Harper & Row, 1974; revised and expanded edition (forthcoming).

Konets prekrasnoi epokhi [End of a Beautiful Era]. Ann Arbor, MI: Ardis, 1977; reissued, St. Petersburg: Pushkin Fund, and New York: Slovo/Word Publishing House, 2000.

Chast' rechi [A Part of Speech]. Ann Arbor, MI: Ardis, 1977; reissued, St. Petersburg: Pushkin Fund, and New York: Slovo/Word Publishing House, 2000.

A Part of Speech. New York: Farrar, Straus & Giroux, 1980, and London: Oxford University Press, 1980 [contents differ from *Chast' rechi*].

Novye stansy k Avguste [New Stanzas for Augusta]. Ann Arbor, MI: Ardis, 1983; reissued, St. Petersburg: Pushkin Fund, and New York: Slovo/Word Publishing House, 2000.

Uraniia [Urania]. Ann Arbor, MI: Ardis, 1984; reissued, St. Petersburg: Pushkin Fund, and New York: Slovo/Word Publishing House, 2000.

To Urania. New York: Farrar, Straus & Giroux, 1988, and London: Oxford University Press, 1989 [contents differ from *Uraniia*].

Chast' rechi: Izbranniye stikhi, 1962–1989 [A Part of Speech: Selected Poems] (authorized selected poems). Moscow: Khudozhestvennaia literatura, 1990.

Sochineniia Iosifa Brodskogo [The Works of Joseph Brodsky], Volumes I–IV. St. Petersburg: Pushkin Fund, 1992–96; revised edition, Volumes I–IV, 1997–98; Volume V, 1999; Volume VI, 2000; Volume VII and *Kommentarii*, by Viktor Kulle (forthcoming).

Peizazh s navodneniem [View with a Flood]. Dana Point, CA: Ardis, 1996; reissued, St. Petersburg: Pushkin Fund, 2000.

So Forth. New York: Farrar, Straus & Giroux, 1996, and London: Hamish Hamilton, 1996.

Discovery (children's book), illustrated by Vladimir Radunsky. New York: Farrar, Straus & Giroux, 1999.

Collected Poems in English. New York: Farrar, Straus & Giroux, 2000.

Iosif Brodskii: Stikhotvoreniia i poemy, edited by Lev L. Loseff. St. Petersburg: Novaia Biblioteka Poeta, Akademichesky Proekt (forthcoming).

Stikhotvoreniia dlia detei [Poems for Children] (bilingual collected poems for children), edited by Viktor Kulle (forthcoming).

The Emperor (children's book), illustrated by Vladimir Radunsky (forthcoming).

Uncollected Poems 1972–1996, translated by various hands (forthcoming).

ESSAYS

Less Than One. New York: Farrar, Straus & Giroux, 1986, and London: Viking Press, 1986 [LTO].

Watermark. New York: Farrar, Straus & Giroux, 1992, and London: Hamish Hamilton, 1992.

On Grief and Reason. New York: Farrar, Straus & Giroux, 1996, and London: Hamish Hamilton, 1996 [GR].

PLAYS

Mramor. Ann Arbor, MI: Ardis, 1984.

Marbles, translated by Alan Myers and the author. Cambridge, England: Cambridge University Press, Comparative Criticism, Volume 7, 1985; reissued by Farrar, Straus & Giroux, 1989.

Democracy! Act I (translated by Alan Myers): *Granta,* Volume 30 (Winter 1990); Act II (translated by the author): *Partisan Review,* Spring 1993; revised edition, *Performing Arts Journal* (Volume XVIII, 1996). The Russian original appears in *Sochineniia Iosifa Brodskogo.*

ANTHOLOGIES

Editor, with Carl Proffer, *Modern Russian Poets on Poetry: Blok, Mandelstam, Pasternak, Mayakovsky, Gumilev, Tsvetaeva* (translated by Alexander Golubov). Ann Arbor, MI: Ardis, 1976.

Editor, with Alan Myers, *An Age Ago: A Selection of Nineteenth Century Russian Poetry* (translated by Alan Myers). New York: Farrar, Straus & Giroux, 1988.

CRITICAL STUDIES CITED IN THE NOTES

Lev Loseff, ed. *Poetika Brodskogo.* Tenafly, NJ: Hermitage, 1986 [PB].

—— and Valentina Polukhina, eds. *Brodsky's Poetics and Aesthetics.* London: Macmillan, 1990 [P&A].

——. *Joseph Brodsky: The Art of a Poem.* London: Macmillan and New York: St. Martin's Press, 1999 [AP].

Piotr Vail, ed. *Peresechennaia mestnost': Puteshestviia s kommentariiami.* Moscow: Nezavisimaia Gazeta, 1995 [PM].

Vladimir Vishniak. "Joseph Brodsky and Mary Stuart." Alexander Herzen Centre for Soviet, Slavic and East European Studies, Department of Russian Studies, University of Manchester, Manchester, England; Working Paper #4, April 1994 [VV].

Notes

Notes appearing in Joseph Brodsky's original collections are identified with [au]; those supplied by the translators with [trans]; those drawn from the work of Lev Loseff, the editor of the *Biblioteka poeta* edition of Brodsky's work in Russian [LL]. Other notes are derived from sources referred to by abbreviations in the bibliography. Transliterations follow the simplified Library of Congress system for transliterating Russian. Sources for the Russian poems refer to the Ardis editions listed in the bibliography, although many of the translations were made from manuscript versions and predate the originals' publication in book form. Many of the translations were substantially revised between first publication and appearance in book form. The dates of composition that Brodsky provided for his English editions have been preserved unless they were known to be incorrect; alternative dates indicated by other sources are provided in brackets. The reader is warned that the author himself was often approximate about dating, and the published dates of his poems are sometimes inconsistent.

A Part of Speech

The translations appearing in *A Part of Speech* were commissioned by the author in consultation with Barry Rubin and Nancy Meiselas of Farrar, Straus and Giroux. They were reviewed and in some cases substantially revised by the author.

The following author's note appeared in the original edition:

Since a translation, by definition, lags behind the original work, a good number of poems included in this collection belong chronologically in *Selected Poems* [translated by George L. Kline], published in 1973. The reason for my putting them into this book, however, is not so much a desire to provide the reader with the complete picture as an attempt to supply this book with a semblance of context, with a semblance of continuum.

I would like to thank each of my translators for his long hours of work in rendering my poems into English. I have taken the liberty of reworking some of the translations to bring them closer to the original, though perhaps at the expense of their smoothness. I am doubly grateful to the translators for their indulgence.

My thanks also to Ann Frydman, Masha Vorobiova, and Stephen White for preparing interlinear versions for this book. And I gratefully acknowledge my debt to Jonathan Aaron, Nancy Meiselas, Margo Picken, David Rieff, Pat Strachan, Peter Viereck, and, above all, to Barry Rubin and Derek Walcott, for their suggestions, proofreading, and assistance with certain references. My special thanks go to the John Simon Guggenheim Foundation, which made it possible for me to complete this collection.

The original edition was divided into two sections: "A Song to No Music," which ended with the poem "Odysseus to Telemachus," and "A Part of Speech."

Six Years Later: *Sem'let spustia* (also appears as *Shest'let spustia*) from *Ostanovka v pustyne*. This translation, by Richard Wilbur, first appeared in *The New Yorker*, January 1, 1979.

Anno Domini: *Anno Domini* from *Ostanovka v pustyne*. This translation, by Daniel Weissbort, first appeared in *The Iowa Review* (4:3), Summer 1973.

The speaker is a fictional deputy in an unnamed Roman outpost.

Cynthia: Cynthia shares her name with the addressee of the love lyrics of the Latin poet Sextus Propertius (c. 50 B.C.–c. 60 B.C.).

"a coal under a cold font": i.e., a baptismal font.

Autumn in Norenskaia: *Osen' v Norenskoi* did not appear in the Ardis editions. It can be found in *Sochineniia Iosifa Brodskogo*, Volume II, p. 351. This translation, by Daniel Weissbort with the author, first appeared in *The Iowa Review* (9:4), Autumn 1978.

Norenskaia is a village of fourteen dwellings in the Archangel region of the USSR, where the author temporarily resided in 1964–65 [au].

"A second Christmas by the shore": *"Vtoroe Rozhdestvo na beregu"* from *Konets prekrasnoi epokhi*. This translation, by George L. Kline, first appeared in *Paintbrush* (IV: 7/8), Spring and Autumn 1977.

Pontus: The Pontus Euxinus, the ancient name of the Black Sea [au]. Pontus was the place of Ovid's exile.

Homage to Yalta: *Posviashchaetsia Ialte* from *Konets prekrasnoi epokhi*. This translation, by Barry Rubin, first appeared in *Kontinent 3* (1978).

I. M. I. Chigorin (1850–1908): Russian chess player [LL].

III. Košice: The eastern front crossed near the city of Košice in Slovakia in early 1944 [LL].

Stechkin: Soviet semiautomatic pistol developed after World War II.

Parabellum: Or Lugar, standard-issue semiautomatic pistol of the German Army during World War II.

IV. Richard Sorge (1895–1944): German Communist and Soviet spy in Japan during World War II; subject of the 1961 film *Who Are You, Mr. Sorge?*. Max Klausen was his radio operator [LL].

V. "apotheosis of the meaningless": A reference to *The Apotheosis of Groundlessness* (1905), by the philosopher Lev Shestov [LL].

Monument: In Prymorsky Park in Yalta there is an obelisk commemorating Lenin's Crimea Decree of 1920.

A Song to No Music: *Pen'e bez muzyki* from *Konets prekrasnoi epokhi*. This translation, by David Rigsbee, first appeared as "Singing without Music" in *Vogue*, February 1975; subsequently revised with the author.

stanza 13. "tongue of native asps": This reference to trees in Russia is taken from an epigram by Ivan Turgenev characterizing the language used by a nineteenth-century Russian translator of Shakespeare [au].

The End of a Beautiful Era: *Konets prekrasnoi epokhi* from *Konets prekrasnoi epokhi.* This translation, by David Rigsbee, first appeared in *Kontinent* 1 (1976); subsequently revised with the author. This version incorporates revisions the author made subsequent to the publication of *A Part of Speech.*

stanza 6. Era of Deeds: *epokha svershenii,* a cliché of Soviet propaganda, denoting the current period of Russian history, the 1960s [LL].

Lobachevsky: See note to "Kellomäki," XI, p. 523.

stanza 7. "five-sixths": The Soviet Union, the largest country in the world at the time, constituted one-sixth of the earth's landmass, a fact often noted in Soviet textbooks [LL].

stanza 10. "fallen from cradles and fallen from saddles": In Russian, a pun on the word *liul'ka,* which means "cradle" and, in a Ukrainian dialect used by Gogol in the story "Taras Bulba," "pipe." In Gogol's story (1835), the Cossack leader Taras Bulba falls into the hands of his enemy while dismounting to retrieve his beloved *liul'ka* [Barry Rubin].

"plenty of saucers, there is no one to turn tables with": A reference to séances.

Rurik: A ninth-century Norseman who, according to the Russian *Primary Chronicle,* was invited by the Russian tribes around Novgorod to come and rule, and is considered the founder of the first Russian princely dynasty [au].

Lithuanian Divertissement: *Litovskii divertisment* from *Konets prekrasnoi epokhi.* This translation, by Alan Myers, first appeared in *The New York Review of Books,* October 12, 1978.

I. "tyrant's brownstone villa": The house of Antanas Snechkus (1903–74), the general secretary of the Lithuanian Communist Party [Tomas Venclova].

"statue of a bard": The Lithuanian writer Maironis (1862–1932), whose tomb is in Kaunas [TV].

II. Liejyklos: A street in Vilnius ("Foundry Street") [au].

Catherine's crosses: Filigreed iron crosses atop the twin towers of St. Catherine's Church in Vilnius.

III. Café Neringa: A popular café among the Vilnius intelligentsia of the 1960s and 1970s [TV].

IV. St. George: The Lithuanian coat of arms, banned in Soviet times, bears an image of a knight with a sword on horseback, reminiscent of St. George [TV].

Vytautas: Vytautas the Great (*c.* 1350–1430), Grand Duke and most famous monarch of early Lithuania [au].

V. *Amicum-philosophum de melancholia, mania et plica polonica:* The Latin title of an eighteenth-century treatise in the Vilnius library. The title means "To a philosopher friend, on madness, melancholy, and *plica polonica.*" According to *Taber's Cyclopedic Medical Dictionary, plica polonica* is "tangled matted hair in which crusts and vermin are embedded" [au].

VI. Palanga: Renowned Lithuanian seaside resort on the Baltic coast [au].

VII. The Dominicans: A Catholic cathedral in Vilnius [au].

"God's whorled ear": The cathedral's curved, baroque interior [TV].

On Love: *Liubov'* from *Konets prekrasnoi epokhi*. This translation, by Daniel Weissbort, first appeared in *The Iowa Review* (4:3), Summer 1973; subsequently revised with the author.

I Sit by the Window: *"Ia vsegda tverdil, chto sud'ba—igra"* from *Konets prekrasnoi epokhi*. This translation, by Howard Moss, first appeared in *The New Yorker*, June 4, 1979.

Nature Morte: *Natiurmort* from *Konets prekrasnoi epokhi*. This translation, by George L. Kline, first appeared in *Saturday Review*, August 12, 1972; also in *Joseph Brodsky: Selected Poems*.

Epigraph: "Death will come and it will have your eyes," from Pavese's poem of the same name (1950).

"Mary now speaks to Christ," etc.: In an epigraph to "Requiem," X (1940), Anna Akhmatova also alludes to an apocryphal conversation between Mary and the dead Christ, quoting the Russian Orthodox liturgy for Holy Saturday in which Christ tells his mother not to weep over his dead body [LL].

X. "woman": In Russian, the antiquated, vocative form of "woman" is used, echoing biblical language [LL].

December 24, 1971: *24 dekabria 1971 goda* from *Chast' rechi*. This translation, by Alan Myers with the author, first appeared in *The New York Review of Books*, December 21, 1978.

stanza 6. "sounding / chimney pots on the roof": In Russian, chimney pots are called chimney "pipes," *truby*.

"Herod drinks": "Herod" in Russian colloquially denotes a brutal person; "my Herod drinks all the time" would be understood as a wife's complaint about her husband [LL].

To a Tyrant: *Odnomu tiranu* from *Chast' rechi*. This translation, by Alan Myers, first appeared in *The New Yorker*, July 17, 1978, and *Bananas* (UK) 11, Summer 1978.

The Funeral of Bobò: *Pokhorony Bobo* from *Chast' rechi*. This translation, by Richard Wilbur, first appeared in *The Atlantic Monthly*, January 1975.

In a footnote to his collection *The Mind Reader: New Poems* (1976), Mr. Wilbur thanks Carl R. Proffer for linguistic aid in translating this poem from the Russian.

I. "mount a butterfly," etc.: A play on Pushkin's comparison, in "The Bronze Horseman," of St. Petersburg's Admiralty tower with a needle [LL].

II. Carlo Rossi (1775–1849): leading Neoclassical architect of early nineteenth-century St. Petersburg; a street he designed in central Petersburg is named after him.

IV. "You were all things": A parody of the Communist "Internationale," "who was nothing will become all" [LL].

"to these round eyes," etc.: A reference to the scene of a knife cutting an eye in Luis Buñuel's *"Un Chien andelou"* (1928) [LL].

Letters to a Roman Friend: *Pis'ma rimskomu drugu* from *Chast' rechi*. This translation, by George L. Kline, first appeared in the *Los Angeles Times*, June 16, 1974.

The Russian has the subtitle "from Martial." See also Ovid's verse-epistles from exile, *Tristia* (A.D. 12) and *Epistulae ex Ponto* (A.D. 17/18) [Viktor Kulle].

Postumus: Latin name meaning "he who was after," usually given to a Roman child born after his father's death. Horace wrote several odes to his friend Postumus [LL].

III. "lies a merchant from Asia," etc.: A paraphrase from Simonides of Ceos (c. 556–468 B.C.), "Epitaph to a Cretan Merchant": "I, Brotachos, a Gortynian of Crete, lie here, where I came not for this end, but to trade" (*Greek Anthology*, 7.254a) [LL].

IV. "If one's fated to be born," etc.: Martial spent his last days in his homeland, Bilbilis, in the far Roman province of Spain.

V. "find yourself a proper husband": See Martial, *Epigrams*: "Find yourself a drunken poet" (XII. 61) [LL].

IX. Pontus: See note to "A second Christmas by the shore," p. 508.

Nunc Dimittis: *Sreten'e* from *Chast' rechi*. This translation, by George L. Kline, first appeared in *Vogue*, September 1973; also in *Joseph Brodsky: Selected Poems*.

This poem is based on the account in Luke 2:22-36, considered the point of transition from the Old Testament to the New. The title in the original, *"Sreten'e"* (literally, "The Meeting," referring to Simeon's meeting with the infant Christ), denotes the church festival celebrated as the Feast of the Presentation in the Temple. Simeon's speech in the fifth to seventh stanzas is the *Nunc dimittis* ("Now lettest thou thy servant depart . . .") found in most Christian liturgies. The date of the poem, February 16 (on the Russian New Calendar, or February 3 on the Old), is the Feast Day of Saints Simeon and Anna, and hence the name day of Anna Akhmatova [au].

Odysseus to Telemachus: *Odissei Telemaku* from *Chast' rechi*. This translation, by George L. Kline, first appeared in *The New York Review of Books*, April 5, 1973; also in *Joseph Brodsky: Selected Poems*.

See Umberto Saba's "Letter" (1947-48), translated by Brodsky before his emigration [Viktor Kulle], and *Itaka* (1993) from *Peizazh s navodneniem*.

"An autumn evening in the modest square": *"Osennii vecher v skromnom gorodke"* from *Chast' rechi*. This translation, by George L. Kline, first appeared in *Confrontation* 8, Spring 1974.

In *Peresechennaia mestnost'* the author identified the setting of this poem as Ann Arbor, Michigan.

stanza 3. "to fish for men": See Matthew 4:19, *et al.*: "Follow me, and I will make you fishers of men."

stanza 4. "like some Eccles/iastes": See Ecclesiastes 12:3: "those that look out of the windows be darkened" [LL].

1972: *1972 god* from *Chast' rechi*. This translation, by Alan Myers with the author, first appeared in *The Kenyon Review* 1:1, Winter 1979.

stanza 3. "those who'll carry you out besiege the doorway": A paraphrase of the Apostle Peter's words to Sapphira in Acts 5:9 [au].

stanza 4. "Well met, then, joyful, young, unfamiliar/tribe!" is a paraphrase of a line of Pushkin addressed to a grove of young trees that have sprung up next to three old pines he used to see during his two years in exile [au]: ". . . I visit once again" (1835). (See *An Age Ago.*)

"Ivan's queen in her tower": A motif of Russian folktales [au].

stanza 6. "even a cuckoo's crooning in darkness": In Russian folklore, the number of calls emitted by a cuckoo predicts the number of years that a person has left to live [au].

stanza 7. "metallic brow": The Russian phrase *mednyi lob* has the figurative meaning of "numskull" [au].

stanza 8. "Remove, dear chums, your faces! / Let me out into open valley!": A parody of a folk song or ballad.

stanza 9. "Dragged my fool": A paraphrase of a standard Russian obscenity [au].

"Had a stable ground, / fashioned a lever": A reference to Archimedes' claims on behalf of the lever.

stanza 10. "Listen, my boon brethren": An echo of Prince Igor's address to his warriors in the *Lay of Igor's Campaign*, the twelfth-century Old Russian epic [au].

stanza 11. "as/with Prince Igor's helmet": In the *Lay*, Igor expresses an urge to drink of the Don from his helmet [au].

In the Lake District: *V ozernom kraiu* from *Chast' rechi*. This translation, by George L. Kline, first appeared in the *Bryn Mawr Alumnae Bulletin*, Fall 1974.

The Butterfly: *Babochka* from *Chast' rechi*. This translation, by George L. Kline, first appeared in *The New Yorker*, March 15, 1976.

Torso: *Tors* from *Chast' rechi*. This translation, by Howard Moss, first appeared in *The New Yorker*, September 25, 1978.

Lagoon: *Laguna* from *Chast' rechi*. This translation, by Anthony Hecht, first appeared in *The Paris Review* 77, Winter–Spring 1980.

VII. "winged lion": Emblem of Venice, symbol of St. Mark the Evangelist.

"northern sphinxes of renown": The two sphinxes of King Amenhotep III on the Neva esplanade, in front of the Academy of Arts in Leningrad [au].

"The classical ballet, let's say, is beauty's keep": *"Klassicheskii balet est' zamok krasoty"* from *Chast' rechi*. This translation, by Alan Myers with the author, first appeared in *A Part of Speech*.

stanza 4. "sang hey nonny-nonny": In Russian, *bobeobi*, a neologism borrowed from Velemir Khlebnikov's "The Lips' Song Was Bobeobi" (1908-9) [LL].

On the Death of Zhukov: *Na smert' Zhukova* from *Chast' rechi*. This translation, by George L. Kline, first appeared in *Kontinent* 1 (1976).

This poem was inspired by Derzhavin's celebrated poem *Snegir'* ("The Bullfinch"), written in May 1800 on the death of Count A. V. Suvorov, commander of the Russian armies under Catherine the Great. The bullfinch's song is supposed to resemble the sound of a fife. The meter of both poems suggests the slow interrupted beat of a military funeral march [au].

Mexican Divertimento: *Meksikanskii divertisment* from *Chast' rechi*. This translation, by Alan Myers with the author, first appeared in *The New York Review of Books*, December 7, 1978.

This poem employs meters that are standard in Spanish poetry. In particular, "1867" is set to the rhythm of "El Choclo," an Argentine tango; "Mérida" is in the meter used by the fifteenth-century

Spanish poet Jorge Manrique; and "Mexican Romancero" has the traditional poetic form of the Spanish ballad [au].

Cuernavaca: I: Maximilian I (1832-67), the brother of the Austrian Emperor Franz Joseph, was installed by Napoleon III as Emperor of Mexico from 1864 to 1867. He was executed by the followers of the Mexican liberal Benito Juárez.

"shake down a rain of pears": In Russian, *okolachivaiut grushi*, a vulgar expression meaning to waste time.

II. "Me and my marmot friend": A reference to Beethoven's song "Marmotte" (Opus 52, number 7), to a text by Goethe [au].

1867: "tango": See Brodsky, "Spoils of War": " 'La Comparsita' [is] the greatest musical work of this century, as far as I am concerned," etc. (XIII [GR]).

In the Russian original there is a section here called "In the Hotel Continental."

Mexican Romancero, II: "to stop an instant that's fair": See note to "New Life," stanza 7, p. 525.

IV: "Guardian Angel": Atop Mexico City's Monumento a la Independencia there is a golden winged victory known as "El Ángel."

To Evgeny: In *Peresechennaia mestnost'* the author identified Evgeny as the Russian poet Evgeny Rein (b. 1935).

Epigraph: Pushkin, "To Viazemsky" (1826). (See *An Age Ago*.)

stanza 4. "Cortés's unicorns": A type of cannon [au].

The Thames at Chelsea. *Temza v Chelsi* from *Chast' rechi*. This translation, by David Rigsbee, first appeared in *The New Yorker*, November 28, 1977.

The author identified this as the poem with which he began to depart from the strict accentual-syllabic tradition of Russian meters, in this case by gravitating to French syllabic forms [PM].

I. Thomas More: A gilded statue of the English humanist Thomas More stands in the gardens of Cheyne Walk, Chelsea, facing the Thames.

II. "Agrippa's water pipe": The consul Marcus Vipsanius Agrippa (63-12 B.C.E.) built the first aqueduct in Rome; in Russian "darken" can mean "overshadow" or "eclipse" [LL].

"an ensemble of monotonous / drainpipe flutes": See Vladimir Mayakovsky, "And could you?" (1913): "And you? Could you play a nocturne on a drainpipe flute?" [LL].

III. "the milk will always stand sedately white": See the closing of George Orwell's *Homage to Catalonia* (1938): "Don't worry, the milk will be on the doorstep tomorrow morning," etc. [Barry Rubin].

A Part of Speech: *Chast' rechi* from *Chast' rechi*. This translation, by Daniel Weissbort, first appeared in *Poetry* (March 1978); subsequently revised with the author; revised I, II, IV, VII, X, XIII, XIV, and XV first appeared in *The New York Review of Books*, December 20, 1979.

The Russian original of this sequence contains twenty poems, in a different order.

"The North buckles metal": "darkens like Scott": Robert Falcon Scott (1868-1912): Antarctic explorer who died in a blizzard having nearly concluded his expedition to the South Pole.

"From nowhere with love": "resting on whalelike backs": A reference to the myth that the world is supported on the backs of whales [au].

"I recognize this wind": "that eager man's campaign": A reference to the *Lay of Igor's Campaign*, see note to "1972," stanzas 10 and 11, p. 512. The language of this poem is characterized by heroic imagery from the Russian-Tartar medieval wars [LL].

"A navy-blue dawn": "that parallel-/ line stuff": See note to "Lobachevsky," "Kellomäki," XI, p. 523.

". . . and when 'the future' is uttered": "a seraphic 'do' ": As in "do-re-mi."

"Not that I am losing my grip": "the usual zebra": A striped crosswalk.

Lullaby of Cape Cod: *Kolybel'naia Treskovogo Mysa* from *Chast' rechi*. This translation, by Anthony Hecht, under the title "Cape Cod Lullaby," first appeared in *Columbia* 4, Spring–Summer 1980.

In *Peresechennaia mestnost'* the author identified this as an occasional poem for the American bicentennial. He elsewhere made reference, regarding the title, to a Charlie Parker recording of "Lullaby of Birdland" that he knew before his emigration.

II. "I beheld new heavens, I beheld the earth made new": These lines are an ironic echo of Isaiah 65:17—"For, behold, I create new heavens and a new earth: and the former shall not be remembered, nor come into mind" [au].

IV. Lobachevsky: Nikolai Lobachevsky (1792–1856): See note to "Kellomäki," XI, p. 523.

VII. "Archimedean laws": See note to "1972," stanza 9, p. 512.

VIII. (and, again, in X): "Preserve these words": Echo of a Mandelstam poem, dedicated and addressed to Anna Akhmatova, which begins "Do preserve what I've said for its taste of misfortune and smoke" [au].

December in Florence: *Dekabr' vo Florentsii* from *Chast' rechi*. This translation, by the author, first appeared in *The New York Review of Books*, May 1, 1980.

The epigraph is from Akhmatova's poem "Dante" (1936) [au].

II. "architecture of Paradise": Michelangelo called Lorenzo Ghiberti's bronze doors of the Baptistery in Florence the "Gates of Paradise."

IV. "the unwitting pen/strays into drawing—while tackling an/'M'—some eyebrows": Alludes to the medieval notion that facial features represent letters in the phrase OMO DEI [au]; see *Purgatorio*, XXIII, 32–3.

IX. "six bridges": Six bridges cross the Neva River in St. Petersburg.

In England: *V Anglii* from *Uraniia*. The translations, by Alan Myers, of "York," "Brighton Rock," and "East Finchley," first appeared in *The New Yorker*, June 19, 1978, February 6, 1978, and May 22, 1978, respectively; "North Kensington" and "Soho" first appeared in *Bananas* (UK) 11, Summer 1978.

The sections appear in a different order in the Russian original.

"Three Knights": "The abbey": "The abbey is a composite image, but the impression is from the Pembroke Rotunda in the City of London" [PM].

"York": "I have known three great poets": Yeats, Frost, and Brecht (see *Later Auden*, by Edward Mendelson [New York: Farrar, Straus & Giroux, 1999], p. 447).

Chester: Chester Kallman (1921-75): Friend of Auden.

Plato Elaborated: *Razvivaia Platona* from *Uraniia*. This translation, by George L. Kline, first appeared in *The New Yorker*, March 12, 1979.

See Richard Wilbur, "Lamarck Elaborated." The author translated Wilbur into Russian in 1971.

I. Fortunatus: Latin name meaning "born lucky."

Mario: Mario Cavaradossi, the hero of Puccini's opera *Tosca*.

Letters from the Ming Dynasty: *Pis'ma dinastii Min'* from *Uraniia*. This translation, by Derek Walcott, first appeared in *The New Yorker*, January 28, 1980. This version incorporates a minor revision the author made subsequent to the publication of *A Part of Speech*.

The Rustle of Acacias: *Shorokh akatsii* from *Uraniia*. This translation, by Daniel Weissbort with the author, first appeared in *The Iowa Review* 9:4, Autumn 1978.

Another source dates this poem 1974-75.

Elegy: For Robert Lowell: First appeared in *The New Yorker*, October 31, 1977.

This poem was written in English [au].

This was the author's first poem in English to be collected in a book. An elegy written in English for W. H. Auden was published in *The New York Review of Books*, December 12, 1974, and reproduced in *W. H. Auden: A Tribute*, edited by Stephen Spender (London: Weidenfeld and Nicolson, 1974, and New York: Macmillan, 1975), but not collected by the author. Light verse in English also appeared in several small magazines in the 1970s (see, "North is South, and another couple" and "East 89th," *The Ghent Quarterly* 1, Summer 1975, and "Four Sonnets," *Empyria*, Vol. 1, Spring 1979).

Strophes: *Strophy* from *Uraniia*. This translation, by David McDuff, first appeared in *Stand* (UK) 21:1, 1979/1980, and *Vogue*, May 1980; subsequently revised with the author. This version incorporates revisions the author made subsequent to the publication of *A Part of Speech*.

IX. "the stick": A reference to the Russian expression to do something "from under the stick," similar to the English "under the gun."

"the Fatal Sister": From Greek mythology, one of the three Parcae, or Fates.

X. "thirty-third letter": In the Russian alphabet the thirty-third letter is Я [*ia*] [au].

XIII. Elzevir: A family of type, named for a seventeenth-century Dutch printing dynasty.

San Pietro: *San-P'etro* from *Uraniia*. This translation, by Barry Rubin, first appeared in *The New Yorker*, April 30, 1979.

San Pietro: A solitary island on the eastern edge of Venice.

I. "in a deaf-and-dumb corner/of the northern Adriatic": The author parodies a line from his own translation of Umberto Saba's "Three Poems for Linuccia" (1946): "in a remote corner of the wild Adriatic" [LL].

Victor Emmanuel II (1820-78): The first king of a united Italy, represented in an equestrian statue in front of the Londra Hotel.

Gorbunov and Gorchakov: *Gorbunov i Gorchakov* from *Ostanovka v pustyne*. A full translation of *Gorbunov and Gorchakov* was not completed in time for *A Part of Speech*. This translation was eventually appended to *To Urania* in 1989, although it belongs with the earlier work appearing in *A Part of Speech*, hence we move it forward here. Cantos II and X also appeared in George L. Kline's translation in *Joseph Brodsky: Selected Poems*. A translation by Harry Thomas first appeared in *The Paris Review* 93, Autumn 1984; subsequently revised by the author and this editor.

In the Russian original, Cantos V and X employ a different rhyme scheme.

Gorbunov (from the Russian *gorbun*, "hunched") and Gorchakov (from *gor'kii*, "bitter") are patients in a "psychiatric hospital" on the outskirts of Leningrad [au].

I. stanza 1. "dreams": The Russian *son* means both "sleep" and "dream" [au].

"mushrooms": In Russian, *lisichki*, chanterelles, a mushroom commonly hunted in the environs of St. Petersburg.

stanza 3. Mickiewicz: The patient shares his name with Adam Mickiewicz (1798-1855), the great Polish Romantic poet.

stanza 6. The Crosses: A prison in Leningrad [au].

"under glass": Reference to prison slang for a cell in which the prisoner can only stand [LL].

II. stanza 2. Khomutov and Hamilton: According to Russian legend, the Khomutov family is descended from the Scotsman Thomas Hamilton, borrowing their name from the Russian word *khomut*, a kind of yoke [LL].

Peter: Tsar Peter the Great (1672-1725) built St. Petersburg on the swamps of the Neva delta.

khariton: An ordinary Russian name.

stanza 9. "Five months spent in a wasteland": See Revelation 9:5-6 [LL].

"Fiery Angel": See Revelation 16:2 [George L. Kline].

III. stanza 4. "Jewish telescope": Reference to an anti-Semitic joke about a "Jewish rifle," which has a twisted barrel for shooting around corners [LL].

IV. stanza 5. "A man ... a well": See Genesis 37:22-24 [LL].

V. stanza 6. Ivan Aivazovsky (1817-1900): Seascape painter [au].

"moved upon the clouds": See Genesis 1:2.

VI. stanza 4. "war/in the Crimea—smoke is all about": A Russian expression denoting an unclear situation [LL].

Ivan Krylov (1768-1844): Satirist and poet, famous for his fables [au].

Liubov Orlova (1902-75): Film star [au].

Galina Ulanova (1910-98): Dancer with the Bolshoi Ballet [au].

VII. stanza 3. Opochka: Provincial city in the Pskov region.

stanza 4. "traitor": In Russian, *seksot*, Soviet bureaucratic abbreviation for "secret informer" (*sekretny sotrudnik*) [LL].

stanza 6. "one leg of the compass": See John Donne, "A Valediction Forbidding Mourning" (1611), which the author translated into Russian, along with several other poems of the English metaphysical school, in the late 1960s.

stanza 8. Karakulan furs: Fur from a sheep native to central Asia.

IX. stanza 6. "the Greek/philosopher": Heraclitus (c. 540–c. 480 B.C.).

Mikhail Lomonosov (1711–65): Russian scientist, scholar, poet [au].

X. stanza 5. "a star that climbs above the field/. . . interlocutor": Paraphrase from Lermontov, "I walk out alone into the darkness" (1841) [LL]. (See *An Age Ago*.)

XI. stanza 4. " 'Hoist-or-heave' ": A reference to a phrase from the jargon of longshoremen, *Podniat' i brosit', vira ili maina*—"It's all the same to us whether we pick it up or throw it back" [LL].

stanza 6. "That palindrome": The Marxist formula "Existence determines consciousness." (See Brodsky, "Less Than One," 1 [LTO].)

"Panmongolism! There's a loaded term": Parody of Soloviev's epigraph to Blok's poem "The Scythians" [au].

XII. stanza 1. "to quote the proverb": The Russian proverb "Pour me some more of that cabbage soup, but this time make it more watery" [LL].

stanza 2. "bromide": Bromide was said to be given to Soviet psychiatric patients to dampen their sexual drive.

stanza 5. "fart/upon his head": A play on a Russian expression of hatred [LL].

stanza 7. "bad infinity": *Durnaia beskonechnost'*, a phrase originating with Hegel (*schlechte Unendlichkeit*), which entered Soviet jargon when it was quoted by Lenin in his *Philosophical Notebooks* [VV]. In Hegel's conception, a "true infinity" is a self-sustaining logical system; a "bad infinity" is an infinite sequence of inferences or connections.

stanza 9. Elbrus: The highest peak in the Caucasus [au].

XIII. stanza 4. "like knights in chain-mail coats": From Pushkin's "Tale of Tsar Saltan" [au].

"a lilac stripe": A "blue horizontal stripe, at eye level, run[s] unfailingly across the whole country, like the line of an infinite common denominator" (Brodsky, "Less Than One," 1 [LTO]).

XIV. stanza 5. "a Kuban Cossack's": Reference to the Soviet romantic comedy *Kuban Cossacks,* by I. Pyr'ev, which produced a popular song about a fierce Cossack, "eagle of the steppes" [LL].

To Urania

Translations, where not made by the author, were commissioned and revised by the author.

May 24, 1980: *"Ia vkhodil vmesto dikogo zveria v kletku"* from *Uraniia*. This translation, by the author, first appeared in *The Times Literary Supplement*, May 29, 1987.

To a Friend: In Memoriam: *Na smert' druga* from *Chast' rechi*. This translation, by the author, first appeared in *The New Yorker*, May 6, 1985.

This poem responds to a false report of the death of Sergei Chudakov, a Moscow poet and raconteur [LL].

"Aesopian chant": I.e., conversation in riddles to elude informers [LL].

"squinchers" and "beavers": In Russian *korol'kov* and *sipovok*, criminal jargon for female sex organs.

Natalia Goncharova (1812-63): Pushkin's wife [au].

"Orenburg shawl": A fine woolen shawl, named for a city in the southern Urals.

"Third Rome": See note to "Eclogue V: Summer," 1, stanza 8, p. 523

"someone's pipe": See Revelation 8:2 [LL].

October Tune: *Oktiabr'skaia pesnia* from *Konets prekrasnoi epokhi*. This translation, by the author, first appeared in *The New Yorker,* October 5, 1987.

Konets prekrasnoi epokhi dates this poem 1971.

A Polar Explorer: *Poliarnyi issledovatel'* from *Uraniia*. This translation, by the author, under the pseudonym "F. F. Morton," first appeared in *The Times Literary Supplement,* October 17, 1980.

Lithuanian Nocturne: *Litovskii noktiurn: Tomasu Ventslova* from *Uraniia*. This translation, by the author, first appeared in *Ploughshares* (13:1), Spring 1987.

Tomas Venclova dates this poem 1973 (74?)-1983. He writes that one could refer to a "Lithuanian cycle" in Brodsky's works that would include "Lithuanian Divertissement" and "Lithuanian Nocturne," as well as other works like "Anno Domini" and "Letters to a Roman Friend" that refer figuratively to the Lithuanian situation. Venclova has also written that the form of "Lithuanian Nocturne" recalls Pushkin's poems addressed to the exiled Ovid [AP].

III. Zhemaitija: Lithuanian name for Samogitia, a historical region of western Lithuania [au].

Gerai: "Okay" in Lithuanian.

IV. Stasis Girenas (1893-1933) and Steponas Darius (1896-1933): American aviators of Lithuanian origin who crashed near Soldin (then part of Germany, now Mysliborz in Poland), after successfully flying across the Atlantic. They were widely believed to have been shot down by the Nazis [au].

VIII. "Magnavox's/ends-*cum*-means demiurge": I.e, Stalin; in Russian, "*makrous*," or "macrowhisker."

"famed Lithuanian inn": From Pushkin's *Boris Godunov* [TV].

"poised to put fingers in/to his mouth": See Isaiah 6:1-13 and Pushkin's "The Prophet" (1828). (See *An Age Ago.*)

"wound of your namesake": See John 20:25-28.

X. "simpleton's cheese": From the fable in Krylov and Aesop, "The Fox and the Crow."

XII. Prince Vytautas (c. 1350-1430): Grand Duke and most famous monarch of early Lithuania [au].

XIII. "Vizier of Woes": Kashchei, an evil character from Russian folklore [TV].

XIV. Laisves Boulevard: Pedestrian boulevard in the center of Kaunas.

Tulpe: A café in Kaunas famous during the 1930s as a gathering place for intellectuals [TV].

XV. "new Clio": See W. H. Auden, "Homage to Clio" (1955).

XVIII. "splits/a round eye," etc.: See note to "The Funeral of Bobò," IV, p. 510.

XXI. St. Casimir (1458–84): Patron saint of Lithuania [au].

St. Nicholas (d. 324): Patron saint of Russia [au].

Twenty Sonnets to Mary Queen of Scots: *Dvadtsat' sonetov k Marii Stiuart* from *Chast' rechi.* This translation, by Peter France with the author, first appeared in *London Magazine* (October/November 1988).

The author referred to these poems as an homage to the sonnet form, particularly the sonnets of French poet Joachim Du Bellay (c. 1522–60) [PM].

I. "a statue": A nineteenth-century depiction of Mary Queen of Scots, by Jean-Jacques Feuchère, one of a series of French queens in the Luxembourg Gardens, Paris [VV].

"ram/at the new gates": A reference to a Russian expression signifying stupid amazement [trans].

" 'all the dead past now lives anew/in my cold heart' ": From a popular nineteenth-century Russian love song [au], set to a poem by Fiodor Tiutchev [trans].

II. Zarah Leander (1907–81): Swedish actress and singer popular in the 1940s. She played Mary Queen of Scots in the German film *Das Herz einer Königin* (1940) [au]. (See Brodsky, "Spoils of War," VI [GR].)

II. the Spartacus: A cinema in St. Petersburg, occupying since 1939 the neoclassical Church of St. Anna.

IV. "Wearing a mackintosh, she went off somewhere": See Alexander Blok, "Of all heroic deeds and fortitude and fame" (1908): "into a damp night you went leaving home" [anonymous/PB].

VI. "I loved you": See Pushkin, "I loved you once: of love perhaps an ember" (1829) [trans]. (See *An Age Ago.*)

Parmenides: Greek philosopher of the Eleatic School, c. 515 B.C. [au].

VII. *muzhik*: Russian for "man," now with a colloquial derogatory meaning, implying a loutish peasant.

"an ugly cretin in a Russian shirt": See Alexander Blok, "Retribution" (1910–21): "now a nihilist wearing a slant-color shirt/turns up arrogantly demanding some vodka" [VV].

"General-Secretary": Reference to the half-paralyzed Lenin and his successors [trans, LL].

VIII. "I'd have displayed you to the haughty Slavs": See Pushkin, "The Monument" (1836): "the proud grandson of the Slavs" [VV].

"shoes of bast": Idiomatically identified with the Russian peasantry.

X. "crippled Hamburg cooper": From Gogol's *Diary of a Madman* (1835) [au], referring to the moon.

XI. " 'I am alone' . . . 'There are a lot of you' ": In Russian, a proverbial phrase used by overwhelmed shopgirls [VV].

XII. Schiller: See Friedrich Schiller's romantic drama *Mary Stuart* (1800) [trans].

XV. "the grooms who'd got/no carpenters to raise the roofbeams higher": See Sappho, *Epithalamia* #2: "Raise high the roof-beam, carpenters. Like Ares comes the bridegroom, taller far than a tall man"; the epigraph to J. D. Salinger's "Raise High the Roof-beam, Carpenters" (1963), which was well known in Soviet Russia.

XVI. " 'Melancholy Days' ": A nineteenth-century popular song, taking its name from a quotation from Pushkin's fragment "Autumn" (1833) [trans].

XVIII. "lack of do-re-mi": Reference to an ironic remark of Pushkin's: "But, gentlemen, is it possible to compare a do-re-mi [meaning opera] with wine?" [VV].

"a mound/of rubbish": See Anna Akhmatova, "The Secrets of the Craft" (1940): "If only you knew from what rubbish/Poetry grows" [VV].

XX. "Katmandu": A bilingual pun: *kat*, for "cut," and *mandu*, "cunt" in Russian.

North Baltic: *Shvedskaia muzyka* from *Uraniia.* This translation, by the author, first appeared in *The New York Review of Books,* February 18, 1988.

The Berlin Wall Tune: Written in English. This poem first appeared in *The New York Review of Books,* December 17, 1981.

Dutch Mistress: Written in English. This poem first appeared in *The New York Review of Books,* January 20, 1983.

Allenby Road: Written in English. This poem first appeared in *The New York Review of Books,* February 18, 1988.

The first of a series of 16-line poems written in English during the early 1980s; see Gerald Smith [AP]; see also "A Part of Speech."

The Fifth Anniversary: *Piataia godovshchina (4 iiunia 1977)* from *Uraniia.* This translation, by the author, first appeared in *To Urania.*

June 4, 1972: the date of the author's departure from the Soviet Union.

section 2. "enchanted oaks": See Pushkin, "Ruslan and Ludmilla" (1820): "For you alone, enchanting beauties . . ." (dedication) [LL].

section 3. striving for the "third shore": I.e., an absurd, futile endeavor, in Russian referring to the expression "fifth corner" (see note to "Constancy," p. 526) [LL].

section 7. "No leader seems quite fit to stop green leaves' ovation": A reference to a common image on Soviet television and newsreels: the leader struggling to quell from the stage the enthusiastic applause of his immense audience [LL].

section 10. "a certain bridge": The Engineers' Bridge in St. Petersburg, which bears images of Perseus' shield.

Polonaise: A Variation: *Polonez: variatsiia* from *Uraniia.* This translation, by the author, first appeared in *The New Yorker,* September 21, 1987.

The New Jules Verne: *Novyi Zhiul' Vern* from *Uraniia.* This translation, by the author, first appeared in *Partisan Review* LIV:4, 1987.

Lines on the Winter Campaign, 1980: *Stikhi o zimnei kampanii 1980-go goda* from *Uraniia.* This translation, by Alan Myers, first appeared as *Verses on the Winter Campaign: 1980* (London: Anvil Press Poetry, 1981) and in *The New York Review of Books,* September 24, 1981.

Epigraph: From "The Dream" (1841). (See *An Age Ago.*)

The Soviet Union invaded Afghanistan in December 1979.

Café Trieste: San Francisco: Written in English. This poem first appeared in *Confrontation* 27–28, (1984).

The Hawk's Cry in Autumn: *Osennii krik iastreba* from *Uraniia*. This translation, by Alan Myers with the author, first appeared in *Paris Review* 103, Summer 1987.

Sextet: *Kvintet* from *Uraniia*. This translation, by the author, first appeared in *The New Yorker*, December 31, 1984.

The author added section VI to the English version, turning a "Quintet" into a "Sextet."

Minefield Revisited: *"Ty, gitaroobraznaia veshch' so sputannoi pautinoi"* from *Uraniia*. This translation, by the author, first appeared in *To Urania*.

Sophia Kovalevska[ia] (1850–91): A celebrated Russian mathematician [au].

Near Alexandria: *B okrestnostiakh Aleksandrii* from *Uraniia*. This translation, by the author, first appeared in *The New York Review of Books*, December 22, 1983.

stanza 1. "a spy": Alexandria, Virginia, neighbors Langley, the home of the Central Intelligence Agency.

stanza 2. "all / four hooves": According to the symbolism of equestrian statuary, if a mount's hooves are all on the ground, the rider died in peacetime. See Brodsky, "Homage to Marcus Aurelius," II [GR].

Tsushima Screen: *"Voskhodiashchee zheltoe solntse sledit kosymi"* from *Uraniia*. This translation, by the author, first appeared in *To Urania*.

"frozen straits of Epiphany": The Russian Orthodox holiday of Epiphany, January 18, comes during the coldest time of the year in central Russia, whence the Russian expression "Epiphany frost" [LL].

A Martial Law Carol: Written in English. First appeared in *The New York Review of Books*, March 17, 1983.

Wiktor Woroszylski (1927–96) and Andrzej Drawicz (1932–97) were writers and Solidarity activists imprisoned upon the imposition of martial law in Poland in December 1981.

stanza 5. "Wujek mine:" A coal mine in Silesia where seven men were killed at an underground sit-in resisting martial law.

Folk Tune: *"To ne Muza vody nabiraet v rot"* from *Uraniia*. This translation, by the author, first appeared in *The Times Literary Supplement*, October 11, 1985.

stanza 4. *Tirpitz*: A German destroyer [au].

Roman Elegies: *Rimskie elegii* from *Uraniia*. The translation, by the author, of "Roman Elegy III" first appeared in *The New Yorker*, July 13, 1981, and *Amacadmy: The Newsletter of the American Academy in Rome* (4:1), Summer 1981; all twelve then appeared in *Vanity Fair* (46:10), December 1983.

These poems appear in a different sequence in Russian.

The author follows the Russian tradition in using the word "elegy" in its classical sense, which is not limited to poems of mourning but describes a number of verses for which the elegiac distich form was considered suitable. In Latin literature, particularly the Augustan lyricist Sextus Propertius, this form became associated with the genre of the love complaint. Goethe also wrote a sequence of *Roman Elegies* (1788–90); Brodsky commended the influence of Goethe's Italian travels on these poems [PM]. See also pp. 319, 363, 399, and 423.

II. "Jewish / *r* ": In Russian a guttural *r* sound is considered characteristic of a Jewish accent.

VI. "I've never built that cloud-thrusting stony," etc.: See Horace, *Odes*: "I have finished a monument" (III:30) [LL].

VIII. "gramophone-dodging mongrel": The mascot of RCA, accompanying the slogan "His Master's Voice" (see Brodsky, "Spoils of War," XII [GR]).

IX. "Lesbia, Julia, Cynthia, Livia": Lesbia was the addressee of the love lyrics of Catullus; Julia was Caesar Augustus's daughter, rumored mistress of Ovid; Cynthia was the addressee of the love lyrics of Propertius; and Livia Drusilla was the second wife of Augustus [LL].

Kazimir: Kazimir Malevich: See note to "Eclogue IV: Winter," IX, below.

XI. Tanaiis: The river Don, mentioned by Ovid in his *Tristia* [au].

To Urania: *K Uranii* from *Uraniia*. This translation, by the author, first appeared in *The Paris Review* 103, Summer 1987.

"Sister Clio": See note to "Lithuanian Nocturne," XV, p. 518.

The Bust of Tiberius: *Biust Tiberiia* from *Uraniia*. This translation, by Alan Myers with the author, first appeared in *The New York Review of Books,* June 25, 1987.

In *Peresechennaia mestnost'* the author dates this poem 1984–85.

stanza 3. holding wolves by the ears: Caesar Augustus said that ruling Rome was like holding a wolf by the ears—equally dangerous to do and to stop doing [trans].

Seven Strophes: *"Ia byl tol'ko tem, chego"* from *Uraniia*. This translation, by Paul Graves, first appeared in *Western Humanities Review,* Spring 1988.

The Residence: *Rezidentsiia* from *Uraniia*. This translation, by the author, first appeared in *The Times Literary Supplement,* July 13, 1984.

Eclogue IV: Winter: *Ekloga 4-ia: (zimniaia)* from *Uraniia*. This translation, by the author, first appeared in *The New Yorker,* March 29, 1982.

Epigraph: "Now the last age of Cumae's prophecy has come; / The great succession of centuries is born afresh" (Guy Lee, trans.).

V. "scamp from popular Russian verses": "the yard-boy, who . . . has got a finger frozen," Pushkin, *Eugene Onegin* (Five:II:9,12) (Charles Johnston, trans.).

VII. Terek: A river in the Caucasus [au].

IX. Kazimir Malevich (1878–1935): Russian suprematist painter [au].

Eclogue V: Summer: *Ekloga 5-ia: (letniaia)* from *Uraniia*. This translation, by George L. Kline with the author, first appeared in *The New Yorker,* August 3, 1987.

I. stanza 1. " 'lower than grass' ": "Stiller than water, lower than grass," Russian expression denoting humility.

stanza 6. "cock-and-hen": A children's guessing game played with meadow grass [au].

stanza 8. Terzaromeville: Moscow is traditionally identified as the "Third Rome" [au].

"knight at the crossroads": Traditional motif in Russian epic songs and fairy tales [LL].

II. *"zh"*: The Cyrillic letter Ж.

III. " 'Manchurian Mountains' ": Popular sentimental waltz tune of the time of the Russo-Japanese War (1905) [LL].

IV. Simonides of Ceos (c. 556–468 B.C.): Greek lyric poet [au].

Venetian Stanzas I: *Venetsianskie strofy (1)* from *Uraniia*. This translation, by Jane Ann Miller with the author, first appeared in *The Times Literary Supplement*, July 15-21, 1988.

The author remarked that he fashioned these poems after paintings depicting cityscapes at different times of day and seasons, particularly those of Claude Lorrain at the Hermitage [PM].

VII. "Perm's citizen": The ballet impresario Sergei Diaghilev (1872-1929) was born in Perm, Russia, and buried in Venice.

VIII. "pupil of Claude": Claude Lorrain (1600-82), French landscape painter who lived and worked in Italy.

Venetian Stanzas II: *Venetsianskie strofy (2)* from *Uraniia*. This translation, by Jane Ann Miller with the author, first appeared in *The Times Literary Supplement*, July 15-21, 1988.

II. Susanna: See Daniel 13:1-27 (Apocrypha).

Seaward: Written in English. This poem first appeared in *To Urania*.

Galatea Encore: Written in English. This poem first appeared in *The New Yorker*, October 7, 1985.

Variation in V: Written in English. This poem first appeared in *The Times Literary Supplement*, November 22, 1985.

Letter to an Archaeologist: Written in English. This poem first appeared in *The Times Literary Supplement*, October 11, 1985.

See *"Tol'ko pepel znaet, chto znachit sgoret' dotla"* in *Peizazh s navodneniem*.

Kellomäki: *Kellomiaki* from *Uraniia*. This translation, by the author, first appeared in *The New Yorker*, January 26, 1987.

This poem was dated 1982 upon its first publication in Russian.

The Russian name for Kellomäki, a village on the Karelian Isthmus to the north of St. Petersburg, is Komarovo.

XI. Nikolai Lobachevsky (1792-1856): Mathematician who proposed the theory that parallel lines converge in infinity [au].

Ex Voto: Written in English. This poem first appeared in *The Times Literary Supplement,* June 26, 1987.

Elegy: "About a year has passed. I've returned to the place of battle": *Elegiia ("Proshlo chto-to okolo goda. Ia vernulsia na mesto bitvy")* from *Uraniia.* This translation, by the author, first appeared in *The Times Literary Supplement,* June 26, 1987.

The Fly: *Mukha* from *Uraniia.* This translation, by Jane Ann Miller with the author, first appeared in *The New Yorker,* March 7, 1988.

III. Junkers: World War II–era German manufacturer of fighter planes and bombers.

VI. "six-legged letters": The Cyrillic letter Ж, which indicates the *zh* sound [au].

XI. "obol": In Greek mythology, the coin placed on the tongue of the dead to pay for a crossing over the river Lethe into Hades.

XIV. "that stayed moment": See note to "New Life," stanza 7, p. 525.

XIX. "the great Halicarnassian": The historian Herodotus (484?-425? B.C.), who was the first Greek to describe snow.

Belfast Tune: Written in English. This poem first appeared in *The New Yorker,* July 13, 1987.

Afterword: *Posleslovie* from *Uraniia.* This translation, by Jamey Gambrell with the author, under the pseudonym "E. T. Huddlestone," first appeared in *The Times Literary Supplement,* October 30–November 5, 1987.

II. Kuzbass: Acronym for an industrial region in Siberia [au].

At Carel Willink's Exhibition: *Na vystavke Karla Veilinka* from *Uraniia.* This translation, by Jamey Gambrell, first appeared in *The Times Literary Supplement,* January 8-14, 1988.

Albert Carel Willink (1900-83): Dutch figurative painter, who described himself as a "fantastic realist."

"Slave, Come to My Service!": This translation, by the author, from the Sumerian, first appeared in *The New York Review of Books,* November 19, 1987.

This text dates back to the eleventh or tenth century B.C. and is known among Sumerian scholars as "The Dialogue of Pessimism." In antiquity it was regarded as a philosophical text; now some argue that it is, rather, a skit. For my translation I used two interlinear renditions: one was taken from *Babylonian Wisdom Literature,* by W. G. Lambert (Oxford, 1960); the other, from *Ancient Near Eastern Texts Relating to the Old Testament,* edited by James B. Pritchard (Princeton, 1955) [au].

A correspondent to *The New York Review of Books* observed that the original languages of this text were the Babylonian and Assyrian dialects of Akkadian. His letter and Brodsky's reply appeared on March 17, 1988.

In Italy: *V Italii* from *Uraniia.* This translation, by the author, first appeared in *To Urania.*

"golden pigeon / coop": See Anna Akhmatova, "Venice" (1912).

"a local penseur": The St. Petersburg philosopher Vasily Rozanov (1856-1919), who argued that Christianity had its orgins in sexual perversion [Viktor Kulle].

In Memoriam: *"Mysl' o tebe udaliaetsia, kak razzhalovannaia prisluga"* from *Uraniia*. This translation, by the author, first appeared in *The New Yorker*, November 9, 1987.

The author's mother, Maria Moiseevna Vol'pert, died in Leningrad on March 17, 1983.

So Forth

Translations, where not made by the author, were commissioned by him and executed under his direction.

Infinitive: Written in English. This poem first appeared in *The New York Review of Books*, July 14, 1994.

A Song: Written in English. This poem first appeared in *The New Yorker*, March 27, 1989.

The author remarked that this poem was a pastiche of Auden's "Songs."

A Footnote to Weather Forecasts: *Primechan'e k prognozam pogody* from *Peizazh s navodneniem*. This translation, by the author, first appeared in *The Times Literary Supplement*, June 30–July 6, 1989.

Star of the Nativity: *Rozhdestvenskaia zvezda* from *Peizazh s navodneniem*. This translation, by the author, first appeared in *The New York Times*, December 24, 1988.

New Life: *Novaia zhizn'* from *Peizazh s navodneniem*. This translation, by David MacFadyen with the author, first appeared in *The New Yorker*, April 26, 1993.

stanza 1. Junkers: See note to "The Fly," III, p. 524.

stanza 7. "no one begs the moment, 'Stay!' ": See Goethe, *Faust*: *"Werd ich zu Augenblicke sagen:/Verweile doch! du bist so schön!"* ("If ever I say to the passing moment/'Linger a while! Thou art so fair!,' " L. MacNeice, trans.) (II. 1699–1700) [VP/P&A].

Angel: *Angel* from *Peizazh s navodneniem*. This translation, by the author, first appeared in *The New Yorker*, January 10, 1994.

An Admonition: *Nazidanie* from *Peizazh s navodneniem*. This translation, by George L. Kline with the author, first appeared as "Advice to a Traveller" in *The Times Literary Supplement*, May 12–18, 1989.

In Memory of My Father: Australia: *Pamiati ottsa: Avstraliia* from *Peizazh s navodneniem*. This translation, by the author, first appeared in *The New Yorker*, March 5, 1990.

The author's father, Alexander Ivanovich Brodsky, died in Leningrad on April 29, 1984.

So Forth: *"Konchitsia leto. Nachnetsia sentiabr'. Razreshat otstrel"* from *Peizazh s navodneniem*. This translation, by the author, first appeared in *The Times Literary Supplement*, October 9, 1992.

Constancy: *Elegiia ("Postoianstvo sut' evoliutsiia printsipa pomeshchen'ia")* from *Peizazh s navodneniem*. This translation, by the author, first appeared in the *Princeton University Library Chronicle* LV:3, Spring 1994.

Clausewitz: A reference to the remark by Prussian military strategist Karl von Clausewitz (1780–1831): "War is the continuation of politics by other means."

" 'Slavic / Glory' ": In Russian, *gei slaviane,* the slogan of the nineteenth-century Pan-Slavic movement, came to be used ironically to denote cheap or sentimental Slavic-style ornamentation [LL].

"fifth corner": Russian police jargon: In an interrogation, four policemen would occupy the four corners of a room and invite the suspect to escape a beating by finding the fifth corner [LL].

Brise Marine: *"Dorogaia, ia vyshel segodnia iz domu pozdno vecherom"* from *Peizazh s navodneniem.* This translation, by the author, first appeared in *The Times Literary Supplement,* February 1, 1991.

Centaurs I-IV: *Kentavry I-IV* from *Peizazh s navodneniem.* This translation, by the author, first appeared in *Western Humanities Review,* Winter 1988.

III. "fairy tale's hut on chicken / feet": In Russian folklore, the home of the witch Baba Yaga [LL].

Epitaph for a Centaur: Written in English. This poem first appeared in *Western Humanities Review,* Winter 1988.

"Epitaph for a Centaur" was composed at the time "Centaurs I-IV" were translated into English.

Axiom: *"Mir sozdan byl iz smeshen'ia griazi, vody, ognia"* from *Peizazh s navodneniem.* This translation, by Jonathan Aaron with the author, first appeared in *Queen's Quarterly* (Canada) (102:2), Summer 1995.

North of Delphi: *Primechaniia paporotnika* from *Peizazh s navodneniem.* This translation, by the author, first appeared in *The Times Literary Supplement,* April 12, 1991.

The Russian title, "The Fern Footnotes," refers to a Russian folk belief in the prognostic powers of ferns.

Epigraph: "Remember me, / whispers the dust," from "The Angels" (1970).

Exeter Revisited: Written in English. This poem first appeared in *The New York Review of Books,* September 29, 1988.

Vertumnus: *Vertumn* from *Peizazh s navodneniem.* This translation, by the author, first appeared in *The Times Literary Supplement,* October 4, 1991.

Giovanni Buttafava (1937–90): The author's translator into Italian.

Parts V and VII of the original Russian have been omitted.

XIII: Ж, Ч, Ш, Щ: The Cyrillic letters *zhe, che, sha,* and *shcha.*

" 'As your head honcho said, / there is nothing that matches abracadabra' ": In a frequently quoted phrase, Lenin, in Gorky's memoirs, says, "I know nothing better than 'Apassionata' " [LL].

Nativity: *"Nevazhno, chto bylo vokrug, i nevazhno"* from *Peizazh s navodneniem.* This translation, by the author, first appeared in *A Garland for Stephen,* arranged by Barry Humphries (Edinburgh: Tragara Press, 1991).

Postcard from Lisbon: *Otkrytka iz Lissabona* from *Peizazh s navodneniem*. This translation, by the author, first appeared in *The Times Literary Supplement*, October 18, 1991.

August Rain: *Dozhd' v avguste* from *Peizazh s navodneniem*. This translation, by the author, first appeared in *The Times Literary Supplement*, August 2, 1991.

Venice: Lido: *Lido* from *Peizazh s navodneniem*. This translation, by Alan Myers, first appeared in *The Times Literary Supplement*, May 14, 1993.

The author elsewhere dated this poem 1991.

Fin de Siècle: *Fin de Siècle* from *Peizazh s navodneniem*. This translation, by the author, first appeared in *The Times Literary Supplement*, August 7, 1992.

stanza 13. "cuckoo's voice": See note to "1972," stanza 6, p. 512.

Mario Cavaradossi: See note to "Plato Elaborated," I, p. 515.

Porta San Pancrazio: *"Pchely ne uleteli, vsadnik ne uskakal. V kofeine"* from *Peizazh s navodneniem*. This translation, by the author, first appeared in *The New Yorker*, March 14, 1994.

The Porta San Pancrazio is on the Gianicolo hill in Rome.

Transatlantic: Written in English. This poem first appeared in *The New Yorker*, August 3, 1992.

"without / even a proper flag to hoist": A reference to the dispute in 1991 over control of the formerly Soviet Black Sea Fleet.

View from the Hill: *Vid s Kholma* from *Peizazh s navodneniem*. This translation, by Alan Myers with the author, first appeared in *The Times Literary Supplement*, November 26, 1993.

In 1991 and 1992 the author served as Poet Laureate at the Library of Congress in Washington, D.C.

Homage to Girolamo Marcello: *"Odnazhdy ia tozhe zimoiu priplyl siuda"* from *Peizazh s navodneniem*. This translation, by the author, first appeared in *The New Yorker*, January 21, 1991.

Girolamo Marcello: A Venetian friend of the author.

The author elsewhere dated this poem 1991.

"I, too, sailed in / here from Egypt": According to Venetian legend, St. Mark, the patron saint of Venice and the founder of the Church of Alexandria, preached in Venice and received a vision that he would be buried there; his remains were brought to Venice from Alexandria in A.D. 829 [PM].

Elegy: "Sweetheart, losing your looks, go to live in a village": *"Podruga, durneia litsom, poselis' v derevne"* from *Peizazh s navodneniem*. This translation, by the author, first appeared in *The Times Literary Supplement*, October 8, 1993.

The author made the following revision to the last two lines of the version published in the *TLS*: "Squinting one day at some faint brushstroke, no doubt, / you'll make out yourself; I'll be another daub." This revision may have been overlooked in the preparation of *So Forth*.

Anti-Shenandoah: Written in English. This poem first appeared in *Antaeus* 75/76, Autumn 1994.

Daedalus in Sicily: *Dedal v Sitsilii* from *Peizazh s navodneniem.* This translation, by the author, first appeared in *The New York Review of Books,* October 7, 1993.

Clouds: *Oblaka* from *Peizazh s navodneniem.* This translation, by the author, first appeared in *The Times Literary Supplement,* May 19, 1995.

Cappadocia: *Kappadokiia* from *Peizazh s navodneniem.* This translation, by Paul Graves with the author, first appeared in *The Times Literary Supplement,* December 23, 1994.

Mithridates Ponticus: Mithridates VI (120–66 B.C.), King of Pontus, an ancient kingdom on the Black Sea. The events described in this poem took place in 92 B.C.

Ab Ovo: Written in English. This poem first appeared in *The New Yorker,* July 8, 1996.

Via Funari: *Na via Funari* from *Peizazh s navodneniem.* This translation, by the author, first appeared in *The New York Review of Books,* February 1, 1996.

Caetani palace: The early-sixteenth-century Palazzo Antici-Mattei stands at the corner of Via Caetani and Via dei Funari in Rome.

"vicious / infinitude": See note to "Gorbunov and Gorchakov," XII, stanza 7, p. 517.

Portrait of Tragedy: *Portret tragedii* from *Peizazh s navodneniem* (second edition). This translation, by the author, first appeared in *The New Yorker,* February 12, 1996.

stanza 1. "the medal's flip side": Russian and Italian expression, "to see the reverse of the medal," as in "the flip side of the coin."

stanza 9. *yi:* The Cyrillic letter ы.

Törnfallet: Written in English. This poem first appeared in *The New Yorker,* August 8, 1994.

Törnfallet is near Lake Vättern in Sweden.

Persian Arrow: *Persidskaia strela* from *Peizazh s navodneniem.* This translation, by the author, first appeared in *The Times Literary Supplement,* December 23, 1994.

Song of Welcome: Written in English. This poem first appeared in *The Times Literary Supplement,* July 24, 1992.

Elegy: "Whether you fished me bravely out of the Pacific": Written in English. This poem first appeared in *So Forth.*

"the poet": John Keats.

Kolo: Written in English. This poem first appeared in *The New York Review of Books,* July 13, 1995.

Lullaby: *Kolybel'naia* from *Peizazh s navodneniem.* This translation, by the author, first appeared in *The New Yorker,* December 20, 1993.

Homage to Chekhov: *Posviashchaetsia Chekhovu* from *Peizazh s navodneniem.* This translation, by Jonathan Aaron with the author, first appeared in *The New Yorker,* August 7, 1995.

Ischia in October: *Iskiia v oktiabre* from *Peizazh s navodneniem*. This translation, by the author, first appeared in *The Times Literary Supplement*, May 19, 1995.

Anthem: Written in English. This poem first appeared in *Queen's Quarterly* (Canada) (102:2), Summer 1995.

In Front of Casa Marcello: *S natury* from *Peizazh s navodneniem*. This translation, by the author, first appeared in *The New Republic*, May 27, 1996.

See note to "Homage to Girolamo Marcello," p. 527.

Palazzo Minelli: A palace in Venice.

"slant bell tower": Probably the steeple of the church of San Stefano in Venice.

After Us: "*Posle nas, razumeetsia, ne potop*" from *Peizazh s navodneniem*. This translation, by Jonathan Aaron with the author, first appeared in *Queen's Quarterly* (Canada) (102:2), Summer 1995.

A Tale: Written in English. This poem first appeared in *The Times Literary Supplement*, February 2, 1996.

The poem is connected with a series of children's poems Brodsky wrote in 1995: "Discovery," "The Emperor," "At the Helmet and Sword," and "Cabbage and Carrot," which in turn recalled a series of poems Brodsky had written in Russian for children's magazines before his emigration. See *Stikhotvoreniia dlia detei,* edited by Viktor Kulle.

Ode to Concrete: Written in English. This poem first appeared in *The New Republic*, May 27, 1996.

At the City Dump in Nantucket: Written in English. This poem first appeared in *The New York Review of Books*, April 4, 1996. This version incorporates revisions the author apparently made subsequent to his last submission of the manuscript to the publisher. The prior version read:

[...] and the seagulls attacking the dump are trying to outnumber

[...]

Here's the primordial alphabet shooting pell-mell, criss-cross.
In no time they'll bill themselves Parker's nephews,
give up fish, preferring human refuse,
scream of money, resemble us!

In their screeching Ws one hears not the hunger but
the prurience of their hooked beaks towards
what outlasts them, these soiled leftovers
of the cardboard flesh and electric blood

as some old anemometer giddily spins its cups
like a tea ceremony gone awry, and the Atlantic
[...]

The poem refers to a photograph by Stephen White reproduced on the jacket of *So Forth*.

A Photograph: "*My zhili v gorode tsveta okamenevshei vodki*" from *Peizazh s navodneniem*. This translation, by the author, first appeared in *The Times Literary Supplement*, October 28, 1994, paired with "A Postcard."

A Postcard: Written in English. This poem first appeared in *The Times Literary Supplement*, October 28, 1994, paired with "A Photograph."

Reveille: Written in English. This poem first appeared in *The Times Literary Supplement*, February 2, 1996.

Blues: Written in English. This poem first appeared in *So Forth*.

At a Lecture: Written in English. This poem first appeared in *The New Republic*, May 8, 1995.

The author's manuscripts were inconclusive as to whether the last word of this poem should be "reflection" or "reflections."

In Memory of Clifford Brown: *Pamiati Klifforda Brauna* from *Peizazh s navodneniem*. This translation, by the author, first appeared in *The New Republic*, December 11, 1995.

Clifford Brown (1930-56): In the author's view, "the greatest jazz trumpet player ever."

Love Song: Written in English. This poem first appeared in *The New Republic*, March 4, 1996.

To My Daughter: Written in English. This poem first appeared in *The Times Literary Supplement*, December 2, 1994.

Flourish: "*O esli by ptitsy peli i oblaka skuchali*" from *Peizazh s navodneniem*. This translation, by the author, first appeared in *The New Republic*, March 4, 1996.

MCMXCIV: *MCMXCIV* from *Peizazh s navodneniem*. This translation, by the author, first appeared in *The New York Review of Books*, June 8, 1995, paired with "MCMXCV."

MCMXCV: "*Klouny razrushaiut tsirk. Slony ubezhali v Indiiu*" from *Peizazh s navodneniem*. This translation, by the author, first appeared in *The New York Review of Books*, June 8, 1995, paired with "MCMXCIV."

View with a Flood: *Peizazh s navodneniem* from *Peizazh s navodneniem*. This translation, by the author, first appeared in *The Times Literary Supplement*, February 10, 1995.

Taps: "*Menia uprekali vo vsem, okromia pogody*" from *Peizazh s navodneniem*. This translation, by the author, first appeared in *The Times Literary Supplement*, January 12, 1996.

Uncollected Poems and Translations

These poems, mostly light verse, were published by the author in magazines and included in early manuscripts of the three books collected here and then withdrawn for various reasons during editing.

Rio Samba: Written in English. This poem first appeared in Brodsky, "After a Journey" [GR].

A Season: Written in English. This poem first appeared in *The New York Review of Books*, February 5, 1981.

Shorts: The author selected two groups of "shorts" for publication. The first four included here, from "Epitaph for a Tyrant" through "To a Fellow Poet," were included in initial manuscripts of *To Urania*; the following eight, from "I sit at my desk" through "New York Lullaby," were published in *Occasional Stiles*, the literary magazine of Ezra Stiles College at Yale University, where the author was a fellow. We reprint these two groups, excluding repetitions, and follow the chronological order of publication for the rest. Beyond identifying the dates of publication, it is difficult to date the shorts precisely, as they were written informally over a long period. In grouping them together and calling them "Shorts," the author was following Auden, first in his *Collected Shorter Poems 1927-1957*.

"Epitaph for a Tyrant" first appeared in *The New York Review of Books*, December 16, 1982. "Abroad" first appeared in *The Times Literary Supplement*, November 17, 1995. "Future" first appeared in *The New York Times*, December 20, 1984."I sit at my desk," "A Postcard from France," "Epitaph to a Tyrant," "Hail the vagina," "I went to a museum," "To a Fellow Poet," "Oysters," "A Valentine," and "I've seen the Atlantic" first appeared in *Occasional Stiles*, Yale University, 1992; the first four lines of "I've seen the Atlantic" were previously published in *The New York Times*, Sophisticated Traveler Section, March 18, 1984, under the title "Postcard from the U.S.," with the concluding couplet, "As for the continent, / I'm not yet on to it."

History of the Twentieth Century: A Roadshow: Written in English. This poem first appeared in *Partisan Review* (LIII:3), 1986; the epigraph was published as a "short" in *Occasional Stiles*, Yale University, 1992. A few inconsistencies of facts and dates in the poem have been noted and allowed to stand.

Isadora: Isadora Duncan (1878-1927): American dancer.

Swiss Blue: Written in English. This poem first appeared in *The Times Literary Supplement*, January 11, 1991. This version incorporates revisions the author made subsequent to publication.

Lines for the Winter Recess: Written in English. This poem first appeared in *The New Yorker*, May 4, 1992.

See note to "View from the Hill," p. 527.

Fossil Unwound: Written in English. This poem first appeared in *The Times Literary Supplement*, September 25, 1992.

Bosnia Tune: Written in English. This poem first appeared in *The New York Times*, November 18, 1992. This version incorporates revisions the author made subsequent to publication.

To the President-elect: Written in English. This poem first appeared in *The Washington Post*, December 13, 1992. It was commissioned as part of a feature commemorating the inauguration of President Clinton.

Robinsonade: *Robinzonada* from *Peizazh s navodneniem*. This translation, by Jonathan Aaron with the author, first appeared in *Queen's Quarterly* (Canada) (102:2), Summer 1995.

531

Once More by the Potomac: Written in English. This poem was first published in *The New Republic*, August 7, 1995. It was commissioned for a special issue on the Balkan War.

Cabbage and Carrot (children's poem). Written in English. This poem first appeared in *The New York Review of Books*, July 11, 1996. It is a version of the author's 1969 poem in Russian *Ssora* (The Argument). See note to "A Tale," p. 529.

At the Helmet and Sword (children's poem): Written in English. This poem first appeared in *Queen's Quarterly* (Canada) (102:2), Summer 1995. See note to "A Tale," p. 529.

"I will win you away from every earth, from every sky" (*"Ia tebia otvoiuiu u vsekh zemel', u vsekh nebes"*) and **"Seeing off the beloved ones, I"** (*"Sobiraia liubimykh v put' "*), by Marina Tsvetaeva: Brodsky's translations from the Russian first appeared together under the title "Two Poems from 1916" in *The New Yorker*, October 17, 1983.

"Seeing off the beloved ones, I" does not usually appear with a dedication, but it is one of a series of poems Mandelstam and Tsvetaeva wrote to each other in the first half of 1916. Tsvetaeva lists several of these in her essay "History of a Dedication" and marked her poems to Mandelstam in a copy of one of her books (See Victoria Schweitzer, *Tsvetaeva* [New York: Farrar, Straus and Giroux, 1992], p. 122).

"Tristia" (*Tristia*) by Osip Mandelstam: Brodsky's translation from the Russian first appeared in *Confrontation*, 27-28, 1984; reprinted in Brodsky, "The Child of Civilization" [LTO]. Brodsky's translation from the Russian first appeared in *Confrontation* 27-28, 1984; reprinted in Brodsky, "The Child of Civilization" [LTO].

See Ovid, *Tristia* (A.D. 12).

stanza 4. "a small translucent figure": A reference to a Russian form of divination, performed by pouring hot wax into water, that appears in Pushkin, *Eugene Onegin* (Five:IV–X).

"Achilles. Penthesilea" (*Achilles. Pentesilea*), by Zbigniew Herbert: Brodsky's translation from the Polish first appeared in *The New York Review of Books*, October 21, 1993.

"End and Beginning" (*"Koniec i początek"*), by Wisława Szymborska: Brodsky's translation from the Polish first appeared in *The Times Literary Supplement*, December 31, 1993.

Index of Titles and First Lines

537

539